THE DIVINE ORDER

and

THE UNIVERSE

compiled by

Bedri Ruhselman

Divine Order Publishing – MTIAD1950

First English language paperback edition published in 2014
by Divine Order Publishing – MTIAD1950

For permission requests, email the publisher at:
divine.order.universe@gmail.com
or write to one of the following addresses:

Divine Order Publishing – MTIAD1950 (UK)
c/o AESOP Publications, 28 Abberbury Road, Oxford OX4 4ES, UK
tel: 44 (0)1865 773862; fax: 01865 389589;
info@aesopbooks.com

Divine Order Publishing – MTIAD1950 (Turkey)
Metapsişik Tetkikler ve İlmi Araştırmalar Derneği, İktisadi İşletmesi
Hasnun Galip Sok, Pembe Çıkmazı
No. 4/4 Beyoglu, Istanbul 34433 Turkey
tel: 0090 212 243 1814; fax: 0090 212 252 0718
www.divineorderanduniverse.org
www.mtiad1950.org.tr
www.mtiad.org.tr

ISBN: 978-0-9928397-1-0

Printed and bound in Great Britain by
Lightning Source UK Ltd,
Chapter House, Pitfield, Kiln Farm,
Milton Keynes MK11 3LW

These spiritual communiqués, which had been issued from the Plan of Sublime Duty and which we named 'Önder [Pioneer]' in 1959, were compiled by Bedri Ruhselman and since then have been preserved in the safes of notaries and banks, and because their time has arrived after 54 years, have now been published. The book in your hands is the faithfully translated version of the original Turkish text.

*
* *

This book is part of the harmony we see, feel around us, and name as nature in a partial fashion. It is a bridge in our universe, between that path of light that we can only name as evolution and which reaches across to the knowledge of mankind. It is the one and only path that connects the limited and narrow matter-life of mankind to a further stage that is wide and comprehensive. It is neither ours nor yours as mankind[1] nor anybody else. It is a gift of the divine order given to mankind. That is, it is a part of nature.

*
* *

This book was given to Earth by those beings in duty to it from the unity of comprehension that we name as unitary, in a form to respond to the evolutionary needs of mankind.

VOYAGERS OF DESTINY

---

[1] The term 'mankind' is used throughout to indicate both men and women. (*Translator*)

Matter is a component constituting the ground for all influences and responding to these influences in varying proportions. Another meaning hidden in this knowledge is: Matter has no ability to initiate a movement or take any action by itself – of not even the most rudimentary nature. There is no possibility of anything occurring or being done by itself in it. That is, matter only awaits the influences coming to it and takes states, forms or situations according to the directions of these influences. Therefore, if we think of any matter that is, let us assume, free of any influences, we have to accept that this matter will not have any form or state. We therefore call that matter which is isolated from all of its states and forms – which is beyond human understanding and imagination – amorphous or primary matter. So, in amorphous matter:

(a) There is no trace of any motion; it is the absolute and complete motionless state of matter.

(b) Since all features and qualities seen in matter are but the manifestations of motion in it, a form, feature or quality of amorphous matter, which means the absolute motionless state, is out of the question.

(c) Since such a state cannot be comprehended – although amorphous matter exists – for humans, this is equivalent to saying that it does not exist.

(d) Since amorphous or primary matter – because of its quality of absolute motionless – cannot make any movement or stir by itself, it is impossible for it to initiate a motion by itself and to display forms, states and manifestations which are

9

the consequences of motion in matter, without any incoming external influences.

Following this knowledge, it can easily be understood that those things that mankind understands and evaluate as matter are the manifestations of various motions created by incoming external influences through the possibilities that exist within the constitution of matter; and not the amorphous matter itself.

*
* *

All these forms and situations, according to their states of fineness, roughness, simplicity or complexity, have sections that may become the focus for various understandings and views. As matter that appears with manifestations of high and complex motion display complex and highly developed states at that level, the ones that display themselves with lesser and simpler motions manifest themselves at that level of primitive and simple qualities.

So, matter displays various values in innumerable degrees of development at various levels, from its primitive states that have the simplest motions to their higher states that have developed the most complex motions. Therefore, the simplest matter means a state of matter which has taken its initial form by separating from amorphous matter through initial motions. In contrast, high or complex matter means the state of matter which has assumed complex states and forms through various compositions and forms of motion.

*
* *

At this point, let us add the following as technical knowledge: the concepts of *fine and crude* states of matter, and *simple and complex* states of matter, should not be confused with each other. Differences in simplicity-complexity of matter are because of the motions that make the constitutions of matter less or more complex or developed. If the matter-combinations of a matter, the values that set up its constitution – namely the motions – are more enriched and complex, that matter becomes more complex and moves away from simplicity to the same extent.

However, the concept of fineness and roughness does not have this meaning. In the case of fineness and roughness, the decreasing or increasing of the combination or value quantity within matter is not the issue. Thus the fineness or roughness of a matter does not show its state of development, that is, its degree of distance or proximity to amorphous matter. Sometimes, with the strong external influences, the bonds between the parts of a matter's mass increase and strengthen; these parts even become so close to each other that their motions become limited. So, in order to influence their motions, it is necessary to send – to the extent of overcoming the influences that are strong enough to compress them – strong influences. These comprise matter, displaying dense, crude states.

In contrast, if the bonds between parts of a matter's mass are weak, the loose bonds of these parts result in larger distances between them. And these parts are influenced by lesser and weaker influences. Therefore, to influence them becomes easier than influencing the previously mentioned rough matter, because the influences to hold them in this state are not strong. Because of this, it is possible to conquer them with more ease. And these are the fine matter that we call fluidic. So, simple or complex matter in every state can be refined or roughened without changing their stages.

As an example of this, we can consider water. Its states of steam, water and ice display differences in fineness and roughness among themselves. However, these three are but water matter, which is in equal distance to amorphous matter and is at the same stage of complexity. Similarly, a complex matter may sometimes be rougher than a matter which is, in contrast, simpler. For example, iron matter is more complex, but denser and rougher, than oxygen.

*
* *

Mankind can see and understand the forms and states of a few rings of matter within certain limits of the motions that lie extended – in the chain of simplicity and complexity – between the lowermost and uppermost infinite points. When these forms and states reach a limit, in the sense of the scantiness or simplicity of their motions, as they are becoming primitive and descending, they start to move away from the perceptive field of human comprehension and eventually vanish completely. Similarly, as the rings of the chain of matter ascend and develop through motions which increase and become more complex, human comprehension again loses them completely after a certain point. This is because no human intellect or comprehension, which is bound to the brain substance of world-matter, can comprehend the quality and quantity of the motions resulting in matter states that are neither below that limit nor above that limit. Therefore, mankind has been unable to afford to understand, other than a few rings in the infinitely extending chain of universe-matter and to make them the subject of tangible study pursuant to themselves. Nevertheless, the main reason that some people reject and deny the possibilities of some high material manifestations is just this.

*
* *

In the path of universe's matter development, transverse from its initial matter state to our astronomic cosmos, there is a dark field which is impossible for mankind to understand. This field is but a coarse, dispersed, amorphous mass. In this crude milieu, there are no formations of constituted matter. After this field, comes a range comprising the initial hydrogen atom that constitutes the beginning of the hydrogen cosmos. Although we use this word because mankind has named the first atom 'hydrogen', in truth the matter we have mentioned and from now on will mention in this context is not the hydrogen atom (H) that mankind knows. This atom known by mankind is a very developed, complex and advanced state of the atom. Mankind do not yet recognise this first hydrogen atom.

The matter-states and forms of our world and of our whole astronomic cosmos with its spheres, systems, nebulae have been made of various combinations of developed states of this hydrogen atom.

Below and above the elements which make up our world there are such elements that are too distant from mankind's field of comprehension. These elements, which are among the most advanced stages of the Earth's atoms, which mankind does not recognise, display substance states which are of an utterly different make-up and quality to the atoms they know. If embodied beings – namely mankind – cannot utilise these states of matter through their comprehension, they often use them automatically through the help of superior beings. As a simple example of this, consider the thought vibrations that pass from one human to another. These thought vibrations are a matter state beyond the matter that mankind recognises and which exists on Earth. Similarly, what is named as *périesprit*[2] and has been named variously by the various spiritualist schools on Earth but has been unable to be explained for ages is, again, one of the matter states that exist on the world but which are not known by mankind. As examples of these, some matter energies that exist on the world but which are again not recognised by mankind are: sympathy, love, antipathy, begrudging, fear, joy, pride, envy, selfishness, which are explained away as subjective psychological states.

*
* *

Universe is a whole. This whole is made of several parts that are different from each other which we call worlds, systems and realms. In the universe, each realm has a particular characteristic. And these characteristics are arranged according to the evolutionary[3] needs of spirits. So, what we call primary matter or matter-substance is an amorphous matter state, qualified by absolute motionless and formlessness, which constitutes the main matter or ferment of this whole universal. This substance, from the moment it first started to move, by becoming more and more complex, created stages accompanied by higher characteristic changes in comparison to each other. We call each of these matter stages nuclei or primary matter of the realms that fill up the matter-universe and which display different attributes

---

[2] *Périesprit*: (French) In classical spiritualism, spirit needs a vehicle composed of the subtlest matter in order to connect to material bodies; this is called *périesprit*, meaning 'surrounding spirit'. (*Publisher*)

[3] *Evolution*: The term means maturation, development and evolving. In our field of research, evolution refers to spiritual evolution which is one of the tenets of experimental spiritualism. It means, in brief, spirits' expanding their fields of consciousness and knowledge through increasing their experiences in the material universe. (*Publisher*)

compared to each other. This is because the primary matter of these realms, which become milieus for manifestations which are more developed from each other, only have the ability to create the motions and forms particular to their own realms. So, the initial matter or atom of each realm is one of the ranges arrived at by the universe's original substance, in the journey ascending from its initial state to the universal whole, and each of these ranges carries the characteristic of that realm in its constitution.

*
* *

The primary matter of any realm is the initial matter of that realm. In this initial matter, there is the essence of all states and forms particular to that realm. The component that creates these states and forms is motion. And the quality and character of the motions are different in a manner to give birth to each realm's own properties. That is, there are separate forms of motions particular to each realm. Therefore, because the atom or nucleus which is the initial primary matter of a realm has not yet revealed the motions of that realm, it is in a motionless and amorphous state. These initial atoms, by displaying and varying, increasing and accelerating initial motions, gradually make up all states and forms particular to that realm.

As matter descends from above to below the appearance of their progress from motion to motionless, from activity to inertia, as an immutable rule constitutes the scientific observation of this truth.

The highest and most developed matter are those that have the most complex motions. In contrast, as matter descends below, in the development hierarchy their motions lessen, they regress to simpler states, and eventually they assume a state which is near to zero in regard to possibilities of motion in that realm.

*
* *

The reduction in the motion of matter as it descends offers another valuable observation. Since this reduction in the motions of matter and their simplification necessitates matter becoming more primitive, the reduction and simplification of influences external to that matter result in the corresponding reduction and simplification of

14

that matter's motions. For example, those who observe the structure of hydrogen and uranium atoms will see the truth of this.

The hydrogen atom is a matter state qualified by the motions of innumerable qualities and quantities. The uranium atom, which is a more complex form of this atom, carries within it many times more complex motions.

Moreover, the influence of a hydrogen atom on its surroundings is less than uranium's. So, the abundance of influences uranium has on its surroundings, compared to those of hydrogen, shows that it is receiving more influences than hydrogen does. Since the influences only manifest through the motions they cause in matter, the motions of uranium atoms are much greater and more complex than those of hydrogen atoms. Nevertheless, here, uranium's sending out more influences to its surroundings reflects the fact that it receives more influences, that is, it is displaying the reactions of the incoming influences accordingly. For, no influence is unilateral and in matter neither does a reaction occur without an action, nor is there an action that remains without a response.

*
* *

All state transitions and all the ways in which forms take place and change are only possible through the motions and diversification of motions. Therefore, the primary matter of our realm which has not yet exhibited any motions should hardly have any state and form particular to our world at all. That is why we call it amorphous – that is, the formless matter of our realm. Thus, primary matter is a reality[4] which can only be conceived and accepted theoretically in the face of our comprehension of the world and expresses an apparent absence; and this reality, in order to take particular forms appropriate to our

---

[4] *Reality*: One's surmise about existence which one relates to and can understand with one's senses and capabilities or the state of this surmise, as opposed to the truth. For each individual, the milieu he or she perceives is their reality. Their general surmise, composed of conclusions they have arrived at through their perceptions, is a reality for him. However, every reality is relative and incomplete compared to truth. In the following pages, you will find a passage on reality. (*Publisher*)

world, needs to gain many values that belong to the earthly sphere and go through many developmental stages.

*
* *

After imparting this knowledge, we proceed to the second important property of primary matter. Mankind may think this: How come that primary matter, despite the fact that it is comparatively inert and motionless – that is, devoid of the motions of our realm – starts to go through some developmental stages by assuming forms that have innumerable motions? In reply to this question, we will also consider the second property of primary matter we mentioned above. Here, we start with an example which everyone can see.

On the table there is a pencil which is stationary and motionless. Although this pencil carries innumerable motion complexities within its structure – compared to the rough matter in the room and in regard to our degrees of sight – it is devoid of any motion, that is, it does not stir. Now, if we push this pencil slightly with our finger, it changes position and slides away slightly – that is, it moves. This observation exhibits how matter starts to move with an external influence. If your finger, which occupies the seat of influence, did not push it, it could not move by itself. This is the first property of primary matter we mentioned earlier.

However, we also observe that when we push the pencil with our finger it immediately responds to this – that is, immediately reacts to an action. If it did not form any resistance against our finger, it would be impossible for it to move. In that case our finger would go through it, like an object moving through smoke. Thus, although motionless in itself, the possibility of responding immediately to any external motion also exists within the pencil. And this constitutes its second property. So, primary matter in its inert state which cannot afford to start to move by itself – or more correctly, has no motion in itself – has the possibility of responding to any influence coming from outside and of moving in the direction of that influence.

And since every motion is an influence against other matter that can constitute a resistance surface to it, that is, that can be

16

sympathised with it, so we express this knowledge with this formula: primary matter, which is motionless, formless and without influence in itself and has no power to move by itself, has the ability to start to move according to the form, direction, degree and intensity of any incoming influence to it from outside and to influence its own surroundings. That is, there is no power in matter to generate energy by itself but it has the possibility to start to move as the result of the external influence and to display energy manifestations.

The reaction, that is, the equivalent motion which has been evoked in primary matter by an external influence, does not continue after that influence ceases. Here, let us return to the above example. Let us slightly touch the pencil, which is standing still, with our finger and start to push it with a slight pressure. When the pressure from our finger stops, we see that the pencil also stops immediately and return to its previous motionless state. So, this pencil keeps its state only as long as the continuance of our finger's influence and the moment this influence ceases, it loses the possibility of movement.

If we give the pencil a powerful flick with our finger, it will move only as long as the influence of this flick continues and when the intensity of the influence disappears, it stops again. While we have given this example, we do not see the necessity of mentioning the technical variations that may come to mind in regard to the secondary resistance motions the surroundings may exert upon the pencil. By adding this reality to the two main properties of primary matter we mentioned above, we may say that primary matter, which is inert and motionless in itself, can only start to move as result of the external influences it receives and that it keeps its motion as long as these influences continue and when they cease it will again return to its motionless, inert state.

*
* *

Therefore, what we see as matter in our world is not the primary matter itself but the various forms and states it has taken since the moment it first started to move as a result of influences. However,

17

these forms and states are but the various manifestations of external influences that utilise the possibilities of motion which exist in primary matter. That is, every influence wakes up one of the possibilities of motion within matter which is latent and unable to wake up by itself. So, we call this transitioning of matter under influences by starting varied motions to take varied states the realisation of the possibilities hidden in them.

*
* *

We have arrived at a very important stage of the topic. Seeing that the original substance of the universe is devoid of motion by itself and in a formless and inert state, and seeing that it is not capable of motion by itself unless it receives influences from outside, then where do these influences that constitute such a vast universe, with its myriad realities by creating such infinite states and forms in that amorphous and inert substance, come from? And if matter cannot start to move by itself, what is the reason for its becoming engaged in infinite states and forms?

According to the knowledge of essence matter and of the disposition of matter, it is not appropriate for rational principles to accept that matter in the universe could breed these influences. There is the imperative to look for these in the truths that exist outside of the universe. And this is actually the situation. We will suffice with pointing out these truths as much as they could be intuited by mankind.

Even if our intuitions about the outside of the universe are weak and insufficient, our knowledge regarding the qualities and compositions of the matter-substance that constitutes our universe never stops compelling us to accept the imperativeness of the existence of supra-substance truths that cause myriad manifestations of this substance. Thus, what mankind calls spirit is also among these supra-substance truths. Therefore, spirit carries a quality that expresses the exact opposite of the main quality of universe-substance, which is inert and motionless.

*
* *

In universe-substances, there is nothing that belongs to spirit. Also, spirit has none of the properties that belong to universe-substances. In our universe, imagining and comprehending the disposition of spirit is out of the question. For, among universe-matter there is no word, no form at all sufficient to explain or identify it in detail. To accept the imperativeness of its existence without trying to study its disposition is the most suitable way to the truth.

Therefore, any similarity in any aspect, any direct relation or even proximity between spirit and any universe-substance is quite unthinkable. And any transition from one of them to another – that is, a direct exchange occurring between them – is also impossible. Between spirit and universe-substances there is an infinite inaccessibility.

*
* *

There is no such thing as the spirit within a body or on Earth or in the universe. Everything in the universe is all matter. And every event, every state and form are but myriad states and appearances of matter.

Spirit is not in the universe. Then where is it? Because the concepts of within and without, inside and outside, are realities particular to the universe, yet it cannot be said that spirit is outside of universe, because the outside of the universe is the inside of another universe. That is, there is no empty field which is outside of the universe. However, looking at these words and imagining universes as spheres within each other is also a mistake. No such thing exists. Actually, accepting universes as ever-widening spheres within each other would mean assigning spaces for them and drawing borders for such spaces, and this is wrong. Naturally, imagining the meaning and objectivity of these words by human comprehension is not possible. It is only possible to intuit this up to a point by contemplation. In order to give this intuition, we will show you an example. However, it is necessary not to take this example literally and to contemplate it in order to gain an intuition of it.

Reflect a projector with white glass into an empty space and let the appearance of the white-coloured light of this projector be the possibilities in a certain universe-substance. This is a whole universe in itself, with all of its truths and realities. Now, change the white glass of this projector with a blue one. This time a blue-coloured projector light will appear. This is also another universe which is completely different in quality and in possibilities than the previous one. For not to deviate into wrong thinking, it is necessary to mention a point with great care, which is that, like the blue projector we have mentioned, it is necessary never to think of imperatives – which again always exist with space – such as the idea that the white projector vanished and the blue projector replaced it, or that these two projectors are joined to each other and have created a mixed light combination, or again that one of these projectors has waned or changed on behalf of the other. Here, both projectors have their own existence without mixing with the other, without engaging in any kind of exchange, without losing anything from all their particular values and qualities – as if there is no other projector light than itself. This situation must be intuited at a deep level.

So, the existence of two universes may be intuited without assigning any space to them. When the projectors here are understood in this sense, they are neither inside nor outside of each other, nor do they occupy each other's space. Now, consider that these projector glasses we take as symbols are not in two colours but in three, five, one hundred and infinite colours and that they all manifest in the same manner. Then you will gain powerful insights about the infinite existence of universe-substances outside the concepts of time and space, without mixing with each other, without any question of relationship.

So, when the situation of spirit in relation to these infinite universes that know no space and limit is being considered, attempting to assign to it a place, a space that is bound to human comprehension on which mankind depends and which is insufficient even to encompass universes, is the biggest mistake. Therefore, regarding spirits utilising all universes as if they are in a deep embrace with them – without thinking of any direct relationship of spirits to any of these universes, without bringing up any direct contact of spirits to their substances even in the most distant manner – suffice it to say that spirits are quite beyond all concepts of universe-substances. To reach any further intuition than this is not possible for our world.

*
* *

The universe is not the only one. Universes are infinite. And the infiniteness of the universes is an imperative of absolute inaccessibility and unattainability. None of these infinite universes carries the quality of any other. And every universe's character emerges with its fundamental substance which is its principle. Our universe's fundamental or original substance is the matter state that is absolute, motionless and amorphous.

Spirit, which is active and in need of evolution, is a purpose for passive universes. That is, spirits meet their needs as they see the reflections of their behaviours over and over upon universe-substances. Therefore, universes are the field that respond to the needs of spirits which we call evolution. We express this symbolically as: universes are milieus – each one particular to their substances – that are useful for the applications of spirits and that reflect the consequences of these applications back to spirits. Spirits which are active evolve by indirectly using – according to their needs – the infinite possibilities of myriad universe-substances which are passive. If the universes did not exist, neither would the sublime needs of spirits that we do not know about be met, nor would the reason for the existence of universes remain if the spirits did not exist. These go together and are always in tandem with each other, to such a degree that, although an absolute and infinite inaccessibility and unattainability exists between these two, they are nevertheless, as it were, closely intertwined with each other.

*
* *

Here, this question comes to mind: seeing that there is such absolute inaccessibility and unattainability between spirits and universes, then how can spirits use all the possibilities of universes – even down to the tiniest particle – and how can spirits and universes embrace each other as if they were intertwined?

First of all, let us say that relations between spirits and universes that are separated from each other with an absolute inaccessibility and unattainability never ever occur directly but instead occur in

21

indirect ways. Here, it is necessary and imperative to state a great truth, which is as follows:

There are high principles governing both; above the myriad universes – which are organised following each other in an infinite sequence, with each one's quality composed of different substances and each more encompassing than the other and containing infinite variations – as well as above the spirits – which have infinite expansion and profundity and which will continue their endless evolution in these universes – and they determine, evaluate and affirm all states and destinies of spirits and universes in both a forward and backward direction. Of their qualities, we can neither know nor have the slightest insight.

For, this great truth is above the infinite spirit realm and the infinite chain of universe-substances; and separated from them by an absolute inaccessibility and unattainability. We cannot afford to say a word or to put forward an idea about the explanation of this truth we call the original principle. For, no power, capability, comprehension or intuition that may allow it exists in our matter-universe and cannot exist. However, we will mention this great truth – which is the unattainability of unattainability – with a symbolic name, as the original principle. Every truth, within the universes, above the universes and among the spirits, are under the governance and order of the original principle. All those occurrences, fluxes and everything can only be realised by its necessities. We leave all divine concepts about this to mankind's degrees of comprehension and especially their ability to intuit.

So, this apparent state of embracing each other, despite the inaccessibility and unattainability between spirits and universes, is realised by the necessities of this sublime principle we call the original principle. The force of the original principle, which on the one hand takes in spirits (these are symbolic expressions), also on the other hand takes in universes. And spirits and universes, in the presence of this sublime principle, are reflected in each other as if being reflected by a mirror. Naturally, this concept of a mirror is again symbolic and this symbol should not be placed with the original principle. Here, the point is to express the smallest aspect of the force of the original principle belonging to the relation of universes and spirits, by referring to the mirror symbol, and we can only express it in such a way.

Now, let us expand this knowledge with worldly language. Influences coming from the original principle set the amorphous universe-substances in motion according to the needs of spirits. And there they form infinite variations of matter-substance. Therefore, in regard to substance comparison, spirit is not within the universe but in regard to its representation and expression within the universe-substance through a subtle[5] matter being, it is within the universe. So, as they will be revisited in the following topics, we have provided here the first knowledge about the aim towards which the forming and transitions of matter are directed.

*
* *

Manifestation of a matter – that is, its emergence with its own particular properties amidst other matter in its milieu – means first of all its involvement in relation to other matter states and forms in certain proportions and degrees; more correctly, the fact that it is within means of interaction with them. So it means that the more the multitude and scope of influences a matter receives and gives, the more that matter manifests and the higher the stages of development it is in.

Of course, there is the order, sequence and ways of a matter's relations with its milieu. The order and sequence are executed by myriad influences coming from above, below, left and right to the matter combinations in accordance with the harmony of sublime principles. And the purpose of this execution is to allow spirits to evolve by utilising matter. Thus, if a spirit no longer needs a matter combination and does not act towards it, all motions of that matter combination – which are seen in the milieu it is in – vanish and all of its values which are particular to that moment cease to be; and we describe this – in mankind's language – as a kind of death or disintegration of that matter combination.

---

[5] *Subtle*: A term used to define that which is fine in density. (*Publisher*)

*
* *

Now, we will indicate the various mechanisms regarding the influences that are continuously coming into matter and causing its reactions; thus we will enter the topic of a very important reality which is directly pertinent to the constitution of matter, which is the duality[6] principle and the reality of value differentiation.

Matter's ability to realise its possibility of manifestation depends on the activity it will exhibit in its milieu. However, no activity occurs without motion. That is, the activity of a matter means that it displays motion. And the emergence of motion in matter is possible through equilibrium changes. Therefore, for motion to occur in the constitution of matter in our realm, first of all there must be two components that provide equilibrium and then, by adding more value to one of these components, the equilibrium must be disrupted in order to be restored again. So, the existence of these opposing components in matter and differentiating the values between these components express the reality of the duality principle and the reality of value differentiation.

Studying the duality principle and the mechanism of value differentiation which are pertinent to the constitution of matter makes it possible to explain the motions in matter.

There are myriad motion complexes in all universe parts, starting with the initial amorphous substance of our realm to those extending way beyond of it. These motions resulting in the manifestations of these parts with infinite qualities and quantities constitute two separate value groups in matter, which are exact opposites in character, but at the same time support each other, in accordance with the principle of equilibrium. In the case of one of these opposite values that remains in equilibrium in the structures of matter combinations receiving more charge – or more correctly, more influences – than the other one in comparison results in the disruption of equilibrium between them; and for these disrupted components

---

[6] *Duality*: A term used to express the opposition and complementary principle in nature and universe. Generally it is seen that it is used to express the physical milieu that contains opposite aspects such as good and bad, conscience and selfishness/self-centredness, altruism and selfishness, positive and negative. (*Publisher*)

of equilibrium to be restored back to a state of equilibrium, the value starts to flux from one of them to another and this condition causes various motions to occur. So, adding more value to one or another of the opposites to a certain degree to disrupt equilibrium creates different states between them. We name this state value differentiation or quantitative transitions.

*
* *

Therefore, every matter combination is but a unit which is the result of two opposite values. If we take only one of the opposites of this matter unit or matter combination which contains two opposite values we see again that this is also composed of two opposite values. This situation goes on like this back to the primary matter. Because of this, it is necessary to name each of these matter combinations as a duality-unit. This term may be defined as a unity that expresses two components.

In order to offer a simple idea about this duality-unit, we will give an example, although it is crude, of a bar magnet. This bar magnet is a unity, a unit that exhibits two kinds of magnetic manifestation – starting from the middle of it, one half is signed (+) and the other half is (-) – which are opposite in character. The point in the middle of this unit where two opposite values with different signs join together is neutral, that is, there is no magnetic manifestation there. By cutting this bar magnet from the neutral point, when we separately examine the halves that fall to the right and left side we again observe that each of them has entered a state of duality-unit on their own which exhibits magnetic manifestation with one half (+) and the other half (-) as opposites. As these pieces are continuously being split in the middle and separated into two parts, duality manifestations go on and on. That is, at each division of the bar magnet, components of magnetism with two opposite characters generate new unities, new units in smaller scale than the previous ones.

So, we name this reality – which is one of the most important laws of our realm – the duality principle belonging to matter constitution; and the value differentiation or quantitative transitions we have mentioned is an additional mechanism of this duality principle. The duality principle and its dependent mechanism of value differentiation form the most important basis, allowing the realisation of possibilities within the occurrences and fluxes of matter in our realm. Without these, neither states nor forms nor material manifestations are possible. For, when these principles vanish, no emergence of motion may occur in matter; and without motions, and the development and transitions of matter into myriad states, in brief, their involvement in the building mechanisms of worlds are not possible; that is, worlds cannot be formed.

*
* *

On Earth, duality always exists. In everything, in all radiations of matter, in the essentials and details of matter, in all psychological states that are actually variations of matter but appear as devoid of matter, in matter called inanimate, in matter called animated, in individuals, in states of individuals in the face of each other, collectively, in feelings and in ideas; shortly, in all conditions of the world observable and unobservable, the duality principle and the mechanism of value differentiation prevail. And in every state of matter that appears as a unity, there are always two components which are opposite to each other and in equilibrium. Existence of these opposite components in a unity is necessary because without this, matter cannot come forth, live; it disintegrates. And in the case of matter that does not exist, existence of anything cannot be talked about.

On Earth and in the whole of our cosmos, everything that appears as one or as a unity is actually composed of two values which are in opposite character to each other and which can never be isolated from each other. But these opposite values are not two independent, completely separate components from each other; they are two components dependent on each other but with opposite appearances that compose the character of an individual unit.

All parts that constitute our world and even the initial matter of Earth – which is one of these parts – cannot be outside the scope of duality principle. We repeat the main knowledge on this as a summary:

1. Unit is the name of duality. That is why we call it a duality-unit.

2. The opposites of duality are not made up of a single value. Again, in smaller scales they are each duality-units.

3. Duality, as will be explained in the topic on constitution of initial matter, is the initial origin and basis of motion.

4. Without the duality mechanism, motion cannot exist and without motion, matter states and forms cannot exist.

5. Duality is the original appearance of the state of spirit and matter.

Regarding the ideas mentioned in the last item, we feel the need to provide further explanation. We have said that in the matter-universe, spirit and matter cannot be in conjunction with each other. That is, the concept of spirit–matter directly interacting with each other in the universe cannot be a real concept. Nevertheless, from this statement, a meaning such as rejecting the existence of spirit and accepting only the existence of matter must not be inferred.

In effect, there is not a spirit–matter reality in the universe that directly exchanges influences between them, sending something to each other from themselves; however, the existence of matter, which constitutes the basis of the universe, is not without purpose and reason. We have mentioned before that the reason for the existence of matter is actually to service a spirit. The expression of this truth is hidden in the duality of matter, such that the purpose of matter's existence is its service to spirit. Servicing the spirit happens through spirit's utilising matter's possibilities of development in all kinds of states and forms. And utilising these possibilities depends on a number of motions that are able to emerge in matter through indirect influences arising from spirit. However, the occurrence of every motion in matter is only possible through the duality principle and the mechanism of value differentiation. That is, were it not for the duality principle and its additional mechanism of value differentiation, it would not be possible for spirit to utilise matter. In that case, the spirit–matter relationship cannot be realised. Therefore duality, the mechanism of value differentiation, is an expression of the necessity of spirit–matter duality. More correctly, when the duality principle in matter is examined in that regard, it becomes the original appearance of spirit–matter duality, that is, its imperativeness – in the face of the sublime principles.

*
* *

So, the duality principle which allows for the animation and occurrence of all matter has been placed in the constitution of matter as the basic structure, as it is set in its components by the original principle. The original principle is a divine principle. So, in this way, duality expresses the situation of spirit – which is not within the universe – and of beings in our universe – that is, of matter – with each other within the matter constitution. So, a being – a body – thus understands that it is not a spirit itself but a reflection of spirit in the universe, and is a being that responds to the needs of a spirit through all its states and situations, and that it reflects the need that represents the spirit. Because of this, when the term 'being' is used, the meaning intended in this regard is spirit. So, duality has been established to make this meaning possible.

*
* *

Life, throughout, is but the persistent observation of the duality principle and its dependent mechanism of value differentiation. The more mankind's comprehension increases and expands in this regard, the better they penetrate the nuances of details concerning the matter and events that are subject to these principles.

At first glance, it is possible to observe duality in rough states as well, because there is also duality in every matter form seen. The appearance of duality is obvious in the wholes and parts of this rough matter. For example, the activities of the human organism are executed through states of reciprocal equilibrium of two nervous systems: sympathetic and parasympathetic. These two nervous systems stand against each other in every organ of the body in opposite directions, such that, for example, in the heart, if the sympathetic system takes upon (+) roles and the parasympathetic system takes upon (-) roles then in the stomach where the sympathetic system takes upon (-) roles, the parasympathetic system takes upon (+) roles. That is, the states of stabilisation of these two nervous systems which are opposite to each other execute main deeds in the continuation of the organism's activities which constitute a whole. As one of these activates an organ and accelerates its duty, the other one which stands against it in an opposite character works to stop and to decelerate the same organ. So, by restraining the influences of the first system it limits its speed which can be detrimental and thus protects the organism. Here, shifting the equilibrium of these two nervous systems this or that way is regulated and supervised by the being who governs that body, according to the necessities and requirements of life.

We see the strongest manifestation of duality in the states of the sexes. A male and a female that came together constitute a duality-unit. They are both opposites and supporters of each other. In this way, their reciprocal states and relations allow the progression and well-being of the family unit on all sides. And the complete disruption of the equilibrium between these two opposites means the disintegration of the family. There is duality in feelings, as well: sympathy–antipathy, love–hate, friendship–enmity, selfishness–altruism etc. Similarly, there is also a duality in concepts: goodness–bad, beauty–ugliness etc. In short, it is possible to see and find duality in all crude states. However, it is also essential to see duality in more complex states.

If the duality principle is not supported by the value differentiation mechanism and stands alone, it will be useless and depreciated. The duality principle and value differentiation mechanism are two mechanisms attuned to each other for the realisation of a certain function and can engage in action through each other's existence. More correctly, value differentiation is the additional mechanism of the duality principle.

*
* *

Let us complete our explanation on value differentiation. First, we should explain what the value is. We have seen that matter states exist only through certain motions. In this case, the state of matter in a given stage means manifestation of the sum of motion complexes that exist in that matter at that moment. And this is a concept which makes that matter exist and which gives an identity to it particular to that moment. So in any given moment, the motion complexes, of matter that resulted in the presence in a milieu it is in, are a sum of values or of quantities for that being. Therefore, decreasing or increasing of the content of motion in a matter's constitution in this or that way means the differentiation of that matter's values, that is, the decreasing or increasing of these values. And this occurs through incoming external influences on one or other of the opposites of that matter unit. For, influence is a motion as well. So, this is the meaning we express by value differentiation or quantitative transitions.

In summary, more incoming influences at one or other of the motion complexes, which are opposites in kind to each other – that is, at one of two opposite values of a duality-unit – requires the value differentiation of that unity or unit. Therefore, incoming influences each have their own values. So, one of the opposites receiving more value than the other results in a disruption in the equilibrium that exists between these opposites. However, in accordance with the duality principle, these opposites must remain in a continuous state of equilibrium. So, in order for this disrupted equilibrium to be restored, a flux occurs from the more valued part to the less valued part; and the expression of this fluxing state of matter is motion. Through these motions that will occur in various directions, myriad transitions and re-creations upon the states and forms of matter transpire.

*

* *

In the duality of spirit and universe, it must never be forgotten that the responding of the universe-parts with complete harmony towards the behaviours of spirits that occur in accordance with their evolutionary needs is realised only by the necessities of the original principle. This principle reflects these behaviours of spirits upon matter-substance and returns the reactions of every matter-parts and whole by reflecting these back to spirits. That is, the needs of spirits are reflected to the universe as influences in accordance with the necessities of sublime principles. Because responding immediately to the needs which are reflected to the universe – that is, acting upon the necessities this influence carries – is the characteristic imperative of matter-substance, the response that matter gives through this imperative is again reflected back through the same channels with the same necessities to spirits. Here, this knowledge states one more time what the concept of necessity is and how vast and profound is the meaning it carries. In our universe, in universes and amidst spirits which are above the universes, necessity encompasses everything. Necessity is the expression of situations that are stated and determined in the original principle.

*
* *

Each word we utter, each statement we use, each example we give, is but the material facilities of our universe and none of these can have an authentic presence amidst the sublime values which are above the universe. Nevertheless, these are sufficient to put forth the materialised expressions of the truths within the universe as symbols and, by this, to give some intuitions. After all, there is no earthly being who can grasp it further than this. After stating this point, we return again to the mirror symbol.

We have said that by the necessities of sublime principles, the needs of spirits are reflected – as if from a mirror – to the universe and the response coming from there is reflected back to spirits. We wish to strengthen the intuition of this enormous truth which we have to put into a world example. By reconciling the mirror symbol here with world time and space, by thinking of the spirits on one side, and the mirror against them and the universe on the other side, considerations should not be carried out by trying to measure the reflections for certain periods of time in accordance with the distances between these. For, in the truths which are above the universe there are no states of time and space particular to our world. Nevertheless, by remaining devoid of time and space restrictions, it is necessary to accept the concepts of mirror-spirit-universe as if they are within each other and to look at the process which is intended by this symbol as if it occurs and ends at the same time – without assigning it a time period in the sense that mankind understands it. We vehemently wish to remind you that, as explained in the mirror example, the moment mankind fails to properly gain intuitions that are free from their accustomed time and space constraint, it is always possible for them to face the danger awaiting them. And this danger is a misconception. That is, this intuition of spirit-mirror-universe symbol we stated should never ever lead one to a concept of pantheism,[7] because the ones who understand well what is written know that such a concept has not been intended. The thought of sublime principles, spirits and universes merging into a single being leads mankind in a direction which is the exact opposite of the truths we wish to talk about; and sweeps away all of their higher intuitions.

*
* *

This is a certain truth that no part or whole of the infinite sequence of universes, which are of substances that have much more abundant possibilities and are superior to one another, and which therefore display capabilities that are able to respond to the more advanced needs of spirits, nevertheless cannot reach the level of spirits. Thus also the possibility of spirits, which originate from whatsoever universe-substance, cannot be thought of. There is an absolute inaccessibility between universes, universe-substances and spirits. This inaccessibility arises from the disposition of spirit and universe-substances. Because, if universes and spirits could give and take something from each other and had there been mutually substantial values which had the same disposition between them, there would not be the necessity of spirit and universe duality; and the meaning of evolution would be vanished. Similarly, it cannot be thought that universe-substances could change into each other through development or by any other means. The change of these substances into each other cannot be possible. Therefore, as it may arise in mankind's minds, a universe, by developing, cannot shift up to constitute a higher universe. That universe only – within vast possibilities that can be said to be infinite – congregates, disperses, and congregates, re-disperses again. This state is an infiniteness which no one can conceive.

If the transforming of universes into each other through time and development was a truth, then there would be no necessity and imperative for universe-substances to exist separately and for

---

[7] *Pantheism*: A belief that non-theistic divinity completely pervades all of nature, forming a unity between the creator and what is created. (*Publisher*)

universes to exist separately. And a single universe would remain forever as a milieu of evolution to spirits. But this state cannot be reconciled with the concept of the endless evolutionary needs of spirit. For, however infinite the possibilities it has, a universe, whose quality does not change and which remains of the same quality of substance, is not sufficient to meet the infinite needs of spirit. Such a concept of the single universe would lead to the need for spirits and universes to be of the same value and on the same plane; and this is completely contradictory to the spirit and universe duality and the idea of evolution. Therefore, the concept of the single universe is not in accord with the concept of endless evolution of spirit. Even if its infinite possibilities are accepted, the intuition of a single quality that will respond to the evolution of spirit which has infinite scope is one thing; the intuition of infinite possibilities of infinite qualities which have absolutely no similarity with each other is another thing. And the state which is worthy of the truth of spirits' endless evolution – that is, the state which is suitable for the truth of endless evolution which for reaching an end is out of the question; that is, the latter state – is the state of existence of infinite substances of which each one is of a completely different quality and which has infinite possibilities of development in particular characters. So, the truth of the endlessness of spirits' evolution can find its essential meaning and value only by undergoing endless evolutionary cycles in each of such infinite substance qualities.

*
* *

It is an imperative to accept the perpetuity of spirit's evolution. For, that unattainability of unattainability, which we cannot mention by name, which even our intuition cannot reach in any way, determines that spirits will never enter the state of total accomplishment, of absolute perfection, and will never ever be able to be free of their evolutionary needs. Therefore, the factor which determines the unattainability of universes for spirits also determines the truth of spirits that are not able to elude the imperative of endless evolution.

The factor which determines the endless evolution of spirits also governs the truth that spirits will never attain the original principle. And the factor that determines that spirits will never be able to attain the original principle is the imperative of the unattainability of unattainability which is above everything – even its smallest relation to everything that is the whole of wholes is out of the question – and which is impossible to express by any name for all that cannot enter our minds, imaginations, feelings, but here, for the sake of exigency, we will mention a word without considering any of its connotations – 'Allah' [God]. Accepting this truth as it is, without hesitation and without making it a subject of discussion, is the greatest of the imperatives and also the only direction of the path of deliverance.

*
* *

Necessities coming from the original principle, oriented to evolutions of spirits, by entering from the uppermost boundary (these expressions are symbolic) of our universe, emerge as influences in the universe; and at the uppermost boundary of the universe, of which we do not know, by filtrating through the unitary which will be discussed later, in accordance with the infinite possibilities of development and capability of matter combinations, as subjecting these and themselves to myriad formations, transformations and deformations starting from the higher to the lower as they descend while expanding, scattering and reaching the points they would arrive at and manifesting in accordance with the needs of spirits, they accomplish their functions of indirect exchange between spirit and substance. Through whatever being, whichever stage each influence passes it exactly carries a necessity. And this necessity contains the evolutionary needs of spirits which the matter or beings are subject to at the stage the influences arrive. Therefore, no particle of the universe is free of these influences.

We repeat: the needs of spirits of which we can never appreciate and know their quality, reason and results, because of the absolute and natural impossibility of our universe and their evolution which we accept as the allotted share to our universe are provided through applications in the universe in accordance with the necessities of sublime principles. In order to execute this purpose, necessities coming from the original principle are distributed across the unitary which occupies the uppermost level of the universe. And there, these influences constitute a unity. So, these necessities which are unified with the unitary, filtrate through the unitary as influences and are scattered to the communities, individuals, matter and beings, to all parts of matter down to the smallest particles as in accordance with the needs of each being and generate myriad transformations, deformations and formations. And through this mechanism of influences, the progress and flow of the universe is achieved. The relations of beings with spirits, with each other and with matter are established and so the development of the universe goes on towards its determined aim.

*
* *

We need to talk here about the concept of being – which we just mentioned – and which we will address again later. Being is a matter unit; more correctly a complex of the influences that carry the necessities of the original principle and pertain to spirits; a matter unit which is synthesised by a given spirit through congregating among matter which as at a certain stage of development to service itself until the end of universe. So each being is an evolutionary vehicle assigned to the service of a certain spirit until the end of the universe. This is such a being that it expresses all necessities of spirit's behaviours which occur in the supra-universe plan. And these expressions are reflected to spirit as if reflected from a mirror. Therefore, the being is the symbol of a spirit, to whom it serves, in the universe. So, because the being in the service of a spirit completely expresses all the behaviours, stirrings and needs of that spirit, we can also look at it as the spirit itself. For, every manifestation that appears on that being is but an expression that is reflected to the universe, representing the appearance of spirit's behaviours – in proportion to the allowance of the matter possibilities it uses. And when spirit is no more, all expressions and manifestations belonging to it will vanish and the being will disintegrate at once.

*
* *

The being has a two-sided function in the universe. One of these is simply as a laboratory vehicle for the spirit; the other is as a symbol of spirit amidst matter. As a result of these two functions, the being also needs a field of application. Therefore, in order to properly reflect reactions the spirit awaits from it, it has to gather the necessary elements of these reactions from its milieu, that is, to procure from the beings and matter in its vicinity. Expanded knowledge will be given later on this topic.

*
* *

Now, here, a problem needs to be solved that may come up in mankind's minds. Seeing that the being is but matter combinations with all of its actions and activities, all of its emotions and thoughts, then what does it gain from serving a spirit which has no direct relation to itself? In other words, what will it achieve from going through bitter and sweet experiences, working, striving so much for the evolution of spirit – without even knowing about the quality and form of this – to whom it serves? And if one day, with the departure of that spirit from the universe, it will go back to its endless darkness as a zero after completing such advanced stages of development in parallel to the evolution of the spirit it serves, will all the activities it executed throughout the development of a universe be gratuitous?

Such a thought that may come arise in the minds of mankind can make them pessimistic and lead them to mental confusion. However, before anything else, if some deep thinking is conducted upon the knowledge we have given above about the relations of matter and spirit, it will be understood that the situations causing such discussions are only appearances and that the truth is not such. Nevertheless this topic needs to be illuminated so as not to leave a dark spot in our thoughts. Let us take first, an amorphous matter. There is no motion, no form in it. But when this amorphous matter enters into the state of being, together with qualities that belong to the whole being, many capabilities and states occur in it, starting with the simplest and increasingly ascending, such as loves, sympathies, antipathies, compassions, acts of conscience, thoughts, judgments. Now, let us explain the relations of these manifestations with amorphous matter which may compel the minds of mankind.

In truth, all ways of humane action, moods, emotions and thinking, beliefs of people to which they attribute spiritual values and con-

36

sider supra-matter are but matter function whose liquidity is in increase. However, until now, mankind should not have to see this truth so openly. Not until they could execute tests and experiences that had to be undergone in these realities safely and soundly. But now, today, truths are explained as they are. For, mankind has attained the strength of learning the truths openly. It is possible to give many examples from the world on this topic. The purest, the most sentimental and ideal emotions, thoughts and acts which appear as supra-matter are only the manifestations of the most fluid material possibilities of the world. Many actions that are given an expressive quality by mankind as emotional acts involving love are the expression of a high possibility to sympathise, of a high-matter fluidity, of a high-matter capability of encounter, interaction and encompassment.

Likewise, all antipathies, sympathies, grudges, cruelties, selfishness, altruism, self-devotion, gratification, bliss, suffering – in short, all values pertaining to all feelings and ideas that are called subjective: imaginations, thoughts, ideals, faiths, creeds, powers of invention and creativity, talents, genius, passions, desires, afflictions, habits and all states that are called psychological: fears, courageousness, treacheries, truculence, feelings of good and bad etc. are the manifestations of energies of various kinds that diffuse from matter that exists on Earth but is not recognised yet by the comprehensions of mankind. Therefore, mankind's mastering these, overcoming these, means their mastering matter, overcoming matter. In none of all these realities called spiritual, moral or psychological has matter been overstepped. What has been used here is always matter. However, to know this has not been possible for mankind until now and this was, as we said, a necessity. This truth will be known by mankind from now on.

We had previously said that there are many other elements above and below of the matter-parts and elements constituting the Earth and these are not yet known by mankind. Similarly, we had also mentioned that in these elements unrecognised by mankind there is a constitution of hydrogen atom of such quality that it exhibits substance-states in completely different capabilities which are above and beyond the knowledge of mankind about all manifestations of energy radiating from an atom. Material possibilities radiate from this hydrogen atom unknown to mankind and are so fluid and powerful as to compel the comprehension of mankind, prepare the possibility for and cause the occurrence of many events that mankind has never been able to comprehend so far.

In summary, spirit is involved with matter. It brings about the state of conscious matter that is called body. Afterwards, spirit is completely bound by the conditions of that body. And within these conditions, all of its states that are called spiritual, moral and psychological – other than its organic activities – are bound by the brain and nervous system, that is, by the possibilities and capacities of the brain and nervous system. We will later explain the roles of states and actions assumed to belong to spirit but which, in truth, originate in matter, in the evolution mechanism.

But so far we have always talked about the side of these states that belongs to matter. If this was all there was, then it would necessitate justifying the anxieties – which we mentioned above – that people fret about. But despite the truths we have just explained, if we bear in mind the essential knowledge about matter – that it is powerless for any motion by itself – things will change. For, this knowledge teaches us that no stirrings in matter are by the matter itself. Matter is absolutely devoid of power to do this. Therefore, any motion, any stirring of a being is the expression of a situation that has not been caused by itself. And there cannot be anything else. Otherwise, it would entail rejecting the main quality of matter and this is not possible.

So, we name all expressions which are not matter the being displays in all of these motions that are matter, the state of spirit in our universe. Thus, sublime manifestations called psychological, such as all kinds of love, thought, conscience that have occurred in a being through infinite motions, combinations, forms and states as matter, are in effect the counterparts of spirit's infinite behaviours which exist in its own plan and, unknown to us, have been translated into ideal, emotional and vital forms in accordance with the matter-possibilities of the universe. Therefore, in belonging to being, it leaves nothing else but matter motions and it makes it clear that all meanings and expressions in these motions belong to spirit.

As an example of this, let us take comprehension. Mankind comprehends. Who comprehends is mankind. In their nervous system structure there are such subtle combinations that these are continuously transmitting and receiving vibrations, energies that manifest as comprehension. And the health or ill-health of the comprehension capability depends on the motions that occur as a result of interventions which are carried out by external influences through the duality principle and value differentiation mechanism upon these very subtle matter combinations in the nervous system which transmits and receives these energies. So, comprehension with its outer appearance occurs in matter and emerges with material vibrations. Therefore, it is a matter.

Nonetheless, at the same time, it is also a counterpart, an expression of spirit's behaviours in matter that is reflected in the universe as if reflected from a mirror. That is, comprehension's state in motion belongs to matter. And its state in regard to expression belongs to spirit. So, this expression that belongs to states of spirit which are supra-universe has been only interpreted and represented by the comprehension mechanism in the universe through depending on the possibilities of matter motions – within a completely material reality.

More briefly, comprehension is the technical expression of a behaviour in matter, which exists in spirit, with a quality that is unknown by the inhabitants of the universe. So, a day will come when the spirit will abandon the being depending on it in the universe for all time and the abandoned being will disintegrate; but what will disintegrate are only the combinations, forms and motions of matter that carry these emotions, ideas and many more of these myriad expressions of which we do not know and which are to come in future. And originals of these states in spirit – of their quality we cannot know – that appear in matter motions will continue their infinite occurrence and flow, together with spirit. Actually, the loss of all those expressions the being carries with the departure of spirit and its returning back its inert and amorphous state at once constitutes the most obvious proof of this truth.

Thus, in this way, we have expressed the fact that states that occur in a being are in effect only material symbols, material appearances each of much vaster and encompassing states and behaviours that exist in the realm of spirits, of whose quality we do not know. That is why when being is spoken of, we remember spirits and understand that events involving beings only belong to their counterparts in the realm of spirits, of whose quality we do not know.

*
* *

It is necessary to separate the concepts of advancement of matter in parallel with those of spirits by mentioning the terms *development* and *evolution*. For, these are separate things. Development is the state for matter in universe; of the increasing of motions in their constitutions, of the complexity of their material combinations, of widening of their fields to be targeted by influences, of increasing their values. And evolution is the state in parallel with developments in beings which are in service to spirits. This situation is a part of the endless needs of spirits – of which we never can penetrate their quality – that need to be fulfilled in our universe and which is expressed by the evolution symbol in our world. So, the meaning of evolution walks in parallel with the meaning of developments which are its expression within matter. Therefore, studying the progress of evolution means studying the forms of development and progress of the being, which is a vehicle to it, and of matter which is the vehicle to this being.

*
* *

Of a spirit that will start its evolutionary application in the universe for the first time, its initial states belonging to this application are reflected in the amorphous states of the universe. This reflection is done by the channel of influences. And influences are the expression and manifestation of the force – which we call necessity – of the original principle which encompasses and governs both the world of spirits and universes, of which quality we will never understand, nor even intuit – upon the spirit–matter states belonging to our universe. These influences, carrying the needs of spirits to universes, bring about motions in matter – which we have previously mentioned – through the duality principle and the value differentiation mechanism. Thus, motions in universe are the symbolic expressions of the stirrings and behaviours of spirits, which are manifested as matter constitutions through the channel of these influences. So, influences belonging to the simple, novice spirits, entering the universe for the first time, allow this initial matter at once to become fields of observation for these spirits.

*
* *

Response of matter as motions to the influences coming from a spirit are again reflected back to the same spirit by returning from that channel of influence. In this way, in depending on the necessities of original principle and by the help of these powers, the indirect relation of spirit and matter is established and spirit gets, for that moment, what it gets from matter. Afterwards, according to the new needs of that spirit, its observations continue via the same ways and manners in other matter either existing at the same matter stage or in a higher matter stage. For the spirits at the initial stage, an evolutionary need of a spirit corresponds to every moment of matter in the developing state. In other words, any state of the development in matter becomes a mechanical application ground for any spirit. The state of spirits here is only to obey those motions. The stage we mention is the initial and crudest stage of the universe; this stage, which is darkness for us, exists below the hydrogen stage we will mention later. All proceedings at this stage are executed, in accordance with necessities of the original principle, but within the scope of the governance mechanism encompassing the universe which is established by the unitary in the uppermost boundary of universe, through ways of which we do not know. We can only say – although vaguely – that the progress of novice spirits that need to evolve at this stage is subject to a mechanical and passive evolutionary principle.

Because the evolutions of spirits at this initial simple matter stage are not easy and fast as the development of matter, spirits at this stage do not remain connected to a single matter. At each moment they change milieus. In this way, as spirit leaves a matter which is relatively more advanced than itself to a more deserving spirit, it continues to progress as always passive, that is, without intervening with matter motions in the simpler matter within the lower matter stages in which it exists with its slow progression.

41

*
* *

This initial stage advances from spirit's first involvement with the universe until it reaches the first hydrogen atom of matter. This spirit has not yet been in possession of a body in the universe, because there are not yet any powers in it to gather universe-matter. Because of this, it will only be subjected to a passive and mechanical progress in the simple matter-states in accordance with the necessities of the sublime principles, which appreciate its first needs in the face of the universe, filtrating from the unitary. During that time, it will not have a material identity manifesting as comprehension, will, consciousness and freedom in universe. Gaining such an identity will only be possible gradually, in conformity with the order of sublime principles – in proportion to its needs – which after cycles as long as infinity it will go through, always as passive and mechanical amidst amorphous matter.

Because of this, for spirits at these initial matter stages, there are no active states entailing will, freedom and comprehension. They have not yet been connected to some matter constitutions in the universe. These novice spirits, while at this stage, for their simple reflections to be developed through mechanical ways, they are made to encounter myriad states and motions of matter by being plunged in and out (these words are not true but symbolic because spirits can never be plunged into matter) of one matter state to another, and if necessary into another matter state. In matter at this initial stage, there are none of the motions and forms seen in our universe. And these are in formless, amorphous, disarrayed states, relative to our realm, which their general ensemble brings out of an amorphous milieu. Following this developmental stage of initial universe-matter, a higher state which we call the hydrogen state – the one our cosmos is subject to – will occur. Now, we give knowledge relating to this stage.

*
* *

Primary matter which is the beginning of our cosmos is composed of matter of the primal, disarrayed milieu which makes up the initial universe stage. We have seen that matter constitutions come into existence in our cosmos through the duality principle and value

42

differentiation mechanism. As a consequence of this reality, the occurrence of initial states and forms of the original substance in our cosmos must be studied together with these mechanisms. Knowledge to be given about the stirrings of the initial atom of the hydrogen cosmos with the world's language and words will rather be symbolic and depend on intuitions. For, mankind actually has no knowledge at all about the forms and qualities of the initial motions in the cosmos. We have said that as human comprehension stops in the realities belonging above our cosmos after a certain point, neither can it probe beyond a certain point below it. However, the bases of the laws and principles that are valid in our matter-universe are one. Here, what changes are not these bases but forms and manifestations of these laws and principles, occurring according to cosmoses. This situation helps mankind to attain some comparative intuitions that they need about various realities belonging to the lower and higher parts of our cosmos, so these intuitions are enough to complement the knowledge about the universe for mankind. Now we may start to explain how the initial hydrogen atom is constituted.

We have previously said that the initial matter of our cosmos is the hydrogen atom and this is completely different from the hydrogen atom known by mankind and is but a very primitive version of it. Again, we have also mentioned that – because it is the initial matter of our realm – this atom, which is so simple and primal that mankind cannot recognise it, is a matter closest to the amorphous state. As mentioned before, in the universe, this initial stage, ruled by the mechanical evolution principle, is only composed of an infinite, dark, disarrayed and amorphous milieu which is the sub-stage of hydrogen atom. Evolution here has been connected to a completely mechanical system. At this stage, matter is not gathered but disarrayed. Because the spirits, which at this stage are only rendering mechanical applications, have not yet attained the power to gather matter. Because of this, these simple spirits follow a primal path of evolution which is endlessly mechanical and impossible for mankind to understand, drifting by jumping from this matter to that matter, without connecting any matter – due to the sublime necessities of original sources – amidst the disarrayed, formless matter of this primal milieu.

And here, as they are evolving passively, after a long cycle that seems like eternity, some of these spirits slowly become advanced enough in their evolution to gather this disarrayed matter. As a ground for the following evolution of a spirit that has reached such a state, an influence comes from the unitary upon a point within this amorphous milieu. This influence, despite displaying characters opposing each other, as one belonging to a spirit that is connected to that matter – that is, belonging to a spirit that attained the state of becoming able to grasp that matter, and another belonging to the constitution of that matter which is in the process of constitution – is composed of two influences supporting, complementing each other, in short, directed to the same target. And of course, both of these are again, a manifestation of the original influence which appears two-fronted in the universe. These two opposite influences constitute a matter unity, that is, a duality-unit. These components are part of the amorphous matter existing in that milieu, immobilised into a congregated state under the incoming influences; because the magnetic field caused by these motions collect this disarrayed matter together. And these motions are the initial motions of the hydrogen cosmos that are arranged by the original influences in accordance with the necessities of connecting a spirit to that atom.

Fields that are composed of such initial atoms bring out the initial states of myriad nebulous fields that make up all the bodies, spheres and systems of the astronomical cosmos. So, a spirit has been connected to the initial atom which originated in this way. In other words, the need of this spirit to connect to this atom has caused the occurrence of this atom due to necessities of the original principle. And the original influence, descending into an amorphous milieu by carrying the necessities of this need of spirit, has provided its connection with this atom.

So hydrogen atoms that are composed of two components, opposing each other but in a state of equilibrium, make up the primary matter in the simple states of our cosmos.

*
* *

44

A spirit that is connected to the initial atom, that is, to the hydrogen atom of our cosmos, will not leave it until a moment when an advance stage of that atom will occur, which we call being. Here, again, there is a mechanical-automatic evolutionary progress. That is, spirits in that first stage of the evolution of hydrogen will continue in their evolution by passively following all successive developmental stages of the primal hydrogen atom which they grasped at first. During that time, they are not prevailing upon the hydrogen atom. For, there exists neither intuition, comprehension nor freedom in them that determines such a prevalence. These are not in a situation to bring out a being from various matters by gathering them. Therefore, their evolution processes are more or less passive and mechanical as the ones in the initial stage. There is one difference in between that while in the stage of amorphous milieu, beings could not hang on a matter at all. For, there they were not actually in a state in which they were able to grasp any matter. They were only rendering their mechanical applications by jumping from matter to matter, under the necessities of original influences amidst disarrayed matter. In the initial stage of the hydrogen cosmos, beings are connected to the hydrogen atoms they grasped.

They cannot jump to another atom than the one they are connected to. And throughout the whole development of that atom, they follow its developmental stages except that meanwhile they are not prevailing on that atom. They only participate passively in its motions and grow accustomed to adapt to these motions. For, these motions are constituted under the sublime necessities of original influences and take on their directions. There, spirits will complete the application cycle which will take a very long time until the stage of being, under these necessities and by becoming captured, that is, by becoming passively led; obeying these motions. Starting from the constitution of this initial hydrogen atom until the occurrence of the initial state of being, the influence which prevails upon the structure of the atom is the prime influence, that is, the influence coming from the original principle and of this, as we have said, a side exists which belongs to the spirit that has connected to that atom. So, in this original influence descending into this atom, there are sides; one material side, belonging to the structure of the atom and also a spiritual side, incoming as belonging to spirit.

Thus, influences belonging to spirits and incoming indirectly, through the channel of original influences, will only render their mechanical applications by adapting to the determined motions of the atom. As they progress towards the stage of being by this application, they automatically do preparations of initial instincts belonging to the states of relations between matter in the face of the causality principle. Evolution in this cycle is very long and arduous for spirits. Of course, concepts of arduousness and length here are relative. Actually, there is no such thing either as length, shortness, arduousness or easiness in the divine order.

*
* *

The hydrogen atom, even though it is the simplest matter of our cosmos, carries more or less a vast amount of energy, because it has acquired many influences and values before reaching this stage, starting from the initial amorphous matter-state of universe. Let us remind you once again that the hydrogen atom we talk about here is not the hydrogen (H) known by chemistry. The hydrogen atom we talk about is a matter combination which is the primary atom of our cosmos that includes all solar systems, stars, nebulae known by mankind through telescopes – in short all astronomical bodies; and the hydrogen atom known by chemists is one of the very advanced and developed states of this hydrogen atom we mentioned as the initial matter of our cosmos.

As it is in all matter in our cosmos, for the hydrogen atom as well, sustaining its state and its presence and continuously making progress is only possible by the equilibrium sums of the many matter-parts hidden within each other in accordance with the duality principle and value differentiation mechanism and these equilibria are governed by the original influences.

*
* *

Now, we will start explaining how the hydrogen atom has developed until entering the stage of being.

We have stated that below the hydrogen state there is an endless milieu of mechanical development and evolution. This milieu, as we have said, is a dark field making up a disarrayed whole, akin to an amorphous state.

The original influences, after constituting the initial nucleus in this dark milieu, by gathering other parts around it, bring out increasingly more complex, more complicated and more developed states. And the original influence, in the centre of the matter constitution which has been brought out in this way, after being used within this constitution, starts again to radiate from that matter to the outside, as its original state is lost and its quality is changed; and we call it the magnetic field of that body.

So, all spheres and constitutions of the hydrogen cosmos, from its smallest parts to its largest systems, occur in this way.

After the initial hydrogen nucleus is constituted as such, by developing in the way we mentioned above, it eventually reaches the stage of the hydrogen (H) atom known by chemistry.

To the initial hydrogen atom constituted under the governance of the original influences as such, until its utmost stages of development – that is, until it reaches the state of being – only the original influence and the influences belonging to the spirit that is connected to that atom arrive. That is, of the original influences – which we will later explain as we talk about influences – the parts belonging to spirits that we call evolutionary values and the parts belonging to matter that we call prime influence, arrive. Therefore, the motions in the structures of these atoms are only under the governance of the sublime original influence. Spirits, by passively drifting, adapting to these motions render their mechanical-automatic evolution. This is a kind of passive adaptation stage of the evolution. At this stage, influences belonging to other beings that we call secondary influences do not arrive at the structures of atoms. Actually, because the freedom and comprehension of spirits are not in question here, the tests and trials belonging to further stages do not exist. They only have to automatically adapt the regularly progressing and increasingly complex motions of atoms. And while adapting these complicated motions of atoms more and more, they are preparing for the stage of being.

However, gathering various kinds of hydrogen atom to bring out various objects is necessary for the development of beings. So, to these compounds and combinations of atoms, known by mankind as 'objects', secondary influences arrive from the beings in duty – again, under the sublime control of the unitary and these render various formations, deformations and transformations in these objects. Nevertheless, unlike what is the case for atoms, no more direct prime influences descend to these compounds. Instead, secondary influences prevail. And of course, these are always under the control of original influences.

*
* *

The structure of the initial hydrogen atom – as just mentioned – continues its development only under the governance of original influences, until it reaches the state of being and elements occur, which are developed states of hydrogen atom, known by mankind by such names as oxygen, silver, platinum, lead, radium etc. Of these mankind could only recognise about a hundred, but their numbers exceed a hundred.

Again, as we have said, the transformation of the hydrogen atom into higher elements occurs only by the efficacy of the original influences. Thus, after ensuring the development of matter up until the stage of being, from that moment on, prime influences do not directly arrive at being; only influences from the spirit it is subject to, or more correctly from the part of the original influence belonging to spirit and influences from beings which are in various evolutionary stages in universe arrive, and we call the former secondary influences. So, with all these influences, that being starts going through the tests, trials and experiences which are necessary for its evolution and encounters many possibilities.

Amidst these evolutionary possibilities, which are gradually developing, increasing and encompassing – in order to accomplish its doings in the universe – that being sets out on its long journey of evolution. As of necessity for its evolution, with the secondary influences arriving from these beings in duty, as we have just mentioned, out of various elements of hydrogen atom endless combinations are constituted and myriad objects are made up. And by various formations occurring through the assembly and dispersion of these objects within infinite variations, large and small objects, matter combinations, bodies, miscellaneous matter that fill up the worlds, and finally worlds and systems are constituted. All of these are done with innumerable secondary influences sent by beings in

48

duty and who exist at every stage, under the light of original influences filtrating from the unitary.

Therefore, secondary influences cannot intervene in the structure of atom. It is completely under the governance of prime influences. However, all kinds of combinations of atom elements can be built or dispersed by the secondary influences arriving from beings in duty, which are naturally in large or small scale according to the degrees of beings that are at various levels of evolution.

*
* *

The structure of the hydrogen atom, which is increasing, developing more and more from its most primitive state, gains as much as motion, power and efficacy. And spirits connected to these, as they adapt to these motions which are increasingly enriched and powered, evolve. Factors that awoke all these motions in matter are influences arriving from original sources. This is because influences render their functions by evoking motions in matter.

In short, the original influences which constitute hydrogen atoms in accordance with the necessities they carry, by continuously collecting parts from surroundings, develop the hydrogen atom up to a higher realm. Naturally, by its development, the energies of the hydrogen atom will radiate and increase, growing stronger accordingly, and as the hydrogen atom develops it starts to diffuse higher and more complex energies, that is, more developed particles. However, all of these constitute matter still belonging to the initial stage of hydrogen atom.

Here, let us mention that this development of hydrogen does not occur in a manner of a sketchy accumulation of atom nuclei within an atom by preserving their separate identities. The values accumulating in the atom under the governance of original influences make up the structure of a hydrogen atom which characterises its quality at that moment by fusing in complete harmony and equilibrium but without becoming united.

*
* *

All matter has magnetic fields. The magnetic field of such a developed atom is not simple as it is in the initial hydrogen nucleus. Because there are many particles in a hydrogen atom which is made up of compositions of hydrogen nuclei and each particle has a magnetic field, the magnetic field of this developed atom is made up of synthesis of the magnetic fields of the parts which constitute it. We call this field magnetic fields synthesis.

These magnetic fields of matter are very important. For, all their relations with each other and with beings are provided through these magnetic fields; and the secondary influences arriving at these fields, according to their intensity, power and direction, can render – under the rules of the duality principle and value differentiation mechanism – myriad changes, metamorphoses, deformations, dispersions and congregations in the structures of matter to which they [magnetic fields] are subject. Similarly, the utilising of matter by beings, who are able to put these into various states, is done in this way. Beings in duty, utilising the Earth's magnetic field which is encompassing and vast, naturally in that ratio – by sending miscellaneous influences to this field – generate large or small natural phenomena on Earth. Like this, influences coming from a being with far superior comprehension, who is influential on these magnetic fields, generate much larger results upon the matter belonging to them. Basically, motions that may influence states and situations of worlds, systems, suns in this way are only the deeds of very sublime plans. And of course, these are controlled in accordance with the necessities of the original principle.

Wherever matter exists, it is imperative that there exists a magnetic field. After all, the knowledge we have previously given about the constitution of magnetic field makes it easy to understand this truth. So, as an atom has a magnetic field, so do all developmental stages of an atom – that is, of elements, of objects composed of these elements, of worlds, of systems, and also of nebulae, of cosmoses, of beings that have magnetic fields syntheses, which are more or less encompassing, more or less complex in comparison with each other. And above all, the magnetic field of the unitary which consists of the whole universe is single. There is no magnetic fields synthesis there. For, in the unitary, the existence of separate and distinctive beings or components is out of the question.

*
* *

So what mankind calls *périesprit* is also nothing but these magnetic fields of matter. That is, magnetic fields of human bodies are what people accept as the meaning of *périesprit*.

So a spirit utilises matter by influencing its magnetic fields through its being which is a representative of itself in the universe and is but an energy complex. And out of this matter, it establishes bodies which are appropriate for its application in the worlds that these belong to; and through these bodies, by influencing magnetic fields of other beings and the matter of that world and by utilising them, it establishes its evolution.

We have said that just as complex magnetic fields synthesis exist for a world, complex magnetic fields syntheses also exist for solar systems and nebulae, which are much more complex than that. Beings do their duty by influencing these realms through the channels of these fields. For example, there exist very sublime beings in duty, comprising of a few solar systems, even a few nebulae, which they govern by influencing their magnetic fields.

*
* *

Matter mentioned so far has not yet entered into the stage of being.

Here, it must be stated that those who have learned the knowledge given from the start should have understood now that terms like the animate and inanimate in the universe are but words and do not carry a thorough meaning. The order and arrangement of indirect relations of matter with spirits both in the initial stages and in the hydrogen stage make it impossible to render discernment such as life and non-life. For, in every matter of universe-stages, various relations of spirits to matter in accordance with the character of that stage and evolutionary system always exist. And in the universe there is no matter that is not dedicated to the evolution of any spirit. That is, there is no matter-state which is not temporarily or continuously under service to spirits. This situation is especially obvious for all matter in the hydrogen stage. A matter considered

51

out of this service is unnecessary and purposeless. And in the universe, there is no unnecessary process at all.

In this case, it is unwarranted to sink into thoughts such as when matter is connected to spirit it is animate and when it is not it is inanimate. For, every matter has a temporary or continuous connection to a spirit. However, even wishing to call beings animate by seeing that matter is continuously connected to a being is not right either. For, spirits also connect to the previous hydrogen atom in the sub-stage of being until its state of being. Therefore, following the knowledge above, the notion of discerning matter as animate or inanimate is meaningless.

*
* *

Spirits, rendering applications in the initial hydrogen states which have not yet entered the state of being, prepare passively and mechanically in this matter.

This matter is not under the governance of spirits that will render applications. They are only each constituted as grounds, allowing the adjustment of initial student spirits in the universe, with influences coming from the unitary in accordance with the necessities of sublime principles.

So far, necessary knowledge has been given about the development of matter and about spirits obeying these developments by a mechanical form of progress. Now, we may start giving knowledge about the transitions of this matter into separate beings; about the transitions of spirits to the automatic or semi-comprehending evolutionary stages in our cosmos.

Constituted matter that has been turned into an initial hydrogen atom had been grasped by a spirit. That spirit is connected to that atom. However, as we have mentioned, it is not in the situation of governing it. Spirit cannot step out of the ordered and organised motions of matter that emerged with the original principle; it tries to adapt to them. In this spirit, there is yet no intuition, even no mechanical instincts at all. All the while, as the hydrogen atom does motions and developments in the direction determined by original influences, and oriented to the evolutionary purpose of the spirit which is connected to it, it services the evolution of spirit. As the result of this development, the hydrogen atom turns into hydrogen (H) as known by mankind. And successively, the elements known by chemistry emerge. This state is elevated to higher states and the motions of atoms become complicated. Regarding its values, its structure enriches. In its structure various groupings, gatherings and systems occur. Its magnetic fields synthesis enters into more complex, more complicated states. In this way, the hydrogen atom, by passing through many stages, transforms into the states of oxygen, phosphorus, copper, silver, barium, platinum, gold, radium, uranium, centurium.[8]

As the hydrogen atom develops in this way, the spirit which is connected to it and adapting to its motions also develops very slowly with a mechanical-automatic tempo. As this evolution of the spirit accrues, preparations for some of its instinctual behaviours pertaining to various motion combinations, in other words, pertaining to relations within matter, are done as well.

Eventually, the hydrogen atom starts to exuberate from the cadre of the highest elements known to mankind. And it enriches its structure with larger combinations – which have started to transmit high energies – that mankind cannot detect or posit. Meanwhile, preparations of the spirit – which is both causing this development and whose evolutionary progress is in parallel to it – for its initial behavioural instincts pertaining to relations between matter combinations, advance. All of these always occur within the great harmony of original influences – which always target the evolution of spirits. That is, as we previously said, original influences that gather the atom from the primitive matter of the amorphous milieu by descending in the midst of matter, reflect the evolutionary necessities of spirits to the atom in the developing state. It provides

---

[8] *Centurium*: The element 100, now known as *fermium*, was almost named *centurium*, but in 1953, scientists at the Nobel Institute in Stockholm produced fermium 250 by bombarding uranium with oxygen nuclei. At the time the discoveries from the hydrogen bomb were classified, so the Swedes, who tentatively came up with the *centurium* name 100, could have got in first, had fermium not been rapidly declassified. (*Source*: Brian Clegg, http://www.rsc.org/chemistryworld/podcast/Interactive_Periodic_Table_Transcripts/Fermium.asp)

for preparations of reaching of the spirit, in parallel with matter, to a higher stage. In this developmental stage of the hydrogen atom, there are no secondary influences arriving at the structure of the atom. Here, only original influences descend to it. The original influences are influences filtrated from the unitary and pertaining to matter and spirits. This situation continues up to the stages of being.

Starting from its initial constitution, the hydrogen atom finally reaches such a stage that it starts to transmit energies that are super-world matter unknown to mankind, in states of very subtle and complicated matter combinations. When the atom reaches the developmental stage of its ability to transmit these high and complex energies, the spirit causing it to reach that level in the face of the original principle also reaches a stage of evolution, after a long cycle of application, at which it can have instinctual behaviours of relations and motions between matter.

Thus, the high hydrogen atom at the uppermost boundaries of world-matter starts to transmit such strong and complex energies that these can no longer belong to world-matter. Nevertheless, these energies are also not in a gathered state but are disarrayed. However, there are immense differences between this desultory state and the desultory state of amorphous matter in the primitive milieu which we previously mentioned. The former were the formless, simple, crude matter with primitive motions which were almost inert. These is, however, powerful and valued matter in states of surpassing value that is constituted by rich matter combinations, with very complex motions and complicated structures. We call the milieu in which they exist semi-subtle milieu. This semi-subtle milieu is a kind of nebulae constituted by high energies that form the echelon of a completely new and much higher realm than both the amorphous milieu below the hydrogen atom and the astronomic nebulae constituted by initial hydrogen atoms; and the constitution of such a semi-subtle milieu that exists higher than the world expresses the slow shifting of the world, in other words, of the hydrogen cosmos up to a higher cosmos.

So, these high and disarrayed energies constitute the most primitive and simplest atoms of this semi-subtle cosmos, that is, of the nebulae of super-hydrogen cosmos. Thus, higher and disarrayed energies which have started to emanate from the initial atoms of this semi-subtle milieu, through their development, have now reached the ability and possibilities of gathering and entering into a state of being which can serve a spirit until the end of the universe. Similarly, spirits that have evolved with them up to that stage – always with the help of the original influences – have also reached the capability of gathering these high but disarrayed energies and make a being out of them.

When this state occurs, original influences, which also consist of the influences of a spirit that has reached the merit of building a body for itself out of these disarrayed energies, descend in the midst of these disarrayed and high energies. There, by gathering these energies around a perceptual point which we have previously explained, they make a gathering out of them. In the original influences there are also influences belonging to spirits evolved up to that stage. These influences are reflected and connected to the being, that is, to the energy ensemble by the original influence. In this way, that energy ensemble which we call being, has been put in service to be a reflector to all behaviours of that spirit and to send all responses of those behaviours back to it until the end of the universe; and has entered into a state of becoming a symbol, a vehicle of the spirit in universe.

In this way, developing from the start of the initial hydrogen stage up to the moment of reaching the stage of being, the prime influences part of the original influences – pertaining to matter – leaves its place to secondary influences. And through these secondary influences arriving from those beings in duty within the vast organisations or from the beings they utilise in various stages, as continuously supervised by the unitary, the being continues on its evolution until the end of universe. With the start of these secondary influences tests, trials, experiences and observations of beings start as well. And beings are put into a completely new, faster evolutionary system. From that stage on, matter, like beings, will develop under the governance of spirits to which they obey and with the help of secondary influences, by subjecting and translating all states and situations of those spirits and by expressing them in the universe.

A being that comes into existence in this way expresses all behaviours pertaining to the evolution of the spirit to which it is in service, to such perfection that it can then be looked at as the spirit itself in the universe. Because of this, seeing that its active state that carries expressions of spirit relative to the states of other matter which is below it and inert and almost amorphous, the adjective of animated has been attributed to this being; and as previously mentioned, this is but a relative expression. For, here the being that is called animated is actually merely the developed higher states of the initial hydrogen atom matter which appeared inert. The only thing is that its possibilities have sufficiently developed in order to express a spirit in universe; and because of this, it has been assigned to the service of a certain spirit.

In short, the initial nucleus, the core state of the hydrogen atom, which is not yet known by mankind, constitutes our hydrogen cosmos, that is, the principal matter of solar systems, nebulae and all astronomical bodies which we can observe by astronomical means. Eventually, it spontaneously starts to emanate some energies (it should be remembered that matter cannot spontaneously emanate any energies; all of these are subject to the influences coming from original sources). And here, let us say once again that when we say hydrogen atom, we never mean the hydrogen (H) atom known by chemistry. As we have said, this hydrogen (H) atom is in a very advanced stage of development in comparison with the atom we talk about, and is a completely different thing from it. Nevertheless, because mankind named the first atom hydrogen, we have naturally named the first atom of our cosmos as hydrogen. However, to repeat, this is actually not the hydrogen atom.

So, out of these high energies of the hydrogen atom which do not have any apparent manifestation in the world, the semi-subtle milieu at one stage higher than the hydrogen cosmos, comes forth. These high states and forms of hydrogen continuing its development in that milieu become the evolutionary materials for spirits which have attained the merit for gathering these high energies by stepping up their application level in matter with the more superior energies they transmit. Spirits – in the way we have said above – build for themselves beings apiece out of these energies to be in service to them until the end of the universe.

*
* *

The being initially constituted as such, in regard to comprehension, is yet in a very simple and primitive state. In this being, there only exists a mechanical instinct that will progress very slowly throughout the almost eternally long period of development that being will spend in the hydrogen cosmos; and after a long time, it will very slowly transform into intuition-instincts; again, after a very long time, into intuitions; and after a long time, separated by very long time periods, into intuition-comprehensions and primitive comprehensions. Only when the stage of human is reached does it become possible for comprehensions to expand and to start to become encompassing in a slow manner.

*
* *

The being that has started to live with initial mechanical instincts is now in the service of a spirit. It will respond to all needs, all behaviours of that spirit and be a vehicle for its necessities that need to be realised among matter in universe. In accordance with the evolutionary stage it has started from this moment on, it will feel the need to do active applications among the crude atoms and their crude combinations – which are not entered into a state of being yet – of hydrogen cosmos. However, the application here is completely different from the mechanical and automatic lives of the spirit which it previously spent within those crude atoms. Back then, it was unable to govern them, in a situation of connecting and subjecting to a single atom; it was participating in certain motions of that atom and going through a cycle of passive adaptation. Now, it has set off an active application cycle to be gradually able to govern atoms, throughout all developmental stages starting from the simplest to their combinations and compositions constituted with various elements via its being in service to it. Because of this, it will continue its evolution by activities such as gathering, dispersing them and making up new constitutions out of them, building bodies, managing bodies; and in this manner, it will complete its forward preparations in this realm.

From now on, this subtle energy ensemble, which we call being, will be the vehicle to it in carrying out all of these assignments. This being that represents all states of spirit in the universe from now on will be used by spirit in order to provide all of its needs within this matter. Spirits, via this being, by adopting various formations and transformations upon the dense matter combinations of the hydrogen cosmos and crude matter within spheres and worlds, will put these into action. For, it is impossible for spirit to govern this crude matter directly. Because of this, the constituted initial being will immediately try to utilise the most primitive matter in its milieu in the face of the new needs emerging in the spirit and by building initially simple composites out of them, will start the application of its governance over these composites.

All of these assignments occur – as it always is everywhere – with the guidance and illumination of the sublime influences helping spirits. So, matter composites which the being can use first will be initially the simplest and primitive cells of plant bodies. These beings will build bodies apiece out of them and only with their simple bodies, that is, with primitive plant cells, will start to live by influencing – at first, it is always with their instincts – other crude matter and crude bodies in various ways. And mankind calls this as incarnation. Because the beings using these cells are still non-comprehending, this manner of their corporeality may be called a kind of incarnation. The being that reached a state of ability to govern a whole plant, after completing necessary incarnations in every kind of cells of plant bodies, will now start to incarnate independently in respective plants, starting from the simplest to the higher plants. After that, the being will be able to manage an independent individual body and from now on, the initial stages of a collective, communal life for it will be set up. We call this the most primitive stirrings of the preparation towards the organisation systems which we will explain later.

As it increasingly evolves by going through infinite embodiments in innumerable plant species the being will complete – after a very long time – this stage as well, and in order to render the application one stage further – that is, the animality stage – it will pass into a semi-subtle cosmos which is particular to it, and after living there for a while, in order to complete the stages of embodiment gradually in animal and human bodies, it will incarnate in the primitive cells of the simplest animal organism and continue its embodiments upwards. Eventually, it will pass into higher cells, that is, into cells constituting the nervous system of animals; and after completing this cycle and acquiring the necessary abilities, it will enter into a state of governing independent animal bodies and start to manage the simplest animal bodies. And following this, after going through many more embodiments in our world and other planets, by becoming a being able to manage a human body, it will start to use human bodies in the world. And starting from the most primitive stages of the human realm, it will be completing its final preparations in the world within a rich evolutionary cycle which we will explain later.

Therefore, throughout a very long period of time which means eternity according to mankind's comprehension, an evolutionary stage needs to be undergone, starting from the initial state of being, that is, from the initial states of embodiment until arriving at the human stage.

*
* *

The implication of 'incarnation' which is a word not carrying a proper expressional power is: being, in order to serve the spirit that owns itself; more correctly, spirit, in order to be able to utilise the matter of a crude cosmos via the being serving itself, is compelled to build and use a vehicle of influence, that is, a crude body out of matter of that cosmos. However, that being is not yet powerful enough to build such immense combinations out of crude matter by itself. Because of this, it will, according to its need (which actually means the need of spirit), build a body for itself out of crude matter and connect to it by continuously sending influences to it. And then the being will do activities among the crude matter and other beings pertaining to the needs of its spirit which has started its communal evolution in that world, through this body it has built. That is, the being will manage that body in accordance with the behaviours of the spirit. After all, that body is built of a calibre to be managed by it.

So, here, there is a being and a body, serving the spirit through each other. One of these is the being, owning a complex matter structure that we have previously mentioned, and following the spirit throughout the universe; which is a very subtle energy complex – the symbol, reflection and expression of spirit in the universe. And the second one is a crude body, made out of dense matter of that cosmos, for that being to be able to serve the spirit, using as a vehicle of inter-influence with matter and beings in the crude cosmos in which it is compelled to render applications. So, the body which has to serve the being that will accompany the spirit throughout the universe is but a temporary vehicle that will remain connected to that being only during a temporary cycle of application in accordance with the needs of spirit at any crude sphere. The being, in the milieu it exists, once it meets the needs of the spirit it serves, leaves its previous body in order to build another body – suitable for its new needs. And this happens, again, with the help of higher influences. So, the being's building a second body in any sphere is named by mankind as incarnation or birth; and its leaving that body is named by mankind as disincarnation or death.

*

* *

Therefore, the being that is born in any sphere of a solar system, within a body suitable to the conditions of that sphere, reaches the last echelon of matter-cosmos after going through innumerable processes of incarnation and disincarnation in various spheres of that system, according to its evolutionary need; and this last echelon, in our system, is human and in other systems, is one of the bodies at the corresponding stage of development. So, spirits evolve in this stage we call the hydrogen cosmos not within disarrayed matter states, passively, nor by mechanical progress – as in the initial stages of development of matter – but according to the efforts they make in the states that are bound to matter, automatic or semi-comprehending.

*

* *

Now that the atoms of our world can make advanced developments in order to emanate high energies which are the basic matter of a semi-subtle cosmos, superior to our cosmos, then our world is not a backward world as has been assumed or thought until now but, regarding its material development, it is one of the most developed

60

spheres with the most advanced matter constitutions of the whole hydrogen cosmos with all its planets, suns, spheres, systems and nebulae. Thus human bodies, used by spirits whose evolutions progress in parallel with the development of the world, are also among the most advanced and developed beings of this immense astronomical cosmos. As a matter of fact, as we will mention later, with a being's forsaking the world completely after utilising all possibilities of our world and accomplishing its applications there, its simultaneous transition to forsaking the hydrogen cosmos as well constitutes the living proof of this knowledge.

*
* *

Let us make a rough diagram of the universe by likening it to thirty or forty concentric spheres which are larger than one another, with their cosmoses entwined. The crudest and most primitive of these is the smallest sphere in the middle which we called the amorphous initial matter stage.

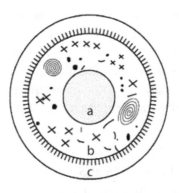

Figure 1

Figure 1 shows the cross-section of the first three of the concentric spheres we mentioned. Here, field (a) shows the initial developmental field of matter which corresponds to the mechanical evolutionary stages of spirits, starting from the initial matter up to hydrogen; which is quite obscured. Field (b) constitutes our hydrogen cosmos with all of its celestial objects. And field (c) is the first echelon, relative to our cosmos, of endless other cosmoses which are superior to our cosmos and which ascend level by level, which we call semi-subtle realm. Following this one, other stages will continue by widening further than one another.

*
* *

In this way, by going through innumerable embodiments in many planets of the solar system in simple, primitive matter complexes relative to the ones in our world but proper for conditions and situations of those planets, the being acquires the merit to build the human body on Earth, which is the most evolved being of our system. And from that moment on, it sets off developmental processes which are in freer states and forms. Comprehension of the being in the human state has rather increased in comparison to previous stages. Its freewill has increased at the same rate as its comprehension. And in accordance with these capabilities, it has started to intuit the meaning of responsibility. Increase in all of these capabilities, has caused it to gain the consciousness of sublime developmental mechanisms called love and conscience. By means of this, under the increasingly strengthening pressures of their intuitions of responsibility, mankind strive to complete the human stage as automatically or semi-comprehending; and for this, they go through hundreds of thousands of refining experiences in their human lives, by living through the ages.

*
* *

A man,[9] if he stands alone in the world, cannot possess refining experience. And when he cannot possess refining experience, he cannot serve the evolution of spirit. Thus, at that point, the imperative of the various communal evolutionary plans in the matter-universe shows itself openly. Therefore, bodily beings need to be in reciprocal interchange with other bodies and matter that exist outside of the body. Out of these relations with them innumerable event combinations occur. Thus, comprehensions pertaining to

---

[9] In this translation, the word 'man' and the personal pronouns 'he' and 'him' are used to indicate both men and women. (*Translator*)

these event-combinations, which are reflected from essence-being to spirit, allow the evolution of being at this stage.

So, spirit participates with matter. It builds the conscious matter, that is, the being. And the being, with the activities of its own spirit and of helping beings, builds as well a body out of crude matter. And it influences matter through this body. And by influencing other bodies other than itself with the crude matter it uses, it steps into the communal plan. And its evolution at the stage of being of the hydrogen cosmos starts to progress from this moment on.

To ensure that no point of this important knowledge remains vague, we will provide some explanations. For example, for the evolution of a very backward man who is destitute of love and conscience, he must encounter opposite values in accordance with the duality principle and the value differentiation mechanism; he must face concepts like love–hate, justice–atrocity, goodness–evil and by this means, he must automatically acquire some knowledge of comparison and restore his equilibrium. Because of this, it is necessary for him to be in relations with other bodies.

A man, with a whip in his hand, lashes a piece of rock again and again; what result can he get from this? None at all. The results he might get from lashing this piece of rock cannot provide any opposite values that would determine his capabilities for love and conscience. He, when he cannot find a body against him, cannot start to perform atrocities and cruelties around him; and when he cannot do this, he cannot acquire opposite values which will spawn the necessary events in accordance with the duality principle and value differentiation mechanism; and as a result of this, he cannot reach the matter developments he needs, cannot evolve.

On the contrary, if that man whips a child, things change. Various reactions of that child or of others around him as a consequence of this whipping will stand up before him as opposite elements and immediately lead him to some knowledge of comparison. In this way, accumulation of the knowledge of comparison with the succeeding hundreds and thousands of events accumulating on top of each other causes the birth of a goodness–evil concept in him, in its simplest form; and by this, conscience starts to develop and becomes alive. Events that will occur as the result of all

63

these acts are reflected to spirit and result in evolution. After that, new and more advanced needs emerge in the spirit.

Spirit, in the face of these new needs, starts to expect more meaningful reactions from the communications its body will render with its environment in a wider field. And this new need of spirit – again, in a similar way to the previous one – is immediately reflected to the body and its response is received from the body; that is, the being serving the spirit, by influencing crude matter and bodies around it through its body, causes the necessary events to occur in the face of these new needs of the spirit. He does good, he does wrong, he steals, he murders a man, he makes a sacrifice; and he sees the response, the reactions of those around him. All of these become an event. And by reflecting each of these events to the spirit via the channel of comprehension, it ensures its evolution. By this means, the human being, who finally reaches the last developmental stage of the world, forsakes the world completely in order to move on to more advanced stages.

*
* *

We had mentioned that developments of matter and their ability to serve the evolutions of spirits are only possible with influences. Now, we need to dwell on influences as much as necessary and to give knowledge regarding them.

In introducing the topic of influences, we will again mention spirit–matter relations. Spirit's need for evolution is a necessity; and matter's ability to respond this need is, again, a necessity. However, neither can spirits directly send anything to matter, nor they can receive something from it. If that was all, the raison d'être of the matter-universe, which is the imperative of the purpose of evolution, would be no more. However, for evolution the realisation of the relation of spirit–matter is imperative in accordance with sublime necessities. So, these necessities are rendered through the manifestations of the original principle, which directly governs and comprises both the spirits beyond universe and the universes, as material influences in the universe.

The realisation of necessities in matter means the execution of the functions of influences by the value differentiation mechanism.

Therefore, it is necessary to give knowledge – to the appropriate degree – about the influences pertaining to these spirit–matter relations which are an enigma of the universe, which has not so far been solved in the world.

Influences using the motion possibilities of universe-substance in infinite numbers and forms –again, in accordance with the evolutionary needs of spirits – and bringing out all the manifestations of the matter-universe – again, with the same purpose, by executing their functions meet the needs of the spirit realm. That is, every motion, every change and every development in matter which is necessary for the evolution of spirits is only provided by these influences.

*
* *

About the original principle which is the great truth higher than the spirits and universes and governing both, we cannot say much. For, this is outside all knowledge, and even of our intuitions. The original principle reflects with its force all the evolutionary needs of spirits for universe-substances and reflects the reactions of the universe-substances in the face of these needs back to spirits. This force put the universe-substances, which brought into existence in the face of the needs of spirits, into service by innumerable vehicles and ways in universe. And this sublime force is manifested in the universe with influences which are in states of the subtlest substances. So, these influences carrying the sublime necessities permeate every point in the universe, from its whole to its smallest particle and do their functions. Matter-substance takes form, develops, assembles, disperses, goes through formations, deformations and transformations in accordance with these functions; and in this way, the whole and parts of universe are consigned and managed in accordance with the needs of spirits. This, as well, of course, is executed through various mechanisms, lower and higher, and with principles of duty within the universe.

*
* *

These influences bridging the way between spirit and universe appear in four groups. Two of these are original influences, directly arriving from outside the universe. That is, they are influences coming from the original principle. The other two are secondary influences that have ensued from modification of the original influences after going through various treatments within matter and beings. We can only understand the advancing parts of the powers coming from the original source, as influence. The true disposition and states of the ones that remain outside the universe are unknown for the universe's inhabitants.

Those at the first part of the original influences are the manifestations of powers reflecting the needs of spirits to the universe and their reactions in the universe to spirits again. These are influences that are coming indirectly, belonging to spirits. And those at the second part are the influences entering the universe from the original principle, for the formation, deformation and transformation of the crude matter which are of necessity and imperative for individual and communal evolution in the universe.

Influences arriving in the universe belonging to spirits and seen in the first part are – although arriving, again, from the original source – expressions apiece of the spirits' behaviours and needs. These powers – sent from the original principle to reflect the universe and spirits to each other, and by this, to ensure evolution – participate in certain structures and mechanisms of beings and bodies which are assigned to spirits.

These influences, when entering the universe, arrive at the unity of beings and necessities at the uppermost evolutionary boundary of the universe that we call the unitary. And from there, as regulated, they head towards a body in the milieu they will reach. Because these influences are directly pertaining to evolution, that is, because they ensure the connection between spirits and beings, we also call them evolutionary values.

As to the powers that arise from the original principle in order to render the evolutionary necessities of spirits and to put crude matter and universe-constitutions into proper forms, they are, by also descending to the unitary from the outside of the universe, apportioned and distributed to the whole and parts of the universe as sublime influences, in order to prepare and enforce cosmoses, spheres, beings and matter in accordance with the necessities of individual and communal evolution; which we call prime influences or prime values.

These ensure the bringing of matter, objects, spheres, systems, nebulae and cosmoses into existence in any matter milieu, by building a nucleus through gathering parts of that milieu around a point and attracting other parts around it and generating matter constitutions.

Influences at the third degree are, unlike first basic influences, not directly arriving from outside of the universe in accordance with the necessities of the original principle, but influences which are transferred to the exterior of the body by the bodies – that is, by the beings that exist at certain stages in universe. Actually, these influences, having come as well from the original sources, are quite altered and have lost their basic value after being utilised by any body and reflected outside of the body, as low quality relative to its actual value. Here, this expression of low quality should not be underrated. For, there is nothing like small and huge scale in any manifestations of the needs of the original principle. The meaning implied by this expression of low quality means the necessities of adjusting influences in accordance with the milieus and aims they will advance in. The sending of high influence into a simple matter combination is not appropriate, nor do weak influences benefit very complex matter combinations. All of these are adjusted by the technical mechanisms being carried out by necessities. It is easy to see examples of these influences in the third degree among the influences mankind have on each other.

Influences in the fourth degree are the values that become crude quantitatively. These are crude influences, stored as completely altered after prime influences used in a matter combination and used in automatic activities, when necessary. For example, the execution of automatic activities within a material system or in a body is done by using these stored influences. The magnetic fields of matter, which we previously declared, are within the scope of these influences.

*
* *

We previously mentioned that a prime influence coming from above brings out matter constitution by constituting a focus in the centre of matter and gathering matter-parts around it and after going through various alterations in that matter, it starts to be transmitted outside of that matter, having been transformed into a low quality energy, which is called the magnetic field of that matter.

Similarly, we have said that the influence matter and bodies exert on each other is possible by the exchange of these magnetic fields as a result of contacts with each other. For example, if a being (a) wishes to accomplish some changes and manifestations in the structure of matter (b), it contacts its magnetic field which contains its own influences with the magnetic field of that matter. These influences which have transmitted from the magnetic field of matter to its structure cause the demanded motions and results occurring in that matter, in degree, direction, form and dosage determined by the being (a).

In the same way, a hypnotist's ability to mesmerise a man and to carry out some modifications on his physical, physiological and psychological states occurs again in the same manner. That is, he influences him by contacting his own magnetic field with the magnetic field of his subject.

Likewise, in a spiritism session, materialisation[10] phenomena called ectoplasm[11] by mankind occur as well, as a result of influences sent by incorporeal beings contacting their magnetic fields with the magnetic field of the medium[12] and transmitted from this field to the medium's body, bringing out material changes, dispersions, gatherings. Again, physical mediums' influence on things – telepathies, sympathies, antipathies, transmissions and other such material phenomena

---

[10] *Materialisation*: In the dictionaries this term is used to express corporeality; as a spiritualist term, it means the appearance of a human form that can be seen and touched during a spiritism session. (*Publisher*)

[11] *Ectoplasm*: A term used for formless subtle matter allegedly emitted from the bodies – especially from the organs such as the mouth, nose, ear – of mediums in a trance state and spreading into the air, sometimes observed with the eyes and touched by hands. (*Publisher*)

[12] *Medium*: In Latin, this word means 'in between, in the middle'. In spiritualism, it means someone who has paranormal abilities and is able to communicate with disembodied beings. (*Publisher*)

among individuals – always occurs through this mechanism. That is, all of these occur by generating various transformations in matter combinations with influences upon magnetic fields, which are connected to them.

We also mentioned previously that the occurrence of great natural events such as an earthquake, the eruption of a volcano, or the emergence of a flood, is ensured through influences sent to the magnetic field of earth by beings in duty.

Other than these influences we have listed, there are some simple influences, simple values which are cruder and pertinent in the secondary degree to these influences. For example, influences like chemical reactions occurring in a body, medicine given to patients; which we call crude charges or crude values because they are even cruder relative to the value differentiations of the duality-unit of an atom, even of a molecule.

*
* *

As matter influences other matter or as influences pass from one matter combination to another body or matter combination, they go through some changes, simplifying as they descend and complicating as they ascend. The reason for this is as follows: As passing from one matter unit to a lower matter unit, because the some part of the values which is the content of the influences is used in the higher unit; that influence descends to the lower unit as partly erased relative to its initial arrival and losing some of its values so this state automatically protects the lower unit from the damage of a strong influence; and this constitutes one of the filtering mechanisms established for the safety of beings and matter in the universe.

These mechanisms are necessary for matter. In order to emphasise their worth, we will consider Earth as an example. Direct and indirect influences, billions times billons, arrive at our world from the Sun, the Moon, stars, other celestial objects and planets; and a network of influences embraces the whole world. It is possible to guess the innumerable amount of the total of influences in hundreds of thousands arriving at each separate particle of beings and matter in the world. Thus, among these incoming influences there are, of course, the ones that can cause great damage to the world. However, apart from the regulation mechanisms belonging to the sources of sublime influence coming from way above, there are some filtering mechanisms, for the secondary influences, established around the world, which are protecting the world from harm by filtering strong influences. The aim of these filtering mechanisms is to ward off influences which are too strong for the world to bear. By means of these various mechanisms, some part of those influences by-pass the world, without reaching it.

Another filtering mechanism is the protecting mechanism established in the atmosphere by the influences coming from the Sun. This alters and renders some radiations and influences harmless, like excess radiations coming from outside or created artificially on Earth which may cause great damage to the world. This operates in such a way that they do not interfere with vibrations coming from the Sun or from here and there – as long as they are not detrimental to the world. However, starting from the moment the dosages of these vibrations exceed certain limits to reach a state that can make the world aggrieved, this mechanism in the atmosphere starts automatically to work and continues to work until rendering those detrimental or maybe deadly radiations harmless and when it has decreased their dosages to a normal level, stops its activity. For example, if there were not such a mechanism in the atmosphere, radioactivity produced in the world could cause many deaths.

These kind of filtering mechanisms besides others exist almost for all objects, all matter. Thus, as influences descend, decreasing of their values becomes a kind of filtering mechanism for the safety of the lower ones.

And the complication of influences as they ascend from lower matter to higher matter is because of this: ascending influences, as they are going up, meet with a wider field of influences, as a necessity of the structure of that level. By sympathising with the influences there and receiving values from them, they widen their constitutions and in this way, become more complex.

Therefore, an influence, as it descends and leaves some part of its values at each stage it stops by, descends while weakening and then vanishes. As going up, it ascends while increasing by receiving new values from each stage. This state is an imperative result of functions performed by the influences as they advance among matter, and as well, a necessity that allows them the possibility of each finding milieus which are sympathetic to them in the stages they stop by as they descend.

If there were not these filters and these mechanisms, there would be various unfusibilities between matter and influences descending to being and matter combinations in order to render necessary changes in accordance with the evolutionary necessities, and these influences could often be detrimental instead of beneficial. All of these influence regulation mechanisms are again under the control of the superior influences carrying sublime necessities.

*

* *

Influences are the states of extra-universe truths which are reflected to matter. Again, these are the influences reflecting the reactions exhibited by matter to the outside of the universe. Influences, after they stimulate a matter, bring out a chain of consecutive influences by causing, with the motions of that matter, motions of other matter and with these, motions of more other matter; which is a kind of automatism. There are myriad deeds executed with such automatisms. However, such consecutive automatic activities also occur only under the controls of descending influences, coming from above, from the beings in duty.

The influences we have mentioned so far in outline enter matter structures in the state of various matter combinations with their endless variations and ensure the innumerable exchanges between matter. All of these influences envelop the universe through and through, as a complicated network, which no human comprehension can grasp. In every particle of these, the sublime necessities of the original principle govern. All of these influences, despite their endless variations, perform their functions as a single power which had manifested in the subtlest matter of the universe within the great harmony of divine order. Everything that had been qualified by mankind as material, moral, corporeal, spiritual, starting from the first particle of the universe to its whole, could only advance in the inclusive order and arrangement of these influences carrying the necessities of sublime principles. For the ones who can intuit this point

71

in all its details, it is practicable to comprehend that no flux or occurrence that is devoid of influences can be possible in the universe.

*
* *

After giving this general knowledge about the flux of influences, it is also necessary to talk about the functioning that occurs between universe-parts; about how this functioning accrues, and finally, about the results brought about in their final targets. Because, for the organisation systems constituting the basic structure of communal evolutionary life in the universe to be better intuited, we must go further in the knowledge of this topic. Organisation systems complement each other with the inter-influence mechanism. Nevertheless, it is necessary to explain that the influences are not isolated but are together with organisation systems and the mechanisms building these systems.

*
* *

The universe is an organisation through and through. However, within this great organisation, organisational forms that emerge as states of organ-organiser start only from a certain stage of the universe and continue until a certain stage. States of organising which remain above and below these occur in the inclusivity of laws and rules belonging to the order and devices of sublime principles which remains outside human comprehension. However, none of these is outside the great universe organisation.

The parts of universe organisations that can be intuited by mankind occur within organ–organiser relations. An organisation works under the organising of its higher organisation. Here, the higher organisation which is in the status of organiser, throws light on the lower organisation. This light has also come to it from a higher organisation. This state continues on up to the unitary. In this way, a projector light, which is shed from the unitary to the whole universe, traverses the duty organisations from upward to downward, which are juxtaposed down to the lowest stages of the plan of duty. Meanwhile, as each organisation does its duty with the light it received from the higher one, it also sends that light to the lower organisation according to the needs of that organisation, which appear as duty. Organisations at all stages and levels of the plan of duty, by the directives coming from the unitary, execute the duties which are their share within the scope of their encompassment and under the light of the directive descending from above.

*

* *

In the path of evolution, described by sublime principles, each organism has some definite duties. All components of that organism, by joining forces – according to their power and merit – are obliged to do these duties. No organ or organiser should abandon or neglect their share of duty. However, the refining experiences of spirits yet at the initial stages of the hydrogen cosmos have not advanced sufficiently to comprehend these truths and imperatives. This state is thoroughly lacking even in the ones which are more or less developed. The ones at this stage have not yet attained the comprehension of duty that carries the share of universe responsibility to various degrees. Because of this, duties of the governance mechanism cannot yet be left to these beings. Therefore, these are not included in great duty organisations. This is a work only belonging to beings involved with plans of duty, which are at more advanced stages of evolution. Nevertheless, superior beings, which are obliged out of duty to help the evolutions of these non-comprehending, even semi-comprehending beings at levels below, help them with the imperative acts which are their share for the preparations for the plan of duty. For this, various ensembles, groupings occur among them in order to prepare for the future organisations. And the beings in duty consign these groups and gatherings to preliminary work, conditionally, which is in some degree automatic or more or less comprehending. As these develop and expand their comprehension they start to gain freedoms that increase accordingly. And meanwhile, they are gradually given intuitions into the great organisation systems.

So this is how a crude matter, upon entering the stage of being and evolving there for a while, and from the moment it starts to build a plant body, entering into an ensemble and starting a new cycle of development, likewise that being starts, as a consequence of a very long evolution and in accordance with the maturation of its sense of duty, enters the path of comprehending its obligations of duty and gaining an intuition of responsibility. And thus it commences to intuit vast and wide paths leading to organisations of the great plan of duty.

*
* *

We have just mentioned automatic duties within a community. Now, we will give further explanation of these automatic activities. On your way back home from shopping, you give the parcels to a porter to carry them to your home. Why does the porter carry them to your home? To help you? No. He has no such concerns. He does this to earn a few pennies from you. So, this is a deed which you make him do automatically. Among various characteristics of automatism, one is, as in this example, to advance someone with some beguiling or diverting compensations for a purpose, which he is unable to understand. Accordingly, a man's advancing automatically along the path of evolution means – for a man who cannot display the power to advance consciously and willingly towards the destination he must reach – ensuring his advancing on the demanded path by either laying down attractive toys before him or waylaying scary or intimidating situations in accordance with his earthly cravings.[13]

These deeds which are orientated to the realisation of great purposes begin with several of such automatisms. And sensual or selfish thoughts and desires that prepare the first steps of this automatism accordingly become the powerful elements of this automatism with their positive or negative functions. As the comprehensions expand and essence-knowledge about the cause and effects of the deeds to be done increases, consequences are gradually seen more clearly and the attractive or scary means of automatism in between cease to function, one by one. A mother no longer has to promise a sweet before washing her child's head. Then, man, by seeing his

---

[13] *Earthly cravings*: The ambition to gratify the attraction that occurs in a spirit/being connected to matter; or, ambition to gratify the selfish emotions due to forgetting that matter is only a means but making it an end. (*Publisher*)

destination directly and more clearly, has begun to comprehend the attainment of that aim and to believe in its exigency, and has thus gained the intuitions of advancing towards the plan of duty.

Indeed, the earth sphere's presence as a powerful vehicle for evolution, as a perfect preparatory school, is because of this. Because of all kinds of materials of a great automatism, which is constituted with programmed and regulated events, its innumerable components of feelings and earthly cravings compelling the consciousness and comprehensions towards the knowledge of duty exist in the world school. And the beings in duty who oversee the life of the world execute this duty of theirs by utilising these materials among humans. Therefore, the world, as it prepares plants to the stage of animality and animals to the stage of humanity through various automatisms, is also full of very rich variations which prepare humans to the intuition of the knowledge of duty and of organisation systems. Tests, trials, observations, experiences, all bitter and sweet feelings complexes, various appearances of sanctions preached by religions such as heaven, hell, afterlife etc. are orientated towards the purpose of preparing humans for the comprehension and consciousness of the great, cosmos-wide deeds which they are obliged to undertake in the universe. Ensuring that mankind learns the true values of world events in the face of the causality principle, and mankind's own state and behaviours in the face of these values, to adapt themselves accordingly and thus to prepare themselves for the knowledge of duty and organisation discipline is one of the essential functions of the life of the world. Only the ones who have attained the aim as the result of this function; and who have embraced the obligation of the deeds they will do in universe can sever their relations to the world.

*

* *

We will now provide knowledge – briefly for the time being – about the activities of organisations which exhibit the technical ways of an immense universe-mechanism. There are boundless deeds that are done in accordance with the necessities of the original principle governing universes and spirits. In the constitution of

75

matter, in the distribution of influences to matter and beings and in the proper utilisation of these distributions, in the governance and supervision of the myriad developmental stages and evolutions of beings, in the effectuation of the innumerable manifestations of crude matter serving their evolutions; in short, in every mechanism of universe, there are innumerable deeds and services, of which each one is a managerial duty that beings are obliged to execute in accordance with their specialisation capability. These obligations – in accordance with the sublime necessities of the original principle – are executed according to the degree of merit of the beings; and beings are accordingly entrusted with and taking on duties.

According to the merit of the beings that have attained the sense and comprehension of duty; groupings, staffing and organisations are constituted in the plans of duty, which are different from one another in regard to the degree and state of duty. These are spread out up to the unitary, as the regulators, supervisors, helpers of each other, and as orientated to the mutual purpose aimed at in the original principles. Among the deeds they will execute are innumerable activities such as serving the evolutions of beings in accordance with sublime necessities, preparing material milieus for them, assisting those still at the automatic stage.

Organisations execute all these duties of theirs, as we have just explained, in accordance with the directives, which originate from the unitary and spread out downwards, in the order of organiser–organisation. Thus, specialisations of beings are involved in the plan of duty in myriad ways, their acquirement of merit for duty, and consequently, their groupings, organisings and systemisations around various duties occur under directives, sanctions and necessities of the original principle, under its light. Thus, the whole of this organisation constitutes the technical side of the immense governance mechanism which is connected to the unitary, of universe advancing unfailingly for the evolution of spirits. Naturally, it is necessary to attain a complete comprehension, to arrive at a super-human level to take on duties in such a sublime mechanism. Actually, the plan of duty begins only after the completion of the hydrogen stage. In order to give an idea about the organisations of duty, as much as needed for now, we would like to explain one of the activity mechanisms belonging to our world, which is smaller than a parti-cle of the particle of universe within the immense universe organi-sation, with the knowledge we have received from the administra-tor of a duty group in this field. The following sentences contain a sublime knowledge which has been given to our world for the first time – as deemed suitable by the sublime sources – by the adminis-trator of a technical administration group, of a plan with duty of the order of world affairs.

'Material phenomena in the universe which are the imperatives and necessities of the principles governing the universe, are the components allowing the evolutionary material and its observation in the universe. For the myriad needs of evolution, starting with the densest matter state to the subtlest matter state, endless trans-formations, deformations and formations occur. These material changes are a result of the channel of directives and power of the beings in duty to the general management of the universe and by the activity and labour of the beings that have taken on duties in certain fields. Perpetual changes, which are the components of the technical content of the universe, are the works of a great number of beings in duty. However, those beings who consign these beings in duty, by increasingly ascending, attend the general responsibility and powers in the unitary. Now, by a directive I have just received, I will explain how the beings who become factors in the occurrence of certain changes, which prepare these, work.

'In accordance with sublime principles, a directive of a soon-to-be change regarding the need-to-be comes to us. After all, other groups with duty which supervise and detect the needs and func-tions for each evolving being of the universe, inform us about the degree of merit and requirement of these beings and the things needed to be done about them. That is, besides the sublime beings giving directives in parallel with the sublime principles, there are other groups with duty and give us complementary information about our activities as well. Let me give an example: imagine a man living a worldly life. He needs a certain change, a certain material for his evolution. He either has acquired merit for it or, due to the necessity of his tests and trials, confusion – in short, his functional characteristics. The group which measures and grades this necessity and determines its time and disposition is another group. The assistance of this group to us is in preparing the characteristics, quantitative value, and timing; in short, all the details of the event that is to occur for that man which we are obliged to have. For example, if that man needs to get ill, the kind, the degree of severity or mildness, the length, the shortness, the means of treatment of the illness are indicated to us.

'Let me go into more detail: if there need to be aggravating reasons in this illness, issues such as sending that man to a place with insufficient means, misdiagnosis by the doctor who will treat it are given in full. Then, for that individual's evolutionary material in this state – if needed – several beings will work; one will prepare the organism, providing the activity of microbes in the organism; another one will influence the mental state of the doctor in that certain moment as required. The fields of these technical activities have many branches but I will list a few important ones. For example, connecting the psychological states of mankind to certain form patterns, and building local, social forms and let me give a final example, governing the mediums, etc. There are a number of activity branches like these, which can be multiplied; each is different from the others in quality and significance. Each works within their cadre, with their techniques. Each of these activity cadres is different from the others. For example, as the group which is obliged to execute the physical changes that occur in nature cannot govern mediums, the group governing mediums cannot execute the duty of the group that builds the social events. After all, the difference in their working grounds entails a difference in working techniques for all these groups.

'Those groups with technical duties utilise a great number of possibilities as they execute certain duties. These possibilities are greatly varied regarding their disposition. By the way, I will be unable to give you technical terms. For, these powers and possibilities that are used are difficult and impossible to express and qualify with words. However, it will suffice to use terms which will express them in an approximate but most suitable way. Powers that are used are electromagnetic powers, mechanical powers, biological powers which are the result of many powers and cosmic powers.

In order to generate these out of spatial possibilities, out of the energies of unconfined beings which have abandoned their bodies, out of the energies emanating from the beings at the higher realms, out of the powers of mankind, out of the powers of the embodied (of course, they are unaware of this). There are many of these embodied ones in the world, such as mankind, animals, plants, etc.

'Thus, energies generated from all of these possibilities and sources, by reinforcing our energy and through the consignment of those beings in duty below us, bring out definite results. Disrupting an object's equilibrium, for example, managing the wind direction (because, sometimes a hurricane that will occur in a certain place by consignment of winds to a certain direction is imperative for the evolution of certain persons), as well as in a local earthquake, bringing out the change in equilibrium which is necessary for the earthquake etc. So, bringing out the necessary conditions for all of these accrues through the energies emanating from the sources I listed and through usage of those energies by beings in duty in definite and appropriate values and forms.'

*
* *

Beings are not introduced immediately into the organisations of duty which begin above the stage of humanity, that is, above the hydrogen atom cycle. For this, it is necessary to have attained a proper level of comprehension in accordance with the necessities of the plan of duty. And this occurs only after a long, even longer cycle of preparation, starting from the most primitive stages of the hydrogen cosmos to its uppermost stages. We had previously talked about the phases needed to pass through for the comprehension to acquire such a merit of duty, starting from the initial state of being to the state of highest-level human beings. At the beginning of these phases, as a start for the most primitive advancement of organisation system, a kind of communal life begins in plants, with automatic-mechanical instincts. These communities become more comprehensive as the lives of beings advance and widen their meaning. In animals, this community is rather clearer. Although a community life has not yet started, meaningful ensembles, expressing the preliminaries towards it, exist among animals.

79

Automatic ensembles of ants, bees, and some animals that live together as a group are examples of these.

These are the organised preparations of those beings which are candidates for communal plans in human life. Naturally, there are superior influences and bonds that connect them to each other. And these come from the beings in duty working at these fields. In this way, ant colonies are organised to collect their winter provision; similarly, bee colonies, as well. Sometimes, in order to protect their nests against the preying eagles, all storks around gather and fight against these monsters as an army. Some wild animals, when they are hungry, make a herd and hunt. These states, which are frequently seen among animals, are brought out by influences sent by the beings in duty to allow them to do the instinctual application of the preparations for a superior communal plan.

Finally come the gatherings and communal lives of mankind, which are again partly automatic and partly semi-comprehending. Here then start the direct and closest preliminary applications of attaining higher duty organisations. And the purpose of human life is to complete the necessary preparations on this path.

Furthermore, there is the reciprocal organiser–organism state of the being that builds and governs a human, with the body of that man. That being, by prevailing on the magnetic field it constituted out of the human nervous system cells, governs the whole body, the organism through these cells. Here, the being is the organiser and the body is the organism.

Activities of all these ensembles, of these organisations, of these systems, of every matter ensemble, of communal systems, of combinations; their relations to each other; in short, each event, each state, everything, is ensured only by this mechanism of influences within the great harmony of the divine order.

*
* *

At each organism, there arrives a great number of secondary and lateral influences from above, from sides, from beneath, that among these there are both positive influences facilitating the duty of that organisation and negative influences which are jarring, disruptive and even destructive in order to strengthen it, to increase its refining experiences, to develop and evolve it; and these cause the occurrences of the applications of this organism for tests and trials, experience and observation. All of these secondary influences come from a great number of beings working with comprehension or automatically for the cultivation of that organism. These beings in duty, connected to the sublime universe mechanism, put many events which are aggravating, obstructing and sometimes precluding – as evolutionary material – on the path of beings in order to make ground for them to display efforts which will allow them to succeed in their duty within their bodily lives. These materials are regulated and ordered in accordance with the laws of the divine order, in order to enable beings to increase their merit, to strengthen and to ascend by shifting to higher states. However, because of their ignorance, mankind always considers these as disasters befalling them.

*
* *

We have said that organisations, as ascending higher and higher, come to an end at the unitary which is in the uppermost boundary of universe. Until they reach the unitary, these organisation components, adapting to the sublime necessities of the original principle, gradually unite, such that, at the time they enter the unitary, their comprehensions have adapted to the sublime necessities at every point and with complete merit, except a few small nuances; and then they continue with sublime, universe encompassing activities, without obeying the imperatives of organiser–organ as they have done downwards, within a single and immense unity of organisation which cannot be grasped by the minds of mankind. This is a truth where the force of the original principle belonging to the universe and spirits joins with all possibilities of our universe. Looking at this side of it, from our point of view, we call it the unitary. For, the powers of the original principle belonging to spirits and universe constitute a unity there with the whole universe.

Therefore, as organisations get closer to the unitary, with the corresponding increase in comprehensions, freedoms and responsibilities, the speed of the progress towards unity increases. States of organiser–organ relations increasingly loosen and eventually vanish. Then, the universal unity that we call the unitary is established. Further explanation will be given on this topic.

*
* *

At the initial sections of the cosmoses, in the initial crude hydrogen stage, there are not yet beings that spirits can govern. Because of this, such an organisation system cannot be of question for them, and even ensembles of these spirits cannot be thought of. Here an administrative system exists which cannot be grasped by the minds of mankind, established by the original influences and allowing the mechanical evolutions of spirits. And under this administrative system, spirits are mechanically drifted on paths designated in accordance with the divine order. Through these applications in this manner, which take a very long time and have been passed through by spirits in passive states, these primitive spirits ascend gradually to the stage of being.

*
* *

A body in the stage of being is an organism, as well. In it, among the particles constituting it, there are organising and systemisations, as well. Because of this – as we have mentioned above – instead of the original principle's prime influences which pertain to matter, alongside the secondary influences, the original principle's powers pertaining to spirits which we call evolutionary values arrive at it from all around.

Of course, these secondary influences are not unattended either; these are also states of the two basic influences we had previously mentioned as entering the universe, which are transmitted outside as altered after passing through beings and bodies. More correctly, these are the magnetic fields of beings. These secondary influences arrive at their targets on time, as needed and as regulated without even the smallest deviation, according to the individual and communal evolutionary needs of spirits and in accordance with the approbation and designation of the unitary. These influences, which are never unattended, are transmitted to the targets which are approved and designated for themselves – as subjected to a great

82

number of administration, control and assistance mechanisms. Although these most often exhibit a scene of disharmony and defeatism with thousands of conflicts, battles, controversies and dissensions among themselves, this state is an exterior appearance. In truth, all these are technical necessities of the compositions and mechanisms that occur to ensure the evolutionary imperatives and their opposite appearances which are deceptive to mankind.

*
* *

Now, let us talk, as much as necessary, about some of the mechanisms belonging to the devices of influences fluxing into matter.

As we said previously, an influence's arrival at a matter means the transfer of some very subtle particles, that is, of values which have very sublime motions from the magnetic field of the influencer matter into the magnetic field of recipient matter. It occurs like this: from the magnetic field of the influencer matter, which has power and merit to respond to the need of the recipient matter, an influence departs. On the other hand, recipient matter or the being assumes an attitude – as if inviting, by extending a part of its own magnetic field – towards this influence which is intended to reach it. More correctly, it starts to send out influences which we call initiator influences. We show the wishes, desires, needs, efforts and prayers of mankind as an example of this group of initiator influences. Prayers may be reflected up above, to a certain distance. The length of these distances depends on the sincerity, rightness and degree of intensity of the wishes the prayers offer above while praying. Some prayers cannot traverse long distances, and remain below. These are weak and because of this they do not encounter beings powerful enough to realise them. And this should be so. Some prayers can reach up to very long distances. These are powerful wishes, coming from the essence and founded on true evolutionary needs. There are more possibilities for these prayers, which can reach powerful beings, to be realised.

In the same way, as these initiator influences start to move, like signals transmitted from an airfield to a plane, in order to meet the first influence on its way, the first secondary influence that needs to land on this field as well starts to come out as comprehending, semi-comprehending, even sometimes automatically from its source and to advance towards the field it will land on. However, as we have said, this first influence is not unattended. Another secondary influence accompanies it from a more comprehending source, to show it the direction of the target it will reach, which we call the guiding influence. This guiding influence is sympathetic to the first influence.

Nevertheless, the guiding influence is rather crude. Even if the consciousness and comprehension of the source it has come out from are superior to the first influence, it does not have the power for homing itself to the magnetic field which is expecting it. However, its attuned state for directly sympathising with the first influence makes it possible to accompany that. If that was all, these could not reach the target anyway. There are two reasons for this: first of all, because the guiding influence does not have the scope of comprehension encompassing the all, it can deviate. That is, there are other magnetic fields with which the first influence can sympathise; because of their needs they can also send a signal for those kinds of influences. However, this first influence should not go to these. So, because of this deficiency of the guiding influence in this regard, it is possible for it to be deceived by the signals given by the other fields and to direct the direction of the first influence to one of these.

Secondly, it is possible for it to encounter a great number of interference influences that have the power to intercept the first influence advancing in its direction and to alter its disposition or its course, even to destroy it. So the guiding influences are not in a state that can withstand these interferences –which are sometimes very strong. The first influence, when it stays unprotected against these offences, can degenerate midway and become dysfunctional or can drift somewhere else or be dissipated. However, in the divine order, derangement of order is never allowed such as states of impending and disrupting of an event, or of giving ill results. Because of this, impediment prevention devices are established. As for that system, besides the guiding influence that comes with the first influence, superior secondary influences come out from the sources of duty. These have a higher comprehension and accompany this consignment. We call them propulsive influences, which means dispatching influences.

Propulsive influences are stronger influences, ensuring the first influence finds its way and protecting it from the offensive, random interference influences and, if necessary, destroying these disruptive influences. It is similar to this: let us take a train, at the front of which there is a railway car and behind it, there is a locomotive; a machinist drives and controls the locomotive. Here, the railway car symbolises the first influence, the locomotive symbolises the guiding influence, and the machinist symbolises the propulsive influence, albeit broadly. And signals given from the station to be reached indicate the initiator influence.

In this way, when this train of influence arrives at the magnetic field of the recipient, because the duties of guiding and propulsive influences are accomplished at the threshold of that field, these accompanying influences leave the first influence at the boundary of the field and separate from it. And the first influence, through the activities it will bring out in that field, as in accordance with its purpose, effects the necessary changes upon the matter structure to which that field is subject, disrupts that matter's equilibrium, causing it to make various motions: displacing it, changing its states and forms – in short, it brings out the miscellaneous events on that matter in relation to its intensity and direction but always by utilising the duality principle and value differentiation mechanism. However, it should be remembered that all of these are always under the supervision of the sublime influences mechanism.

*
* *

Influences that are received from higher places are very important. For, each of these influences contains sublimating values. And matter, by gradually receiving these sublime values, becomes able to sympathise with the matter and influences of the higher plan which are richer in value. And one day, by shifting to the combinations at the higher level, they start to inter-influence with them in the same plan, that is, in the higher plan. What this means is that matter ascends one level up by transiting into matter combinations at the higher level and the development continues on like this. On the other hand, if there are more influences coming from below and influences cannot be received from above to the required degree, then things reverse. That is, because the influences coming from below are relatively simple, they are not in a state to feed all motions in the relatively more complex structure of matter. If these cannot be fed from above as well, some part of these motions begins to be erased. And that matter cannot exchange any more even with other combinations in the level it exists; and becomes mixed with the matter of one level down which can only sympathise with it; and this means the regression and erasure of its values.

In that case, the ascent or descent of a matter combination – more correctly, of an organism – depend on the qualities and quantities of higher and lower influences coming to it; and this depends on power of the being who manages it, to be able to fine-tune the influences to come, to invite the necessary ones into its organism and to keep clear of the unnecessary ones. That is, these acts are under its responsibility. For example, if the organiser, the being who manages that body, cannot fine-tune the billions of influences arriving at each part of an organism and if because of this, organisers of some parts invite influences more than necessary, then excess influences start to flux into these organs and consequently, excess activity is seen in that group in comparison to parts in other groups. These excess activities gradually require that organ to have contradictory motions against the general order of the organism. And this situation finally causes that organ to enter a rebellious state which knows no order in the organism and which we call a cancerous organ.

Therefore, the canceration event points to the need of an organ within the organism to make a much further advance in its development than it currently is. And, for excess or deficient activities in some organs in certain situations, the day comes when that organism to which these organs are subject will begin to collapse and disintegrate. If this happens in the crude internal organs of mankind, mankind talks about organic maladies or deaths. If it is seen among the particles belonging to the nervous system, they talk about psychological illnesses or cognitive disorders. All of these are the result of inability of a being to fine-tune the influences arriving at its body for certain reasons or under the influence of sublime necessities; of which the leading ones are states pertaining to the destiny of that being, that is, states which resulting from its merit and needs.

*
* *

After giving this general knowledge about influences, we will talk about the influences arriving at a man.

What is called man is a body constituted by a being that collects crude matter together in the Earth sphere for utilising as a vehicle for itself in order to serve the spirit it is connected to.

The being can constitute this body only with the help and directives of the sublime beings in duty. We have said that actually the being is also composed only of very subtle particles concentrated in a point of the universe; and a complex of certain energies or influences carrying all expressions of the needs of the spirit throughout universe. However, we would like to make it clear that the concept of 'point' mentioned here should not be thought of as a fixed, frozen space in comparison with the concept of space in the world. This is a concept which is hard and often impossible to understand and to explain under these physical conditions. Let us say on this topic that it should not be understood in the physical sense but in the perceptual sense. This is such a point that wherever comprehension is posited, it is there. So, that point is both at a given space in the universe and also everywhere. Whoever thinks about this topic, will start to intuit many things in this regard. This intuition will be beneficial not only for this topic but for solving many other problems as well. Knowledge of perceptual space or spherical space on the following pages will be preparing mankind in a better way for this intuition.

So, the being is an ensemble of influences or energies gathered at a point that must be accepted in this sense. And these belong to a spirit. A being that is composed of such very subtle energies or influences, which cannot be measured by the superficial concepts of time and space as understood by mankind, cannot directly influence the crude spheres of the cosmoses. However, spirits also need to encounter – during their various applications – the matter of these crude spheres. For, the being who will serve the spirit, in other words, who will be able to execute the necessities of subservience to spirit, needs to build a body for itself out of the matter of that sphere. So, in accordance with this necessity, helper beings in duty, by going into action, assist it. The being becomes connected – through the influences coming from its spirit – to this built body and governing it; and this is called incarnation, as we have previously said. It happens like this:

First of all, in the sphere where the application is to be done, a family unit duality – that is, the coming together of a man and a woman to constitute a unit – is required. After this need is fulfilled, by the assisting beings in duty, the seeds of man and woman are united to make an impregnated ovum. The being makes connection with this impregnated ovum. Here, the being, by intervening in the magnetic fields of the beings belonging to brain cells, consigns them to build the brain of the embryo, more correctly, its brain cells. The human being, while it has been in the spatium,[14] was already keeping these hundreds of thousands of brain cell beings together and influencing their magnetic fields. In this way, brain cells beings build their bodies, that is, brain cells with the human being's influence and help. The being constructs the other parts of the nervous system via this brain which has also been constructed. After this is accomplished, it generates all other formations of the body via the nervous system. While constructing the body, materials of the mother are utilised. That is, bodily materials of the foetus which is in formation are taken out of the materials constituting the body of its mother.

The being prevailing over the human body is influential and governs directly over the magnetic fields synthesis which is constituted of the magnetic fields of hundreds of thousands of beings belonging to brain cells. That is, the body is managed by the brain cells. However, this management is under the governance of the

---

[14] *Spatium*: Interval; the place to which the spirit/being leaving the body passes; this place is in a structure able to compose the most suitable forms, in accordance with the spirit's/being's imagination and free thinking. (*Publisher*)

energies ensemble which is the being of the body and belonging to a spirit, of the human being.

At the initial terms of the embryo, influences are sent to the brain cells ensemble, only as much as necessary. The being does not leave the perceptual point of gathering that is particular to itself, which we previously mentioned, and does not spread out into the body with its general ensemble. By always preserving its state of gathering as a complex of energies or influences in that perceptual point, it only sends the necessary quantity of some part of its influences to the magnetic field of the brain cells; it connects to it by some part of its influences. During the development of the embryo, the evolution of the foetus and finally, at the moment of man's birth, the quantity of influences it sends and connects to the magnetic field of the brain cells increase as needed. And at the moment of birth, a significant amount of its influences become connected to it.

According to worldly understanding, seven-eighths of this energies complex which exists in that perceptual point become connected to the body and only a small part of it remains freely in that perceptual point. And this is what mankind calls incarnation. As it is seen, neither does the being enter the body nor has it spread out with its whole to the organs of the body. It preserves its wholeness, throughout the totality of bodily life, in the perceptual concentration point which we have explained. It sends a great part of itself out and connects to the magnetic fields synthesis of the brain cells.

It should be remembered that, in all of these, there again exists the assistance of sublime influences. Mankind calls the influence fields which are connected to these brain cells – unknowingly, only upon their observations – as consciousness. However, because the parts of the being which remain free and unconnected to brain cells remain unknown to them and to those around them, mankind has not been able to acquire clear knowledge about it.

*
* *

However, on the other hand, the being managing the man is a whole. Although it has left a small part of its own energies outside of the magnetic field of brain cells, that part, as well, in accordance with its wholeness and the necessity of its evolution, is not completely separate from the body but in a close relation with it. Nevertheless, its freedom is not complete. Actually, by means of the close relations between these two parts, that being utilises the activities that aim at the evolution of its parts connected to the body in world and by this way, the imperative of embodiment is realised.

*
* *

The out of the body state of the being does not directly impact on the consciousness of mankind. For, man can only become conscious with a certain part of the influences sent out to him by the being and he tries to comprehend himself incompletely. Although, having some vague intuition of the parts that are not coming to him, he has nevertheless no clear comprehension about these. So, what mankind calls inner being, essential self, essence-being, and sometimes intuit through a deep contemplation, are the relatively free states of his true being outside the body. We say relatively because although it is free, it is still obliged to follow all states of the body, to render the necessities of those states in accordance with the imperative of its duties in the world. This is its duty. Unless, with the death of the body, its connected parts become unconnected; it cannot use its free parts with complete freedom. For, indirectly, it cannot free itself completely from the imperatives of the body via its connected parts. There are compulsory fields of occupation which will always preoccupy it with its activities on its body such as digesting, concluding the impressions it receives from the body through its parts connected to the body – in accordance with the evolutionary imperatives particular to that moment – and reflecting these to spirit.

*
* *

As for the necessities of evolution, the being once in a while reflects a few parts of the values and acquisitions existing in itself to the brain. And mankind has noticed these influences – again, without properly understanding their disposition – which are reflected from these free parts of their beings to their brains and has termed them the subconscious. Therefore, consciousness in man is the manifestation of these

90

parts reflected to the body, more correctly, to the magnetic fields synthesis constituted by brain cells, through the direct connection made by the being. There is also – as we have said – a superconsciousness field of the being belonging to its unconnected parts that have stayed in a perceptual gathering point outside of the body and are not connected to the magnetic field of the brain, which should be discussed in two parts. One of these is subconscious. This field comprises the parts containing impressions pertaining to the past lives of the being. The second part we call higher conscious, containing the influences constantly received from its spirit and other beings by the being's part which has stayed free. So, as a result of their relations of consciousness with higher consciousness; relations and exchanges are built between the influences mankind receives from other beings of the spiritual plan and their consciousness; the brain connects to the higher consciousness through the spiritual influences it receives. That is, impressions belonging to the spiritual plan arrive at it via the higher conscious channel.

*
* *

Therefore, there are innumerable nervous systems which take the influences from the consciousness field which is the basic centre and consign these to necessary places in order to be used; which are not centres in themselves but stations. And even the influences spreading out to the organism do separate functions; their source is one and they are always inter-related. Influences come from the superconsciousness and arrive at the field which is directly connected to the magnetic channel of the brain cells of the being. And from there, in accordance with evolutionary necessities, they are sent out to the nervous stations in order to be used in required places for the survival of the body.

Therefore, mankind is always facing both the influences they receive from their beings and also the influences they receive from their surroundings. And man lives in the equilibrium of the influences coming from his essence-being and the influences he receives from his surroundings in the world.

*
* *

91

What happens when the body dies? When death, which mankind calls, again mistakenly, disincarnation occurs, the beings of the brain cells leave their bodies, that is, the brain cells they incarnated into. However, they do not disperse. Because the being that needs to leave the body does not remove its influence over them, even after it leaves its body. With the influences it continues sending to the magnetic fields of these beings, it keeps them together and under its influence in the spatium, as well. Naturally, it also receives influences from them.

At the initial stages of the spatium, as we will later explain, all influences and connections of a being coming from above, below and the surroundings are severed, except the influences coming from its own spirit. It is only encircled within its own being and the impressions of its subconscious, especially belonging to its last life. And during this time, because it is continuously in relation with the beings of its brain cells; it can collect and make compositions out of the impressions which also exist in those beings, pertaining to the world. This activity, although most often causing much suffering, offers it the possibility to do the required contemplation. After acquiring the necessary results with this contemplation, its awakening and the increase in its comprehension are ensured again by the influences coming from above and the surroundings. Then, it enters a state of ability to understand its true being.

Naturally, in the mean time, beings of the brain cells have also evolved of their own accord. By this means, after subjecting it to some very long applications and processes and its completing the preparation for entering the world once again, it is given the right to choose forms and conditions of its life within a field of available possibilities which are most suitable for its evolution in the world. The scope of this field, that is, the field of choices offered to it, depends on the degree of freedom it has acquired in accordance with its comprehension. If its comprehension is too narrow, this field would be very narrow for it and in some cases, a very limited, almost nil field of choices are left to it. If its comprehension is expanded enough to encompass the whole world, then there remains no need to reembody and do applications in the world. So, in this way, after it prepares its surroundings in the world in relation to its freedom of choice, it consigns the beings of brain cells which it kept under its influence – by influencing their magnetic fields – to the mother's body, in order for them to build a foetus brain in that mother's womb. And the process we previously explained begins afresh under new conditions.

*
* *

However, it should never be forgotten that because it is an imperative that all of these deeds should advance in accordance with the divine order, the constant supervision and control of sublime influences and administrative energy complexes which allows these is always present here – as it is everywhere.

We would like to point out as well that the beings of brain cells, which are under the influence of the being always governing the man, will not stay connected to it forever. For, they do the necessary preparations for themselves as well, in order to acquire the power to manage a human body a piece independently. And as they complete their preparations, they will separate themselves from the influence of that being one by one and will cease to be a brain cell. For them each to enter the stage of independent human beings, they need to separate from the world and go through applications in some interval milieus outside of the world. Only by this and after reaching a state of ability to manage a human whole, again by influencing the magnetic fields synthesis of the brain cells of a man, do they start to render their evolutions, in the world as humans, that is, through the human body.

*
* *

After this knowledge, the expression of the embodiment of human being should be understood in this wider meaning and should not be thought to be in a narrow frame such as the concept of incarnation, which means entrance in the flesh. The term of incarnation may be used for simpler beings which are consigned to connect into cells by force. However, it is not true for a human being.

Therefore, the relation of a man with a body occurs in the form of its governance upon the magnetic field of its brain cells and

93

sending out its influences via this vehicle throughout its organism. And this is ensured by a major part of the influences that are sent out from that perceptual point we have mentioned to the body. And a small part of its influences always exist, more or less freely, in that point outside of the body.

*
* *

Influences in the body render all physical, physiological, biological and psychological functions of the body, under the control of the being governing the body and in accordance with the sublime evolutionary necessities. Here, nothing impedes, even slightly. The functions of these influences are not separate from the general function of the universe. They are realised in the great harmony of it and cannot digress from this harmony.

After all, the divine order has arranged all states and situations of the whole universe and connected it to such an ordered mechanism that in spite of their endless appearances, the events of the universe flow away as a single procession. For the ones who can see this truth, a single body and the whole universe are two inseparable mechanisms.

*
* *

A great number of influences arrive in each particle of the universe, with all its beings. Human comprehension is unable to grasp even a particle of the influences complex that arrives in an object constituted by billions of particles; in a solar system constituted by billions of objects; in a nebulae constituted by billions of solar systems and in a cosmos constituted by innumerable nebulae; and finally, in the universal whole constituted again by innumerable realms besides the hydrogen reality.

So, it is this unity of influences fulfilling the necessities of the divine order in the universe, establishing the harmony of universe within these necessities and embracing it that gathers together all motions and states and which explains the relation of spirits with universe and the imperativeness of the evolutionary flow.

*
* *

We explained how various transitions and the acquisition of higher values of the matter combinations play a big role in the development of matter. Since the sole purpose of spirit's connection to universe is evolution, it becomes an obligation for the being serving the spirit to utilise these transitions and, because of this, to encounter innumerable matter combinations. Matter combinations have myriad forms and degrees in innumerable spheres. Besides the possibilities of a sphere, especially like the earth sphere, which has particularly rich matter constitutions, the riches of possibilities belonging to matter combinations of innumerable spheres are the abundant materials beneficial to the evolution of spirits.

However, for a being to benefit properly from this abundance of material, it is necessary for it to live in these innumerable combinations which are quite different and in different degrees from each other and, afterwards, to change them and be able to pass higher parts and to leave the matter combinations it has used in the lower part where it has been; otherwise it cannot reach the higher combinations and remains in its simple state. However, the purpose of its application in these matter combinations is always actually to reach up and ensure the accomplishment of the evolutionary stages of the spirit with matter, which it serves. In this case, a being will first make a close connection with a body built out of the matter of a sphere according to its need; will prevail over each particle of it by its own subtle vibrations and then will use it in accordance with the needs of the spirit it is connected to; it will thus send the vibrations of events brought out by relations with crude matter combinations and relations between these combinations and other bodies in that sphere, via the channel of its comprehension; as we have mentioned, mankind calls this connection of it with the body incarnation.

After its work has finished in the body, the being does not need to stay there any more, because this would be against its own evolution. Therefore, when its work is completed, the being will leave the body and enter into other matter combination possibilities. And a being, after utilising all possibilities of a body, should engage the applications within the conditions of another and more superior matter complex, as well. However, for this state to be realised, it needs to separate from the conditions of former matter complexes, to leave its body; which mankind calls disincarnation or death.

95

*
* *

Death is a quantitative expression of the value differentiation in a certain moment, under the harmony of the divine order. That is, after a worldly body has served properly as required by the spirit throughout its worldly life, its purpose in serving that spirit as a vehicle ceases to be. Consequently, values in that body must decrease. For, in the divine order, it is an imperative to terminate all processes which are no longer necessary. And, by this imperative, the influences – that is, the values descending to the worldly body which has accomplished its all functions and turned out useless in the face of the being that caused it to animate – will terminate. By the termination of these influences, some part of the motions in its combinations begins to be erased. Meanwhile, by the intervention of the influences coming from below, that body cannot preserve its former form and state any more. It starts to disintegrate and disperse; and the qualitative appearance of this state is death. And it occurs with the cell beings in the brain starting to forsake their bodies. For, brain cells forsaking their bodies means that the being who governs these cells is severing its relation to the body.

The being, who benefited from this body throughout its earthly life, needs to be cultivated and fed with more suitable combinations on the values and mechanisms of the higher influences in order to continue further developmental and evolutionary stages.

In the series of embodiments in a world, as the deaths and the births of the being continue, its work in that world finally ends. So, as the amount of higher influences belonging to the body which needs to be forsaken there forever is decreased for the last time, on the other hand and at the same time, the amount of influences and values of a body belonging to another cosmos are increased. Therefore, the being serving the evolution of spirit will leave that milieu with its last death in the world and will pass to a higher milieu, encompassing and with abundant possibilities. So, for the evolution of a spirit, as for the birth of a being, that is, its subtle material vehicle in the universe, is an imperative and a necessity, also likewise for this subtle being to be able to serve further evolution of the spirit, its leaving the crude milieus which became useless and passing to the higher milieus it needs is the imperative of an equally powerful necessity.

*
* *

All forms and states result in human death: illnesses, seizures, murders, accidents, natural events are only to fulfil these imperatives of necessity in the most suitable manner for the ensuing development and evolution of that being. After learning this truth, there is no meaning to deem the death and the states causing death as disasters in themselves. Here, the whole issue is, during this transition from a lower milieu to a higher milieu that is called death, the necessity of man's having properly completed the deeds expected from him and not having digressed from the higher realities of his conscience which was his sole guide as he successfully lived through his life. As he does this, by obeying the higher realities, he does not lose the right way, as well as ensuring the further developments of his conscience and so benefiting to that extent from its strengthening guidance. Therefore, conscience in the world is the most powerful support and redeemer of mankind in the path of evolution.

WORLD, DISHARMONY, HARMONY

In human life, the developmental mechanism appearing as conscience is not particular only to this stage. It is a preliminary developmental and evolutionary mechanism which all beings in the world are subject to. Therefore, it is necessary to define and understand conscience with this general value.

Conscience is a preparatory mechanism orientated to the realisation of duty, which is the purpose of all acts and actions for beings.

Since the purpose of all beings is evolution and the meaning of evolution at the stage of humanity is preparation for the super-world plan of duty, the conscience mechanism, of which the definition is based on the concept of preparation for duty, must be all-inclusive for all beings in the world. On the other hand, there is a unity between the development of comprehension and conscience. However, the comprehension of beings varies greatly according to their levels of development. So, among beings with varying comprehensions, their understanding of conscience and conscience applications will accordingly be different.

*
* *

So far, only the state of conscience at the stage of human has been studied and its states and situations corresponding to its other stages have been left out of the account. This situation has not allowed mankind to study the consecutive flow of conscience in stages starting from initial plant life to human life. However, studying conscience within the whole of world life is necessary for understanding the knowledge of evolution better. Conscience, with its general and comprehensive implications, should be studied under the light of the duality principle and value differentiation.

101

*
* *

We have previously explained in detail that everything happens in our whole cosmos through the duality principle and value differentiation mechanism; and no particle, no event or concept can be excluded from this principle. And, conscience, a powerful mechanism for evolutionary preparation in the world, also obeys this principle. Therefore, conscience is a duality-unit. We have mentioned that the duality-unit comprises two opposing components. We will explain these opposite components of the conscience duality.

The existence of opposites in any duality-unit is necessary for its function. When there are no opposites, the purpose of existence of that unit cannot be realised. Therefore, one of the opposite components of the conscience which is aimed at ensuring development, the higher one, is directed towards a sense of duty. On the other hand, its opposite, that is, lower component, is the earthly cravings, hindering the former's advance along the path of acquiring a sense of duty. Consequently, we will call the former the duty preparation component and the latter the earthly craving component.

So the conscience mechanism, which works for the preparation of beings in the world to the plan of duty, has two opposite components: one is directed towards duty and the other is directed towards the earthly cravings, and the conscience mechanism works through conflicts, struggles and states of equilibrium which occur as the result of these two components' continuous value differentiation, that is, as one or other opposite receives superior values and influences. And the beings' advancement takes on various forms in accordance with these states of equilibrium. These conflicts and states of equilibrium exist in all stages of all beings in the world, according to their powers of instinct, intuition and comprehension.

*
* *

Mankind cannot comprehend the presence of this duality in plants, animals and even some human beings. Because the form of this mechanism, understood by mankind, appears only in mankind. For conscience to take this form, comprehension must reach the

102

level that is seen in mankind. Because of this, the duality of development that is seen in levels below human will of course not be similar to the form of conscience in mankind. Nevertheless, this duality of development exists in all beings in the world, starting from the most primitive ones which have entered in a more or less independent and free state. And their development – albeit very slowly – depends on the workings of this mechanism. Because the fragments of some breakthroughs of life in the very primitive state are seen in beings using plant bodies, it is possible for mankind to expand the scope of the duality principle of his comprehension as far as to them. However, because the form of this mechanism seen in mankind as conscience has been perfected and taken to its fullest form, for not confusing the minds by extending this term to the beings below human, it is suitable to generalise the term as the developmental or evolutionary mechanism when we talk about all beings and not name it as conscience – as it is in mankind.

*
* *

Now, let us state the equivalents of concepts entailed by developmental mechanism such as comprehension and freedom in the simple beings in the world, such as plants and animals.

In every embodied being there is the simplest and most primitive state of comprehension and freedom, particular to it. We have explained this above. However, comprehensions and wills at primitive levels carry completely different meanings than those accepted by mankind. Especially in plants, these are too simple and primitive to be sensed; almost in states of instinctual leaps, which is abundantly sufficient for the life needs of the beings in that stage. So, in plants and animals, even if not in the form of conscience known by mankind, there is an equivalent developmental duality. Nevertheless, we repeat that it should not be considered in the form of duty-self duality in the human realm.

This duality, which we accept as only a simple developmental mechanism in primitive beings, is naturally attuned to most primitive instincts. For example, let us take plants. Comprehension and

103

freedom of will in plants is so primitive and simple in comparison with mankind that it has no objective but rather a subjective character and it is almost impossible for human comprehension to grasp it. Because of this, development in them appears to mankind to be mechanical, but this is an illusion. For, beings in this stage, unlike the ones in crude matter, are not subject only to the influences coming from the unitary and are obliged to adapt the motions they bring out in matter. In these beings, the needs of instinctual leaps have emerged and simple applications of these have started.

Actually, as it takes its food from the soil through its roots and spreads it throughout its body, its utilising and spending these in its body by obeying the capillarity feature in physics indicates that its instinctual leaps are primitive almost to a degree that it is obscure to mankind. This state expresses the simplest form of that plant's intervention in crude matter for survival. It is also valid for other survival functions of the plant. So, only with the condition of preserving this meaning, we say that development in plants is automatic. Because of this, they each have as well, although very simple, a developmental mechanism consisting of automatic and simple interventions which are sufficient in this primitive state of animation and this, as well, is realised in a duality-unit whose name, in the life of mankind, is conscience. After all, if we do not accept this view, we cannot explain the advancement of plants and animals in accordance with the developmental mechanism particular to embodied beings in the world.

This situation is a little bit clearer in animals. For, their comprehension and freedom of will are a little bit more developed, that is, up to a degree which can strike the eye of mankind. Because of this, it is possible for many to observe this duality-unit mechanism in animals with some small effort. When a dog is set free between a piece of bone and a stick – which it was beaten by – it becomes confused. As the memory of beatings with the stick is relived in its spirit, the indecision in leaping or not leaping towards the bone it will go through for a while, corresponds to a simple and short inner struggle within it. And this situation indicates the form and way of working in animals of the mechanism we call conscience duality in mankind. This mechanism works automatically in animals.

For example, the feeling of hunger directs an animal to over-come its feelings of fear or laziness which prevents its duty of searching for food. It overcomes this feeling because its hunger compels it to make efforts to search and explore its surroundings for food. And this, similar to the conscience mechanism of man-kind, prepares it for many grounds and possibilities for applica-tion. It cannot find food, it starves, it gets beaten in the places it goes, it fights with its fellow animals, and eventually it may get killed. These exist together with a great number of automatic con-flicts, albeit temporary, in the being of that animal.

Similarly, intense influences, connections of love coming from above, charge it with the duty of feeding and bringing up its new-born. In this way, the efforts it will make are in the face of all in-coming influences that advance with the duality-unit, which is the equivalent of the conscience mechanism in mankind; and what prepares animals automatically for the conscience duality in man-kind is this duality-unit. As to mankind, here, the same mechanism naturally starts to take on the form called conscience with its higher – that is, more comprehending – character. Reality of conscience in mankind has three stages as well: automatic, semi-comprehending and also more or less comprehending.

The automatic stage of conscience still belongs to the initial times of mankind. There may be those who mistakenly define such people as not having had their consciences developed yet. However, this judgement is wrong within the encompassing knowledge we gave pertaining to conscience duality. And this situation is the result of mankind's inability to see duality openly. However, regardless of how the conscience mechanism at the initial levels of humanity is vague and appears automatic, it has still enriched with more or less comprehending acts in comparison to those in animals.

For example, in the comprehension of a woman at the initial stage of humanity who is attached to her baby with a great love, there are more or less powerful feelings, intuitions and even fragments of knowledge pertaining to the obligation of motherhood. She does not feed her baby like an animal does, solely by obeying her blind in-stincts. She accepts the necessity of taking precautions as much as her mind allows and of enduring some self-sacrifice for her baby not to get sick, not to be disturbed, not to die; and makes efforts on this path. She does not shake off her growing child as animals do. Again, as much as her mind allows and her knowledge permits, she comprehends the necessity of occupying herself with the training and education of the child and so more or less attains the intuition of obligation that she owns motherhood to her child on this path.

However, on the other hand, she may not be doing these things! That is, the state of freedom and independence, which separates the humankind automatism in its initial stages from the automatism of the animal realm indicates that the sense of responsibility and comprehension which do not exist in animals has started to rise in mankind – even if as a state of intuition. The rise of this sense of responsibility is the beginning of the most important emotions which are factors in the acceleration of human development. For, these have great roles to play in terms of the states of equilibrium between the opposites of conscience reality directed to duty and earthly cravings. By these means, a human being – through the necessary automatisms – will be prepared for the sense of duty as myriad tests and trials, sufferings, torments, observations; in short, innumerable events taking place in his or her field of comprehension.

*
* *

As the stages of humanity progress, emotions, knowledge and comprehensions belonging to the conscience reality increase. And to that degree, the boundaries of freedoms expand. However, on the other hand, as his comprehension expands mankind starts to intuit better the things he should and should not do; he feels the necessity of obeying these and when this is the case, he starts to feel the necessity of limiting his freedom by himself. In this way, the conscience mechanism is gradually comprehended better and to that degree, man evades automatism; and this allows him to get nearer to his sense of duty, step by step. Eventually, after quite a long time, the equilibria of conscience duality reach the threshold of the intuition and knowledge of duty.

*
* *

After summarily giving the general scheme of the developmental mechanism belonging to beings we now begin to explain how it works, how it should work in the mankind's life and in which ways it makes progress.

When following the development of the conscience mechanism in mankind, it is not correct to put some states and capabilities such as love, altruism, earthly cravings, conscience in an order as it has been done generally. For example, it is wrong to arrange an absolute sequence in which the stage of altruism comes first, then the stage of love or of conscience definitely following it. Here only, throughout the life of mankind, components of conscience, which are both opposing and complementing each other and directed to duty and earthly cravings, advance against each as the two opposites of a whole.

Therefore, the conscience mechanism, which puts into effect the preparation for the sense of duty in the world, exhibits a state of a two-sided whole which sometimes leads in the direction of earthly cravings and sometimes in the direction of duty; and the capabilities we listed above take the states of equilibrium, within this whole on its positive and negative sides, which are adjusted to the suitable situations and needs of its every level; and of the opposites ensuring the equilibrium, the higher one is directed to the plan of duty and the lower one is directed to earthly cravings.

For example, if the sense of considering others is a higher reality which is more converging to the plan of duty, the selfishness which stands against it as the opposite constitutes the lower reality. However, it should be remembered that actually both of these are but a two-sided appearance of the same value which displays opposing qualities in accordance with the duality principle. We will explain the meaning of these opposites better as we continue to talk about the topic of conscience. Therefore, the conscience is a powerful mechanism which convergences on human comprehension towards the knowledge of duty, in a complete state of duality-unit with its both positive and negative sides. This mechanism prepares the instincts at the stage of plant to the automatisms of the stage of animal; the automatisms at the stage of animal to the stage of sense of duty in human life and mankind to the comprehensions of the intuition and knowledge of duty, that is, to the plan of duty.

*
* *

This developmental mechanism that has reached the stage of humanity is left to man's comprehension and freedom of will which has more or less emerged. In this way, to whichever opposite of the conscience duality man directs his efforts through the comprehension and freedom of will he is obliged to use, to whichever opposite he adds more value; the equilibrium disrupts in the favour of that opposite. For, orientating to a matter combination means sending influences to it; and the influences that are sent are the corresponding values and entail value differentiation in favour of that side.

*
* *

Now, we will elaborate on the conscience mechanism's way of working. In any level of development, conscience duality's higher reality, which we call positive, and lower reality of earthly cravings, which we relatively call negative, stays in equilibrium in man. That is, the values they contain preserve the status quo among them. Nevertheless, this equilibrium here does not always stay fixed: it is disrupted every moment. However, as we have previously said, all disrupted duality equilibria are inclined to be restored, to be balanced again. In accordance with the duality principle, opposites of the disrupted equilibrium never stay in that state. Whichever side of the equilibrium is disrupted by receiving more values, in order to restore it, from that opposite to the weak one, starts a flux of values. And this entails the increase of the value level of the opposing negative side up to the level of the positive opposite. In this way, the new level of equilibrium which is restored between the positive side that increased its level by receiving higher values actually enters into a superior state in comparison with the previous state; and this means that the duality-unit has passed on to a higher level, that is, comprehension in the conscience mechanism has converged on the knowledge of duty a little bit more. On the contrary, if more values are sent to the negative opposite, that is, to the earthly cravings; although the process is the same as before, the direction is reversed. In this case, the duality-unit, that is, the conscience, starts to shift a level down. And shifting of the conscience to lower levels means the beginning of its losing its higher values; about which mankind uses terms like silencing or blinding the conscience upon looking at the appearances. Thus, for the former states, they talk about strengthening of the conscience.

However, general evolutionary principles do not consent for any being's constantly going downwards. If this is the case – that is, if a man shifts the equilibrium always downwards by continuously sending values to the opposite and enters into a state of inability to free himself from abusing this comprehension and freedom of will – then beings in duty, who are obliged to help him, consign him to a necessary automatism by immediately sending him strong influences. That is – a more or less similar thing occurs in the initial stages of humanity – they try to ensure his comprehension and will to be directed automatically to the higher opposite by putting before him some attractive or repulsive critical events. Naturally, this state which carries with it a more or less a compelling character, does not occur with ease, unlike the way it does with free will. On the contrary, the suffering and troubling qualities of innumerable events that will be brought forth as the imperatives of automatism would prepare for him many struggles, pains and even, if needed, tortures and deaths, until they direct the will of that man into the path so that his will may acquire the power to orientate to the required opposite side which he could not use in his free state.

*
* *

Now, let us pass to the opposite components of the conscience which orientate to duty and earthly cravings. Two components appearing opposite to each other in the conscience mechanism in any level are the higher and lower rings, interlocked and particular to that level, of the chain of realities which are sequenced from below to above and arranged in accordance with the imperatives and necessities of the needs, in a preliminary quality for preparing a man with the knowledge of the plan of duty. We define the reality constituting the lower ring as directed to earthly cravings, and the higher ring to the duty. This chain, as it extends from below to above, is from past to future. When we say that the lower one is directed to earthly cravings,

109

we mean the reality which has been lived, and when we say the higher one is directed to duty, we mean the reality which will be lived. Thus, each component of the conscience mechanism contains the lived and to-be-lived realities of man's life. A reality which completed its cycle stands against a higher reality which has the quality of converging the man a little bit more to the plan of duty. And this is why we call it the earthly cravings. However, it should be remembered that this lower reality which hinders the higher one for that moment has been the higher reality of the previous level, which prepared that higher level of conscience.

*
* *

For mankind, reality is their believing the presence which their feelings are concerned with. Therefore, since the feelings always change, there is no constant reality. As the comprehensions expand and increase, feelings and realities change and become encompassing, as well. So, the state of the ascending and changing realities from below to above in the conscience mechanism points to the speed of the reaching and advancing of the being towards the plan of duty. This is because realities advance together with comprehension. The more comprehensions increase, the more realities expand and become correspondingly more encompassing. That is, presences with which the feelings are concerned with increase and the powers of internalising, absorbing these also increase; and so, higher and further realities are attained. A man, climbing a mountain, can only see a small part of the terrain when he is at the foothill. As he climbs higher and ascends, the terrain unfolding before his eyes widens correspondingly. And when he reaches the summit, then he sees and comprehends the whole scope of the plain. Therefore, as comprehension increases, the scope of realities also increases.

Reality is a knowledge at the same time. The things which concern the feelings and of which their presence is believed are sensed and known. Therefore, in the world there is no constant and unchanging, absolute reality for every level and stage. Everybody has his own particular sense and belief. And in accordance with these senses and beliefs, there are different realities with different qualities and scopes. Situations which have not yet entered the reality of the mankind who are at lower levels, can be reality for the ones at the higher level.

Similarly, as realities ascend they also contain the simpler realities of the lower levels. These simple realities which enter into higher realities lose their identities by gradually dissolving within their scope. Thus, for example, small details, indentations, rises, ditches, shrubs, small puddles etc. that are seen in a few acres of terrain by man when he is at the foothills gradually vanish within the wider field of increasingly widening horizons as he ascends to the summit. Nevertheless, they stay within that field as the constituting components, pieces of this whole which occurs.

Therefore, as the realities join to each other and widen, it is necessary not to be stuck with the old realities. As long as it is not done, unless we are not willing to abandon the details of the scenery of the few acres seen from the foothills, it is not possible to ascend higher and widen the scenery. And the riches, magnificent sceneries of the wide field that is to be observed from the hills cannot be appreciated. Actually, as long as we are stuck in that narrow, lower place, the need to look for this scenery, these beauties, does not emerge at all. Therefore, in order to ascend, to converge the aim – in short, to take the path of acquiring the required merit and comprehensions necessary for the plan of duty – it is necessary not to be buried within the earthly cravings of the lower levels and to shake off and abandon their weight.

*
* *

Shaking off and getting rid of realities is not done by arbitrarily discarding a reality. Here, this point should be understood well. A reality's leaving its place to another reality is not an arbitrary thing. It is, above all else, the result of a developmental imperative; this is because, to be able to abandon a reality and to pass into a higher reality, it is necessary to obey all necessities of that reality, to be governing it and to assimilate it thoroughly; that is, the results of that reality should be internalised with all its necessities by the essence-being and become the essence-knowledge. Otherwise, the real place of a reality which has not yet assimilated and internalised in

111

the conscience mechanism is the higher component of that mechanism, after all. For, it is not a lived but to-be-lived reality – that is, it is not an acquired but a to-be-acquired reality. Therefore, it is necessary to completely obey its necessities so it can descend to becoming the second plan, the plan of earthly cravings as a lived component. And the state which will determine this is the need.

*
* *

When a man, after living thoroughly in a reality, encounters there the points which start to dissatisfy him and needs to look for the superior one; then the reality he is in becomes a component which needs to fall back to the second plan, which enters a state of earthly cravings. So, in this way, events occurring through struggles are made for shaking off a reality which is old and which needs to be left behind and the lessons learnt from these events cause the comprehension to expand and consequently the evolution of spirit.

In this way, realities go on continuously from below to above. That is, the component of any level which is directed to duty constitutes the earthly craving component of a higher reality and its component directed to earthly cravings constitutes the duty component of a lower reality. Let us repeat that these realities do not follow each other in an unchanging order. They follow each other by changing in accordance with the evolutionary need and comprehension capacity of the person. Let us give an example here. Imagine a level at which manslaughter by vengeance is allowed and there is a man who believed and accepted the necessity of vengeance by blood feud as a duty in killing a murderer who killed that man's father or relative. That belief is a knowledge, a reality of that level. However, there is such a level of knowledge above it that what is valid there is the knowledge and judgement of not having desire to revenge someone who has done wrong to him and this is a situation that requires responsibility and correspondingly, of responding to atrocities always with forgiveness and tolerance.

Imagine that what is determined for the man who has lived in the previous reality is to get through his reality and to pass into the reality of the higher level and, because of this, to come back into

112

the world again. That man, having come into the world, has put all possibilities of struggle in his plan to assist him in getting rid of his old reality. However, he is still under the influence of his old reality. Therefore, when he is back in the world, facing the powerful bonds of the revenge reality of the earthly cravings constituting the negative pole of the conscience mechanism, that man may not converge on the higher reality which suggests forgiveness, tolerance, even love. And he starts to have difficulties in pulling himself through from his old reality of revenge. Because of this, if he remains all alone, he will not move an inch from his place and pass into the higher level.

Nevertheless, we have previously said that this situation can never continue like this. And also, we have mentioned the presence of millions of influences which will arrive at the higher opposite from above and at the lower opposite from below of a duality-unit. Besides, there is also his life plan, sketched as he comes into the world; and as how he promised to stay true to this plan in the world, the beings in duty in assisting him around that plan will of course do their duty, as well. Therefore, for the purpose of developing the powers that man needs to reach the higher realities, these helpers will do whatever needs to be done. So, with this help and intervention, that man is uprooted from his old reality and by jumping to the higher level's knowledge of forgiveness, tolerance and compassion, he gives up his old reality of revenge, manslaughter. In this case, internalising the higher reality is possible by becoming disentangled from the bonds of the lower reality.

*
* *

As studying the realities regarding the knowledge they concluded in the essence-being, it is necessary to remember that they complement each other. In this regard, each reality is the piece of a whole which successively goes to the point that is needed to be reached by each reality's preparing for a higher reality. And actually, the refining experiences of a human being are but the impressions of these realities which have accumulated in the essence-being as knowledge. That is, as a past reality prepares the future reality, the impression of the past reality remains present as well within the essence-knowledge of the future reality. In fact, in this way, future realities widen as they gradually include the conclusions of past realities, and their scope increases; and causes the increase of refining experience of the being. For example, individual earthly cravings which complete the level where crude self-centredness reality exists, becomes social selfishness in a higher communal plan reality, with a superior and encompassing character.

If at the former level, a man only strives for his individual interests, at the second level he starts to work for the interests of a small community, of a family which depends on him. And this earthly craving, as the levels ascend, increases and widens by encompassing a community, a society, a nation, mankind and even all beings; and as it orientates towards them it is necessary to call it consideration of others, not selfishness. Nevertheless, it remains in a state of earthly craving in comparison with a higher reality than itself. This situation indicates the states which are widening in scope and developing by the gradual feeding of the conclusions of the previous earthly cravings in the essence-being by the conclusions of new elements, that is, the conclusions of the higher opposites.

So, a reality of earthly craving which entails efforts to achieve a higher reality by standing against it, at the same time, is in a state of candidature to be mixed within this higher reality and vanish into the higher identities. Therefore, within the most advanced and highest realities' syntheses that have turned into essence-knowledge, there are the conclusions of the earthly cravings belonging to initial realities which have adapted to this knowledge and dissolved their initial dispositions within there.

*
* *

Now, we will elaborate upon the problem of how realities prepare mankind for the plan of duty. The part of man that will pass into the plan of duty is not his body with its flesh, bones and neurons. The body needs to be buried in the earth with all its formations at the end of every world life-cycle. However, there is another part of the man, not his body, which advances from his initial human life to the knowledge of duty which is a super-human plan; and this is his being, as we have previously explained. That is, what advances throughout the whole universe as gradually developing by using myriad matter in order to serve the spirit it is subject to is his being. And bodies are only vehicles for this being. Thus, all these realities and all components constituting these realities prepare not the human body but the being which uses it for the plan of duty. And the meaning of these is that world realities that have evaluated according to the human brain do not pass into the essence-being in the same states and forms. And if this was the case, there would be no necessity for the body and the being could directly live in the world. So, what are the real values of the realities – those evaluated by the human brain, that we see and know in the world – which pass into the essence-being and which need to be lived through for its preparation?

These values that pass into the being are not the crude states and forms of the realities which have been adjusted to the world matter. These values are some conclusions which these realities bring about in the essence-being as states of sublime and subtle matter combinations suitable for the subtle structure and the needs of the being. It is even not right to call these impressions. This is because this word does not convey here the complete meaning. So, these conclusions or impressions, whose disposition is very vague to human comprehension, are deep traces that cause the development of beings. And the meaning of the phrase of these traces deepening is the expanding and gradual encompassing of the essence-comprehension belonging to that being and ensuring its evolution. Actually, because the essence-comprehension is identical with the being; the expanding and gradual encompassing of comprehension is the development of the being in itself.

*
* *

As to the manner of occurrence of the realities in the essence-being; as lived realities and all good or bad events which are connected to these realities make mankind happy or sad with their various appearances, they actually cause some formations and transformations in the essence-being – by values suitable to the constitution of that being – which cannot be understood by man. In this way, within very sublime matter syntheses, they put into effect their subtle combinations which are in completely different forms and manners than their appearances in the world, by becoming enriched as they gain values. These are true essence-knowledge of the spirits that serve their evolutions.

So, as material forms and states – as we have just mentioned – of the realities among crude world matter continue by following and preparing each other, their conclusions – their companions – in the essence-being feed the essence-knowledge gradually accumulating in states which have much deeper and subtler meanings than their expressions in relation to the crude cosmos. These are real evolutionary values. Those who compare the concept of evolutionary values we previously talked about with the concept here will expand their intuitions a little more concerning in what manner spirits benefit from the universe. The essence-comprehension that expands with essence-knowledge – that is, the true comprehension belonging to the being which is above the milieu of body, and reaching to the end of universe together with the being – benefits from the manner of crude appearances of the realities it lives indirectly via the channel of the body in the world. And by this, it continues its services belonging to the evolution of the spirit it is subject to.

So, after this knowledge is grasped properly, the possibilities of confusion and bewilderment by mixing the meanings of terms like realities both lived and forgotten have been cleared away. For, here, there are two screens which have become targets for events. One of them is the crude matter gatherings we call the physical and the other is a subtle and complex being serving a spirit by utilising this gathering. Crudeness of the body is good for receiving crude realities and allows the possibility of increase of essence-knowledge in the being. So, what need to be forgotten when they are completed are the crude appearances of the realities addressing the crude bodies. And this is an imperative of the superficial comprehension of time, which we will explain later. For, in accordance with this imperative, for a value to be put into effect, the old value needs to leave its place to it. On the other hand, the aspects of the realities addressing the essence-being are the subtle meanings in the essence-being, which are the companions of their crude appearances. These are, as we previously said, value parts which prepare and join each other; and these parts expand the essence-knowledge synthesis.

We repeat that in studying the topic of living the realities and forgetting them, it should be remembered to discern the material memories which depend on the human brain, on chronological value and systems in accordance with the superficial time compre-hension from the impressions of these realities which are deepened in the being and included within the essence-knowledge synthesis. This is because, as forgetting the former ones is necessary for a body which is subject to the superficial time necessities, the firm establishment of the latter among the essence-knowledge for a be-ing that lives with spherical time comprehension is as natural and imperative. And it is even the necessity of the original purpose.

*
* *

Now we will study a little more the relations between the dualities of the conscience mechanism ensuring an increase in essence-knowledge.

We have said that in the conscience mechanism, the two oppos-ing appearances of which one is directed to duty and the other is di-rected to earthly cravings, consist only of realities following and preparing each other. According to its order, the same reality can be directed both to earthly cravings and to duty. Where it needs to be obliged to, it is directed to duty and where it needs to be left behind it is directed to earthly cravings. Therefore, just like the conclusions of earthly cravings– that is, the essence-knowledge brings about the riches of the past by locking on each other and preparing the future ones, likewise, the future ones pave the way for the ones to come, who are directed to the plan of duty. Here, in order to be able to ex-plain the respective states of the opposing components directed to duty and to earthly cravings, with more material similes, we go back to the example of the bar magnet we have previously given.

Let us hold this bar magnet with its (+) side is up and its (-) side down, in the direction of a plumb line.[15] In this state, the bar magnet's

---

[15] *Plumb line*: A line with a plumb attached to it, used for finding the depth of wa-ter or determining the vertical of an upright surface. (*Publisher*)

exact higher half and exact lower half contain equal amounts of opposite magnetism to each other. Now, if we lengthen this bar upwards, that is, if we add magnetism to it from the higher part, the neutral point of the bar shifts and moves a little higher. Because some magnetism is added to the (+) side, a flux of magnetism will start from (+) to (-) and the equilibrium line moves up. If we do this from the lower part, the result reverses: the equilibrium line shifts a bit lower. This is a rough example, but it is useful in giving an intuition.

This experiment indicates that although one is signed (+) and the other is signed (-) the component on both sides of the bar is the same substance. Naturally, the conscience duality we symbolise with the bar magnet does not display such a simple state. That is, there are differences too great and too complex between its components to compare with the components of magnetism. Because of this, the reality differences here are not as simple as the (+), (-) poles of the magnet. However, we give this example to impart a rough intuition of the workings of the conscience mechanism. So, if we hold the conscience, which we symbolise by a bar magnet, in the direction of the plumb line, with its higher component directed at duty in equilibrium with its lower component directed to earthly cravings, the value degrees of these components in the face of human comprehension, that is, again within the conscience mechanism itself, are equal to each other. And their equilibrium line, relative to the bar magnet symbol, is in the exact middle.

If we lengthen this conscience bar upwards starting from its higher half, that is, if we add values to the higher parts near to the duty reality, the charge of the bar increases towards that part. And the previous equilibrium line remains below. In this case, respective equilibrium state of the directions of duty and earthly cravings becomes disrupted. However, the law of equilibrium cannot stand this disruption. As with the magnetic phenomena, until the equilibrium is restored a flux starts from the increased value side to the decreased value side, from the duty side to the earthly craving side. This flux, of course, means that some value parts of the higher reality pass into the lower reality. Naturally, these values we mention – as explained above – are not for the aspect of reality that addresses the body belonging to matter and forms but for the aspect addressing the being preoccupied with essence-knowledge. These are essence-knowledge values and they are put into effect after myriad applications of the conscience mechanism.

So the start of this flux from (+) side to (-) side causes the disrupted equilibrium line to be restored to a level that is a little higher than the previous one. More correctly, some parts of the duty component values, by mixing amidst the earthly craving components, have elevated the level of earthly cravings a little. In this way, the level of essence-knowledge and comprehension of essence-knowledge reaches upward. Therefore, as the values belonging to the duty side of the conscience mechanism increase, the values of the higher direction flowing in the direction to the earthly cravings, entail a shift of earthly craving direction towards the duty direction and the ascent of the equilibrium line between the two directions towards the knowledge of a plan of duty.

*
* *

We would like to point out that what people must do regarding comprehending world values is to feed the component of the conscience duality orientated to duty and to retroject the component of earthly cravings. For, as the values are added to the duty component, the gains of the conscience equilibrium within the essence-being will increase quickly; and as the higher components are neglected by becoming attached to the earthly craving components, the increase in essence-knowledge will decelerate by becoming subject to the automatic advance through other channels, with gradual and arduous applications at great lengths.

Therefore, to shorten the path of development and lessen the arduous intervention imperatives as much as possible, it is necessary to attain a level of comprehension as soon as possible to be able to discern the higher and lower components of this mechanism so that comprehension and effort of orientation upwards may be possible. Because of this, we must elaborate on comprehension whose significance is obvious.

*
* *

119

We mentioned above that the conscience mechanism exist in pre-human beings – naturally, in the most primitive forms – in states of instinctual dualities and it starts to take its comprehending form at the stage of humanity that only starts with human life. The reason for this is, no doubt, that the power of comprehension has reached its degree particular to the level of humanity. The conscience mechanism at the stage of humanity is adjusted according to the comprehensions. The development of the conscience mechanism in mankind exhibits varying levels, from the simplest level of comprehension to the highest comprehension. All of these indicate that comprehension has a very important status in the development of the conscience mechanism. More correctly, the development of conscience means development of comprehension. In the initial world beings at which the comprehension exists in states of very simple instincts, conscience mechanism exists only according to that level. For example, in plants, which mankind recognised as the initial beings in the world, there exist automatic instincts which are at the simplest state of comprehension. And this, of course, displays a state which is a far cry from the levels of comprehension mankind has. And because of this, they cannot be defined as comprehension. However, these instincts represent comprehension sufficiently in these beings for their life needs. In this context, let us elaborate on the true meaning of comprehension.

*
* *

Comprehension is a power interconnecting the endless matter systems in the matter-universe. However, by making this definition it should be remembered that as for everything in universe, the cause of this power is also outside the matter-universe. So, by this power, relations between matter can be established. And out of these relations the beings which are the symbols, that is, the representatives of spirits, are manifested. Likewise, by this power, through the critical comparison of relations between plans, developments and evolutions are ensured. Here, there are great truths expressed about comprehension. In order to penetrate these truths, it is necessary to ponder upon these words.

*
* *

We have explained how the initial components preparing the comprehension occurred during the constitution of the beings. Here, spirits were constituting these beings by gathering the energies transmitted in a disarrayed state by the developed hydrogen. The constitution of beings through these high energies, which are but high-vibration complexes, triggers instincts which are the most primitive state of comprehension to manifest in these disarrayed energies. Here, secondary assistance is given as well to spirits constituting these beings. For, as previously mentioned, from the moment the being is constituted, the influences coming from above and around it, which we call secondary, takes the place of the original influences.

Let us elaborate on this topic. We have said that comprehension is a power gathering matter systems together. This means that in the initial constitution of the being, hydrogen atom energies have reached such a stage of development that spirits, with the help of secondary influences as well, have attained the possibilities to use their instincts – which are the simplest state of their powers that mankind can only express and symbolise by the word 'comprehension' – by utilising the states of matter at this stage. Here a sufficient degree of knowledge is given about how comprehension begins.

Ferment of the being is comprehension. And the initial being that constituted connects, from its initial moment on, the other simpler matter combinations and systems together in accordance with the gradual development of this ferment existing in it – that is, of comprehension – and brings about new and newer combinations and systems. We have said enough about the birth and significance of comprehension and will proceed to its role in the conscience mechanism.

*
* *

First of all, we would like to state that the role of comprehension in the conscience mechanism is intrinsic to the disposition of this mechanism. For, actually establishment and connections of relations between the opposites of the conscience mechanism occur through the comprehension mechanism and it is even an act belonging to the

121

function of comprehension. Naturally, this act occurs rather through the interventions of assisting influences at the moment of being's initial constitution and gradually, as comprehension develops, these interventions lessen and governance of the being emerges and, at the further states of development of comprehension, it completely prevails over conscience.

Proper appreciation of the interrelations between the conscience realities; establishment of supporting systems for them with sublime components by discerning the duty components with elevating quality towards the higher, from the earthly craving components; and by this, elevation of the equilibrium of conscience mechanism increasingly towards higher levels – these are the acts belonging to the function of comprehension. Therefore, the more perfect comprehension becomes, the more efficient this function works and consequently, the easier and faster the convergence of the conscience level becomes towards the knowledge of duty.

For example, a man who has such a wide and encompassing comprehension knows better if he should direct his efforts to the duty component or the earthly craving component. And when he complies with the duty component which is positive, he starts to appreciate what kind of sublime matter combinations and systems he can build onwards; and this means his increasing convergence – with his comprehension – towards the plan of duty.

On the other hand, as he chooses the earthly craving component which is the opposite of duty and as he goes downward he sees and understands what kind of dissolutions and breakdowns will occur in the high ordered relations within the constitutions of conscience and what kinds of values can be lost from the richness of developmental combinations of matter. For, appreciation of these is among the acts included in the comprehension's scope of power as the builder among the matter combinations and systems.

Therefore, comprehension is such a great power that it is both its own guide and also its own prime mover at all preliminary levels on the path of preparing for the knowledge of duty throughout all the lives it will go through, within the dictates of conscience duality. And this expresses that among other components of matter universe, it is the closest vehicle to spirit.

*
* *

Now, we come to the essence-knowledge feeding the mechanisms of comprehension and conscience which takes such a significant role in the preparations belonging to the plan of duty in the world. First of all, let us say that essence-knowledge, as it feeds comprehension and conscience, is also enriched by comprehension and conscience.

Essence-knowledge increases its value by comprehension itself and also with the help of external interventions. As to the topic of these external interventions' strengthening essence-knowledge, knowledge has been given previously on this, to which we now return.

Interventions helping the increase of essence-knowledge, in relation to conscience, reach their targets by utilising innumerable states and situations of myriad matter combinations, that is, a great number of events. Events, as filtered through crude knowledge of comparison, exit from consciousness to unconsciousness and stay there. These are under the command of essence-knowledge. And they exist there, in the unconscious, throughout the lifetime of mankind. These have not yet passed to the subconscious.

Events cannot directly pass into the state of essence-knowledge. For, there are yet inconsistencies among them. These events that occurred in the consciousness, after their initial comparative accounting is done with the relatively crude material impressions in the unconscious, are pushed to the unconscious. Although these are under the command of the essence-being, they have not yet been its own possessions, have not yet turned into essence-knowledge. For this knowledge in the unconscious to pass into the state of essence-knowledge they need to adapt to essence-knowledge, and to reach the ability to be included within the essence-knowledge synthesis. However, the comparative accounting of these in the unconscious has been done not with subconscious knowledge but with unconscious knowledge; and this is not essence-knowledge.

Because all connections of the being to outside will be severed when it passes to the spatium following death, this knowledge will be compared with subconscious knowledge and accounted by the being; and after that will pass to the subconscious and be appropriated by the being. For, this act will harmonise the knowledge in the subconscious with the knowledge in the unconscious and will mix these within the synthesis of subconscious knowledge.

So, the knowledge that stays unconscious throughout the whole of a life enters the subconscious only after going through the great accountancy following the death event and after it has been represented by the being, it can then enter the subconscious. As to the topic of how knowledge is collected in the unconscious; this is accumulated by subjecting world realities which are comprehended or not by the consciousness to the knowledge of the comparison mechanism in relation to conscience, which is broadly done during sleep, and is then pushed to the unconscious.

*
* *

In short, comprehended or not, events the consciousness has encountered are concluded by the knowledge of comparison in the unconscious and these conclusions stay in the unconscious. There, these have not yet become the essence-knowledge of the being, and therefore they do not belong to the subconscious. Nevertheless, this knowledge is under the command of the being and whenever necessary, it can be taken out to the field of consciousness. And only after the great accounting that is done following death, does it mix with the mass of essence-knowledge in the subconscious.

Sources and means feeding essence-knowledge vary greatly. We will state some of the most important of these. Communal situations like knowledge, religion, nation, family and the states strengthening these situations; and finally communiqués,[16] inspirations, knowledge given to mankind and mediums directly by beings in duty at various levels and events arising from all of these are among the powerful materials strengthening essence-knowledge and converging the being with the plan of duty. These are lived through within the world realities and, as we said, after some acts, they mix with the essence-knowledge repertoire of the being. Now, let us elaborate on essence-knowledge.

---

[16] *Communiqués*: In experimental spiritualism, this term is used to express messages containing significant and valuable knowledge through spiritual connections at sublime levels. (*Publisher*)

*
* *

Essence-knowledge comprises deep impressions – which cannot be comprehended by mankind – that are attained by comparison, by discernment of the assets belonging to the past lives starting from the most primitive cycle with previous assets; and which are appropriated by the being – not by man. As, on the one hand, they ensure the evolution of the spirit to which they serve with the forms of comprehension, on the other hand, they widen the being's field of development by preparing ground for new knowledge. These assets are gained by situations within the world comprehension technique.

It is possible to collect these situations within the concept of an event. Man lives in the midst of the events surrounding him; he becomes the hero of those events. In some cases he does not live it himself but follows and observes the situations of other people and beings living in them with a keen interest. So, because of the necessities of their lives in the world, the relations belonging to the event combinations either mankind directly live in or indirectly see in others are the whole sum of the knowledge which are expressed by world comprehension; and these concepts are separate from essence-knowledge and the materials becoming vehicles for the constitution of essence-knowledge. However, the conclusions and impressions of these, after they go through various mechanisms in the spatium life following death, are transferred to the essence-being and are appropriated by the being as essence-knowledge.

And consciousness, as previously explained, continues to collect new knowledge materials from the world by directly encountering the crude realities of the world, more correctly, these events. After stating the differences in this way between essence-knowledge and events which are evaluated as knowledge in the world, we will continue our explanation by using the meaning of the word knowledge, without mistaking these.

*
* *

To make the study of knowledge belonging the world easier, as a simile, we can call the direct ones, that is, the ones acquired by living in the midst of events, stem knowledge and the indirect ones, that is, the ones acquired by observing others, branch knowledge, both of which are powerful vehicles, causing the development of essence-knowledge according to their capacities. For example, if the knowledge a child gains who puts his hand in a fire by feeling the pain of the burn himself is the stem knowledge, the knowledge he gains by observing the suffering and reactions that occur out of his friend's burning his hand becomes branch knowledge. And by this example, we have said that stem knowledge will give shortcut results in comparison with branch knowledge in the constitution of essence-knowledge. On the other hand, there is no possibility of mankind living each event by themselves and gaining only direct knowledge. So, the shortages arising out of this impossibility are complemented with branch knowledge.

*
* *

As knowledge feeds essence-knowledge, in between there are some assisting principles that provide strengthening, and one of these is the causality principle.

In the universe, no event is without a cause. All events, relations, influencing, integrations, transitions, disintegrations of universe; in short, all formations, transformations and deformations of matter occur in accordance with the necessities of the great evolutionary cause, and as the cause and effect of each other and as interconnected. And this is a manifestation of the great causality principle in universe. After all, as we state at every point of this book, all motions are based on causes and arrive at effects. No occurrence without a cause and effect can be thought of. Mechanisms belonging to the integration and disintegration of all relations in the universe work in accordance with this principle. No event is unattended and self-contained. Every event is connected to other events, directly or indirectly. In this way, the whole universe with all of its parts is woven with an immense network of connection, and the knot points of these connections are the cause–effect necessities of the causality principle. Each event is the effect of the higher one and the cause of the lower one. Of whichever event the cause is unseen, this is because the cause of that event has not been known.

*
* *

The causality principle is a strong support of the knowledge of comparison which is used by comprehension that takes the most significant role in the transformation of events into essence- knowledge. After giving this short explanation of the causality principle, it would be helpful to mention the reciprocal situations of comprehension and the knowledge of comparison.

Knowledge of comparison is the way of adapting comprehension to the causality principle. Comprehension develops as much as it is able to adapt to the causality principle in universe. Comprehension that remains alienated from the causality principle displays that much deficiency in consigning and appreciating the endless relations that exist among the endless combinations in universe and remains accordingly in backward and simple states. To a child who cannot comprehend that his hand will burn if he puts his hand in a fire, the authorisation to play with fire is not given. This is because his comprehension has not yet attained the merit for such a deed. His comprehension has not yet adapted properly to the causality principle belonging to the relations of this matter. And the thing that will allow this adaptation will be his knowledge of comparison. For that child to enter the knowledge of comparison he will experiment a few times to hold fire in his hand and his hand will get burnt each time. Each time his hand is burnt, some intuitions about the causes and effects belonging to the relation of fire and hand will gradually emerge and with the help of his knowledge of comparisons, these intuitions will become knowledge. In this way, the comprehension and consequently content of essence-knowledge will increase. We call this procedure refining experience.

*
* *

This knowledge we have given indicates that the causality principle and knowledge of comparison which increase essence-knowledge render their functions only via events. In the absence of events, neither can the causality principle be studied nor can the knowledge of comparison be understood, nor can their connection to each other be of question. Therefore, to continue on the topic of knowledge of comparison, it becomes necessary to elaborate first on events.

One of the first, even the very first, of the basic materials which are necessary to acquire knowledge and essence-knowledge and consequently to attain evolution is events. It is necessary to live directly or indirectly in the midst of events.

Manifestation of events depends on a great number of causes. However, above anything else, events occur in accordance with the laws of cause and effect. Actually, to be able to bring about essence-knowledge, events depend on the degree of comprehension that can be employed in adapting cause–effect relations in them through comparison. Fire burns the child's hand; the child has felt this pain. The burning of his hand has been because of his holding the fire with his hand. If the child can comprehend the cause–effect connections between the events gathered around this feeling of burning, the result he will get in regard to the essence-knowledge will be one thing and if he cannot, it will be another thing. That is, knowledge is established and reflected to the spirit according to comprehension's adaptation to the cause–effect connections in that event. The events ensuring knowledge in accordance with the needs of that being are arranged by the assisting beings and put on the path of man, or for the same reason, assisting beings have the same being to do it by sending influences to it. That being causes these events by itself, by its own acts. For, the order and sequence of these events preparing that person's knowledge are subject to a great number of individual and communal plans and various orders which can only be executed by superior comprehensions and powers.

When a man needs to take part in a required event, assisting beings activate the earthly craving components of his conscience or they have him encounter events outside of his choices and so direct him to various acts. And this is to make him taste the bitter results of his selfish acts and, in this way, to prepare values for his essence-knowledge through leading him to the knowledge of comparison. For example, if a man needs to feel the sufferings a murderer feels, such events are put in his path so that he cannot contain himself in the face of these and kills a man. Therefore, causing such an event with a serious result by himself is not a thing that has come about arbitrarily or accidentally, since his ability to enter the knowledge of comparison necessary for him to reanimate the developmental preparations he decelerated is possible only to the degree that he is able to comprehend that he himself has acquired the merit for the events. And the thing that will allow this is his killing a man. May he kill that man so that his repertoire of knowledge and comprehension – which has not been valuing the duty component of his conscience more than it does for the earthly craving component, more correctly, which has been too weak to afford it – may get sufficiently strong and enriched by the knowledge of comparison he will engage because of this event and after that, may he meet the possibilities of acceleration in his development by directing his will towards the duty component.

On the face of the thousands of similar needs of the being, these forms of help and intervention occur and myriad events are brought about. Beings in duty therefore assist in bringing about various similar events in the evolution of those humans who have not strengthened sufficiently to orientate to higher components of their conscience duality – more correctly, who have not been able to free themselves from the influences of their lower level knowledge and so remain weak in elevating the equilibrium level of their consciences. Thus mankind, under the anguish and suffering caused by these events, learns important lessons out of the knowledge of comparison in which they engaged; and each of these lessons sows the seeds of their essence-knowledge. By that means, that being prepares its comprehension for the higher values belonging to the realities and development of higher levels. That is, it converges toward the knowledge of duty of its super-human stage. Because of this, mankind has been from time immemorial considering these painful events, regarding tests and trials as redeeming factors accordingly, which is correct. Thus, we refer to the lessons learnt from the results of these tests and trials as refining experiences. Each of these is an evolutionary material.

*
* *

We have said that both the causality principle and the flow of events under the light of this principle – by directly or indirectly having mankind live in the midst of these events – leads to the knowledge of comparison. As a matter of fact, knowledge of comparison emerges as a significant component in the increase of essence-knowledge.

The most efficient assistant of knowledge of comparison is pain and suffering. Here, it is necessary to point out that suffering has a significant role in acquiring essence-knowledge. The obvious point is that knowledge of comparison most often feeds essence-knowledge and comprehension by the way of suffering. Sufferings to be experienced in the spatium are valuable assistants of the knowledge of comparison the being will engage in during the accounting of their unconscious knowledge. We will give a world example about this. This example contains all the subtleties of this topic.

Let us take sexual selfishness, which is the hardest to overcome and can encompass many stages according to its degree and is the subject of many tests and trials; of many advancements and of many degenerations in the world. A man loves a woman just to satisfy his flesh and his bodily desires. And he is to overcome his material selfishness in the following way. The day will come when the woman he loves has had enough of him and loves another man. And, in facing this trial, this man is defeated to his earthly cravings to the degree that he will kill his lover. The reactions he will give continue varying on gradually up to the end of the stage.

Now, let us take another man in a similar situation, who is in the more or less advanced stage of his conscience. His lover has abandoned him and started to love another man. This man, who has been advancing to the heights of his stage of conscience, will accept this without resentment and maybe he will not hesitate in giving his help to that woman in this regard. So here, the comparison of a murder and a virtue, of selfishness and altruism are face to face. The man who murdered, if he is not in a state to attain the knowledge of comparison by his own comprehension (because he murdered then it means that he is not) then the assistance of external interventions will start to arrive at him so, in this way, may he attain the comprehension of this comparison. And only by this knowledge of comparison will the result emerge and that man will be able to spend the efforts to overcome earthly cravings. As such, imagine that he murdered her with a knife. Following the murder, he will be imprisoned.

Here, we would like to list a chain of comparison tests. This man, first of all, will engage in a mandatory comparison by the suffering of his dissatisfied sexual desires and pleasures. As a child got his hand burnt before a fire, he will start to feel the initial bitter results of his desires, not unlike fire. In this way, he will encounter a comparison that will teach him the factors causing his suffering. Let us say this has not chastened him. The prisoner will get old in the prison. His hormones, power, sexual activity will weaken and he will become powerless in his potency. When he is in this state, this man will not feel his selfishness only in particular relation to his flesh and nerves but now can only imagine it. If he has not learned sufficiently from the previous lessons, if he has not benefited sufficiently from the knowledge given by events, then this prisoner will be knifed by another prisoner during a fight, or he will have such an accident that some sharp object like a knife will sink into his body. And he will then feel an intense material suffering because of this.

Here, the subject of our example will naturally engage in a mandatory comparison. Because he is devoid of sexuality, he is not directly a prisoner of his flesh. He now has mandatorily passed through that reality. Moreover, he survived an accident which made him relive the memory of murderer's test by comparison. Now, in the face of this situation, it is not possible for this being not to learn a lesson and not to attempt spending efforts to acquire necessary knowledge.

Now, we give an objective observation of the above example: a rich, middle-aged man, seeing that the young girl he has had a love affair who has grown tired of him and turned away from him, and all the things he had done to regain her attention are in vain, has resorted to violence and waits to catch her and then mutilates her body with 25–30 knife wounds. Following this murder, he evades capital punishment and is confined to the ward of a mental institution reserved for mental patients who have committed murder; and stays there twelve years. One day, he is attacked by another mental patient with whom he gets along very well in the same ward and during his mental agitation this patient mutilates his body with a hoe at 25–30 places.

This observation, again, displays all the sequence of the comparisons. Of course, sufferings and pains are felt in degrees and will be felt by both the child who burnt his hand in the fire and by these men who killed their lovers out of frustrated desire and died respectively in a prison and in a mental institution, encountering similar murders to the ones they committed. This will engage them in the powerful knowledge of comparison; and this knowledge will prepare their essence-knowledge and comprehension – which are necessary for them to reach further levels – in the way we have outlined above.

*
 * *

So, knowledge advances together with comprehension. Because of this, their development should be explained together. In the development of comprehension there are two paths. The first one is man's advance by making the states within his constitution a subject of study. We call this a direct development of comprehension. The second is the advancement by comprehension's observation of events external to the body – more correctly, by comprehension's studying the events caused by itself. And we call this indirect development of comprehension. Among the main components used in indirect development of comprehension are the events, works and deeds caused by mankind itself in its surroundings which will increase its refining experiences; and most of these are brought about by the helps of external influences.

These events appear, especially at the initial stages of development, as heavy, arduous, difficult, the cause of suffering and very long-term. They bring out seemingly never-ending and inexhaustible emotions. In the meantime, man works in hardship; struggles with various impossibilities of nature to earn a morsel of bread; fights with monsters; tussles with his fellow mankind. In this challenge he sometimes wins, but is mostly defeated. He feels the anguish of these in his self; so his gruelling life continues for ages. Because we previously talked about how all of these events feed and increase comprehension and essence-knowledge in mankind, about the ways developmental mechanisms elevate their equilibrium to higher levels, we do not see any reason to repeat these here. In this way, on the one hand, these events cause increase of essence-knowledge, on the other hand they consign the comprehensions to intervene with developmental mechanisms. And this leads to the emergence of newer and newer events, tests and trials, experiences and observations and so the tempo of the comprehension's advance gradually accelerates.

As comprehension increases, meaning of the events around emerge more and more. And by this, comprehension vibrations filtered through matter combinations belonging to human brain begin to draw conclusions from these innumerable events, to build myriad kinds of combinations out of these event parts and from these, world knowledge generates. As comprehensions develop, this knowledge increases and widens their scope, as well. Many branches of knowledge are constituted like arts, literature, science, medicine, philosophy, music, painting, economics, politics, religion. All of these are the results of the new matter combinations built by the comprehension increased in the developmental mechanism. And naturally, they are particular to the world and obliged to remain in the world in order to render only the necessities and imperatives of the evolution in the world. These occur under the influences and controls of the plan of duty governing the world. Therefore, while in the world, the expansion of essence-comprehension is related to its states bound to the brain which it uses as its vehicle to become more complex, enriched and to have new constitutions towards the sublime subtle matter states.

After all, we have previously mentioned that conclusions brought about by event matter in the essence-being, that is, essence-knowledge, should reflect back to spirit via the channel of essence-comprehension. And because of this, a being who comes into the world with the need for evolution, works to benefit from world events possibilities as much as possible. This benefiting of comprehension occurs both through the form changes of the body and by the innumerable matter transitions of the cosmos the body lives in. We have named the first of these direct development of comprehension and the second indirect development of comprehension. In the direct states, as it registers developments as the result of applications it has done by generating formations, transformations and deformations directly in the body; in the indirect states, it expands through its applications upon the results of innumerable external events that either comprehension itself does by means of body or arranged by the higher beings in duty.

All formations in the universe are attuned with the needs of spirits. Transformations within a scale occur through various mechanisms. And in this way, comprehension – which is the subtlest matter state in the world – prepares itself directly and indirectly within these mechanisms for the most suitable manner to be able to serve spirit. And for this, it influences and intervenes its own body and as well as the external realm through its body. By the developments it will generate both in its body and in external matter, ensuring its development and the increase of essence-knowledge. And it should be remembered that all these deeds occur through influences, mechanisms and the duality principle technique on which we have previously elaborated. After explaining the knowledge as one of the components feeding and accelerating the development of essence-knowledge, we will also give some knowledge on the love component.

*
* *

As a matter of fact, the love that causes many events and tests and trials in the life of the world is one of the most powerful factors, playing a role in direct and indirect ways both in the constitution of essence-knowledge and in the development of conscience. If love did not exist, the ways of acquiring essence-knowledge and opportunities for the conscience mechanism to generate results in positive and negative directions would be quite reduced, and consequently the possibilities of observations and knowledge of comparison would be quite limited. This is because love helps to increase essence-knowledge directly with the events it generates in positive directions by supporting the higher components of conscience, that is, by a conscious comprehension; as well as helping the increase in essence-knowledge indirectly and automatically by way of knowledge of comparison arising from the suffering and tormenting results it causes, when necessary, by activating the lower components of conscience mechanism.

For example, the loves we mentioned above that caused much sufferings and knowledge of comparison by sending one man to prison and the other to a mental hospital to be eventually killed, set examples for indirect developments with their influences taking effect in apparently negative ways, although in reality, they are positive. Other than two previous examples of love, here we give an example of its influence that is seen in a positive way.

An inexperienced young man loves a woman for great and noble purposes. And he has been advanced greatly in the stage of conscience. However, the woman rejects him by not seeing in him the qualifications she requires. The young man, determined to attract her affections and attention, starts right away to work on increasing his qualities and adding values to himself. At first, he does this by the automatism of love. As he succeeds, the scope of love begins to expand and its meaning to change. By this means, he feels more the need to cultivate himself and strives for creating works beneficial to mankind. He begins to love everybody and to be loved by everyone. Love becomes generalised and loses its initial simple and one-sided form within the endless directions of a general and encompassing interest; and so he increases his essence-knowledge with the myriad conclusions he encountered as he advances in the path of his initial love, and enters into a state of being which is active at the level of a high equilibrium of conscience and is prepared for the knowledge of duty.

*

* *

When love is mentioned, it should not be interpreted in its narrow sense. Love in the narrow sense, as mankind understands it, is a small though significant part of the great role and immense concept that love plays in the developmental mechanism. That is, the love we mention here has infinite facets and forms. The vast meaning of the roles of love in relation to the conscience mechanism – or more correctly, developmental mechanism – must be dwelled on. It is only by doing this that its value in evolution can be stated. Therefore, let us explain love in this general sense.

Love is an attraction felt towards anything. Everything, every reality in the world can attract mankind and beings in every stage of development – depending on situations and person – towards itself in various manners. Therefore, at every level love can be felt towards anything. So, love is such a general and encompassing topic. Even the physicochemical interests that matter displays towards each other are perhaps the most material and primitive preparation for love seen in superior beings. These are a necessity for the particular needs and imperatives of the beings in that stage. Plants importing food from outside into their structures; absorbing oxygen and carbon dioxide of the air and mixing these with their sap; and even turning some towards the Sun or absorbing and digesting animals into themselves are manifestations of this attraction in the disposition of various instincts seen in most often physicochemical appearances.

We start to see these attraction states of love manifesting in plants through various simple mechanisms, in animals as less materialised states which are more or less closer to the ones in mankind. Among animals it is possible to observe the varieties of friendly interests with their cubs, partners, family and friends and even with others than their own species that sometimes take on the complete scenery of love. As to mankind, the high and rich manifestations of love that is felt with a rather expanded comprehension appear at this stage.

*
* *

Here, it is necessary for us to elaborate on the true nature of love. In order to properly explain the relation between love and the body it would be helpful to revisit the knowledge of matter combinations in the earlier pages of this book. Before anything else, we would like to state openly that the knowledge we will give about the love component's constitution mechanism in the body which is known as an emotion, as previously said, contains the constitutions of all feelings and enthusiasms that manifest in the body and which are called psychological. In the light of this knowledge, it becomes possible to explain the constitution of all emotions existing in the body and their relations to it.

Love that finds its highest form in the developmental stages of mankind is but the manifestations of the high and subtle vibrations, energies transmitted by some very subtle matter combinations of the body. Either by a man's own refining experiences, that is, by the necessities and conclusions of his essence-knowledge and plan applications; or by the intervention of beings in duty as a direct subject of a test and trial, some matter combinations and systems in such a high and subtle order that the vibrations and energies emanated by these subtle combinations put into effect a very powerful and attractive field, a magnetic field around him.

However, by looking at the crude meanings expressed by words here, it should not be understood that we meant an ordinary magnetic flux. These are much more subtle than the magnetic waves we know and of a higher degree of quality which cannot be compared with them. And this field attracts other vibrations that may sympathise with itself. And in the same way, it is attracted by the magnetic fields to which other vibrations are subject. So, the words of bodies loving each other and loved by each other express these meanings. As long as these subtle matter combinations constituted for this or that reason continue, the vibrations they emanate continue as well. As they change, depending on the form and degree of this change, the quality and intensity of vibrations vary as well. When these combinations dissolve, vibrations are no more and the manifestation of love ceases, as well. It is known that all of these acts occur through influences coming from above in accordance with necessities.

Now, let us imagine the reverse of it. There is another man whose body also builds some subtle matter combinations but within different orders. Although these are rather quite subtle and fine in comparison with other physicochemical matter combinations, they are still crude compared with the former love combinations. And the vibrations they emanate are antipathy and hate vibrations. They also, as they receive the vibrations of hate and antipathy emotions, are interested in their surroundings and send out

the same vibrations to them. In this way, while sympathetic emana-
tions are transmitted from the whole bodies of the former, antipa-
thic waves constantly spread out to surroundings from the bodies
of the latter. Sympathetic transmission has superior subtleties and
powers and if turned towards the matter combinations transmitting antipathy, these vibrations which are more powerful than
them can erase and dissipate those combinations. For this reason,
those who love and who can be loved have a much more powerful
and efficient status than who bear hostility and grudges. This is
very helpful knowledge that will be beneficial in the developmental application on the communal path.

*

* *

Love – since it is used in positive and negative ways – is an important developmental vehicle which increases essence-knowledge by
causing endless event variations in the conscience mechanism. And
in this regard, it also, as is valid in all powers in the life of man –
continues and in due course of time dissipates or degenerates in
accordance with the needs and necessities entailing embodiment.
And beings fill their repertoire of essence-knowledge and spirits
benefit out of all these states.

In this way, because love is always inclined to sympathise with
the higher components of conscience by its higher side depending
on its power and character, this causes the constant elevation of its
equilibrium line, as long as the heavy transmission of simple and
crude combinations are not mixed with these love vibrations for
various reasons and especially because of some mandatory and
necessary tests and trials, and of the needs of observation. For example, of these many crude matter combinations like jealousy, selfishness, pride, self-esteem, bullying, passion of money and of fame
which are toxic for love can mix with love combinations, by these
means, influences coming out of these crude matter combinations,
and orientating powerfully and intensely to the subtle love combinations of the body, start to partly erase their higher values and
consequently to degenerate these combinations by gradually affecting them. In this case, because the hazy, mixed and slowed down
energies transmitted from those combinations will begin to comply

with the lower realities – as always occur in such situations – they lead to some painful events resulting in the automatic workings of the conscience mechanism.

*
* *

Love, through its various kinds of variations, co-mingles with the conscience mechanism. For, it has myriad sides of which some are directed towards duty of conscience and some are directed to earthly cravings. Especially at the initial stages of mankind, aspects of love that are mixed with selfishness prevail. We have mentioned above these forms of love mixed with these crude combinations. These lead to a great number of consequences resulting in inconveniences, anguish, troubles, suffering. And sometimes love transports man directly to the higher realities with its pure and sublime manifestations. On this side of it, there are manifestations of high, subtle matter combinations, accelerating the development especially such as relinquishment, self-sacrifice, altruism, helping, compassion. And we have given above an example of this.

While love supports the conscience's components directed to duty, with its side of altruism and ensuring a fast and comprehending advancement in the developmental mechanism, with its selfish side it also decelerates the advancement tempo of development by its negative powers, activating the earthly craving components and puts man into troubling, suffering conditions. By this means, it causes the increase in essence-knowledge in either case through opposite ways. For example, through love a man is helped, to save someone who fell into sea self-sacrifice is displayed, a starving man is fed, tears of sadness are wiped away and at the end of these the man finds a feeling of relief, peace, even happiness. And this is the manifestation of a fast development in the consciousness. On the other hand for love many hearts are broken, a betrayal is punished, getting rid of a rival's body is imagined, harm to someone is done and consequently, resentment, unrest and tribulation begin in man. And this expresses the pressure of a man's decelerated development. As the ones in the former group are the powers directed to higher components of the conscience mechanism and the ones in the latter group are the backward factors feeding the earthly craving realities in that degree, both of these may be found in mankind, depending on their developmental levels and they generate results accordingly.

Therefore, according to how low the levels are, the materials and vibrations of selfishness mixing with love at that level are also that low. And on the other hand, whatever the developmental levels are at the levels of the higher equilibrium, the love component enriches with pure and virtue vibrations accordingly. And this developmental state eventually becomes such that these virtuous feelings felt towards mankind reach wide-encompassing and higher degrees such as serving them, risking to help them – at all costs – in every way for their well-being and development. And then, earthly craving components and realities of the conscience shed selfishness and begin to advance on the paths of altruism. The equilibrium levels of the conscience mechanism are now established in the high and comprehending fields of altruism. That man assumes a duty, a debt to himself to endure all kinds of self-sacrifice for the ascension of others. Then, love in him begins to become the love of duty; and this is an indication of his arriving at the threshold of the plan of duty.

And, the high equilibrium level which has reached to these fields of the conscience mechanism is the highest grade man can gain through the world school. A man who has attained that rank will get his diploma with flying colours and will pass to higher plans as a stronger and happier being by taking on duties with the highest power of essence-knowledge he acquired in the world. After he has reached this state, conscience duality will be no more, replaced by a duty duality in a higher order; and from that moment on, the being will have entered into a true and objective evolutionary mechanism. For, as we will state later, the progression of evolution before the stage of duty has been realised within rather subjective conditions. This concept will be explained in more detail when the more explanation about time is given.

*
* *

We see that repeating some points summarily would be helpful to make them well understood. Conscience, reality, comprehension, knowledge, love – in short, all values manifesting in the world are only material appearances that have taken their forms within the possibilities of brain substance. True values of these are in the powers hidden within the essence-being. And their functions within the world possibilities work only for the path of service to essence-being. Therefore, they are world forms, states and appearances which can be measured by superficial time comprehension that is only valid in the world. And the values in the essence-being which they feed and are agents of their developments are the true values gaining in value by the comprehension possibilities, which we may call infinite, of spherical time which the essence-being is subject to; and these values indicate the degree of spirit's evolution in universe. These subtle combinations that gain in value by the spherical or perceptual time technique cannot be defined or qualified by the superficial time comprehension of the world.

So, all words stated in all knowledge pertaining to the conscience mechanism such as comprehension, knowledge, reality, component, love etc. should be taken within these concepts and with their own values. For example, the side of love that is mentioned expresses its values belonging to the world. A man who thinks with world time can never penetrate its state and meaning in the face of perceptual time which belongs to the being. Likewise, it is also not possible for mankind to comprehend the love combinations in the subtle realm which follows the world and is subject to spherical or perceptual time technique. Only the beings that completely left their bodies by ascending will understand the true meanings of these when they pass to that realm. If these sentences are to be visited after seeing the knowledge of superficial and spherical time, it would be easier to intuit the degree of the scope in the vibrations which are the counterparts of love in the being and which advance with the spherical time technique as compared to the human love depending on superficial time comprehension. And it would be possible to make an intuitive comparison between the primitive state of love on the face of one-surfaced, simple human comprehension and the endless scope of love impressions in the super-human realm that contains infinite imaginative surfaces, that is, its magnificent state shining within essence-knowledge.

141

*
* *

We have discussed the knowledge and love of the factors enriching essence-knowledge. However, besides these, there is another component as well, playing a powerful role in the increase of essence-knowledge, which has not yet been appreciated by mankind. These are the influences sent to the beings of mankind by those beings in duty at various levels of evolution in the world. These influences increase communal knowledge values acquired both individually and usually through these individuals – in ways and forms which cannot be guessed at by mankind. And we call people who receive these influences mediums.

For mankind, mediumship means acquiring sensitivity to receiving universe influences and universe vibrations. In the world, the most significant of the influences effectuating mediumistic reactions is sublime intuitive influences. In the make-up of mediums, the possibilities and power enabling to easily express the influences sent are more. This rule is valid for physical mediums, as well. However, the difference is that, in the former, incoming influences are very subtle vibrations pertaining to the sublime comprehension combinations. As to the physical mediums, incoming influences are directed to a crude matter and brought about various formations, transformations, deformations or simpler motions as a result of the reactions in that crude matter. Thus, in a general view there are two appearances of mediumship, one intuitive and the other physical.

*
* *

Before we start to explain the mechanism of mediumship, some preliminary knowledge needs to be given so we will begin by stating these. For this, first of all, some states of the human brain must be mentioned.

Brain is the prevailing organ of the body, constituted by atom ensembles; and put into effect by molecules containing higher functions and motions of these. Throughout the human body, there are cells. And each has certain particular frequencies of motion. The more the motion of a cell, the higher is its degree of power and activity. Most active cells in the human body are brain cells.

Actually, by means of this excess of motions, brain cells can receive impressions belonging to the world. Likewise, the parts in the brain where the motions of molecules are the greatest (which represent the consciousness centre) are the most fluidic and powerful parts. Thus, consciousness centres have high frequencies which correspond to their high functions.

Brain cells have, in the accustomed states, certain frequencies particular to them. These can increase for various reasons. And when increased, their activities and powers increase as well. So, the beings sending influences to mediums, govern the functions of these as they wish by increasing the motions in the centres they want to use either directly or via the channel of consciousness. Let us give a comparative example with relative numbers. Imagine that frequency of consciousness centre's molecules in accustomed states is 40,000 per second; when in a trance state, that is, when the medium is under the influence of a being, these frequencies elevate to 60,000 or 70,000 per second. So, with this increase of frequencies in the consciousness centre, activity there increases as well as comprehension expanding. Expansion of comprehension depends on the increase of this frequency. And the increase of the frequency occurs as and when the being sending that influence deems suitable.

So, by increase of motions, the medium's ability and comprehension to express the meanings of influence received increase as well. Mediums convey these meanings to the outer realms via the means mankind can understand, by speaking or writing or another way. We call these intuitive mediums. There are also physical mediums. Here, the incoming influences are either cruder than the vibrations of matter which will receive the influences or suitable to it. If cruder, when these influences pass through the medium and enter that matter, and because it cannot feed its higher combinations as we previously explained, this entails their erasure or disintegration and this, in turn, puts into effect the phenomena called materialisation.

If the incoming influences contain vibrations suitable to the structure of that matter, then the medium's efficacy in that matter increases and paves the way for possibilities of various formations and manifestations. In this way, materialisations, phantoms, apports,[17] states and motions of innumerable physical appearances of things called by many names are brought about. Phenomena observed by mankind within the group of physical mediumship belong to this mechanism that these are put into effect by executing the value differentiation mechanism and duality principle in matter and consequently, with the occurrence of states like motions, displacements and finally, dispersion and gatherings of molecules.

Although this is not an exact number, there are approximately 90 or 100 centres in the brain. And of these, there are 900 or 1000 secondary centres, that is, stations which have regular functions in the body. So, the influences coming from the essence-being to the brain are distributed from the consciousness centres of the brain to these centres, and from there – according to the needs – to the secondary centres or stations.

*
* *

Now, we will talk about the mechanisms of states such as sleep, dreams, obsession[18] and mediumship which are observed in mankind at certain times, respectively. However, in order to explain the basic technique of these mechanisms it is necessary to repeat some preliminary knowledge. This preliminary knowledge is pertaining to the connection and relations between the being and brain.

As we previously mentioned, seven-eighths of the human being is connected to the human brain. That is, seven parts of the being are connected to the brain and one part is free. The parts connected to the brain occupy a region constituted by certain brain cells we call the consciousness centre. The consciousness centre governs other centres and they, in turn, govern secondary centres. In this way, governance of the being over the body is ensured by centres and stations influencing each other by degrees, starting with the

---

[17] *Apports*: In physical mediumship séances, the paranormal transference of an object from one place to another, or the appearance of an object from an unknown source. (*Publisher*)

[18] *Obsession*: (1) In spiritualism, a disincarnated (disembodied) being's influence over an embodied (man) up to a degree of governing him. (2) The state of being besieged; used specifically of a person beset by a spirit from without. (*Publisher*)

consciousness centre. Previously, we termed the part of the human being connected to the brain consciousness and the part remaining free superconsciousness. Thus, the consciousness centre which the being is connected to is a region of a brain, constituted by the molecules with the most motions. The whole body is governed from this centre. The consciousness centre is always in relation with the outside, that is, with the being. The increase or the decrease of this centre's activity depends on the increase or decrease of its motions by the influences arriving at it.

As to the free part of the being that is not connected to brain, we termed it superconsciousness. It is necessary to divide this into two sections. However, let us say this: that the being is a subtle energies whole which cannot be subject to dividing or separation, in the sense that mankind understands it. Therefore, layered or concentric sections in it cannot be thought; that is, unlike it is for the brain, regions cannot be designated for it. However, in regard to some functions we have to explain here, an imperative for expressing such separate states of activity in the being with the symbol of regions. So the dividing we do here or the names we give belong to the states expressing these functions. Otherwise, in fact, there are no divided, separated parts or regions in the being.

So as not to be mistaken, we would like to explain this situation with an example. Although this example is rough in comparison with the state of the being we would like to explain and is, again, a reality belonging to our world. However, it will help the issue we would like to explain above to be easily intuited. Imagine a certain volume of hydrogen remains gathered, without dispersing in the vacuum, for example. This mass is constituted with a large number of hydrogen atoms. Now, let us divide these atoms into a few groups with distinct characters in regard to some deeds we assume that they carry out. So, each group will have a distinct function. For example, the function of some atoms is to catch the light vibrations; the function of other atoms is particular to heat vibrations; and the function of other atoms is to detect electrical vibrations.

Three kinds of atom characters separated in regard to their functions exist at this hydrogen ensemble in a complete disorder and are not gathered as groups in distinct places. In this way, these atoms that do not have particular regions are nevertheless separated from each other in regard to their functions. However, the being we mention does not display such a material state as a hydrogen atom ensemble. Nevertheless, although applying this example directly to this issue is not correct, it is possible to gain an intuition out of it. For, it is certainly understood from the knowledge we have given so far about the being that even thinking of a certain mass in a certain place for the being is not appropriate. Therefore, without subjecting the being to distinct and separate regional locations, there are influence complexes with distinct and separate functions in it which we cannot comprehend.

In this way, we have said that the free field of the superconsciousness, that is, of the being which is not connected to body, is divided into two parts; more correctly, it has two distinct and separate functional sides. The first of these is the part we call higher consciousness. This is the side of the being which is open to the outside. Influences coming from the spirit of the being enter from this side of the being. Likewise, influences coming from above and from the beings around land at this second part as well.

The second part of the superconsciousness field is the subconscious. This is, again, the being's closed front to the outside in regard to function. No influence arrives at the subconscious field from outside. And it does not send any influences to outside. However, here is the repository for all accumulating acquisitions of the being throughout the whole universe. Therefore, all impressions of past lives exist in the subconscious; essence-knowledge is preserved here. So, as we previously said, only acquisitions which became essence-knowledge and owned by essence-being can enter here.

Higher consciousness and subconscious have communication with the consciousness. These can inter-exchange with each other. However, the communication of the subconscious and higher consciousness or to put it another way, of the superconsciousness with the consciousness, does not occur directly. There is also an intermediary function acting as a bridge which we call the unconscious. Thus, the unconscious is the being's third field of function which intermediates the exchange between the consciousness and superconsciousness. However, the unconscious has another function as such. Impressions belonging to the knowledge which comes from the outer realm, world, daily life, to the consciousness but which has not yet become essence-knowledge, are gathered in this region – that is, in the unconscious – and stay there until death. So, the unconscious field (naturally, what we mean by the term 'field' can be understood) is at the same time a knowledge repository of the consciousness. Consciousness can, when necessary – without descending to the subconscious – take and use the required material from this unconscious. These are the results of the knowledge belonging to the last world life of the being, that is, to the life man goes through. This knowledge, after going through a comparative accounting, as we have previously said, is pushed to the unconscious; and this accounting is rendered by the conscience.

Unconscious knowledge, again as previously said, becomes essence-knowledge and nestles in the subconscious only after death, by going through the great accounting as the being compares these with subconscious knowledge. Events that occur in the consciousness within daily life pass to this unconscious field during sleep. Actually, fields of unconsciousness and of consciousness are very close to each other and in a frequent communication.

*
* *

After explaining these divisions regarding function, let us explain the way ordinary comprehension occurs in the light of this knowledge.

When a man looks at an external object, for example, at a pencil, vibrations belonging to that pencil go to the optic centre by passing through certain stations starting from the points around the optic system. And when it reflects from there to the consciousness centre, the initial material comprehension occurs. This comprehension is the world comprehension completely belonging to the superficial time activity to which the brain is subject. This influence goes to the higher consciousness from the consciousness via the channel of unconscious and there, comprehension belonging to the being occurs, which is outside of the world reality and cannot be understood by

147

mankind. The being knows this pencil within an encompassing comprehension.

Let us repeat that the material comprehension occurring in the consciousness and the subtle comprehension occurring in the being are not the same. The qualities of these comprehensions, depending on the matter milieus they are made of, become dense and subtle according to the relatively dense consciousness and comparatively very fluidic higher consciousness. Comprehension connected to consciousness manifests in a crude manner in accordance with the material structure of the consciousness centre; unlike in a compassing and complex manner as it is in the being.

The above example we give about the comprehension of the pencil is a simple schematic. The way we mention may be much more complicated than this. Other related centres and stations can also be involved with this journey of influence. Likewise, some influences from the unconscious can be involved. These adopt innumerable states in accordance with innumerable necessities.

*
* *

Now, we will explain sleep. For comprehension to occur, the consciousness centre should be free and high in frequency up to a degree so it can invoke the impressions existing in itself. In the state of mankind we call awake, consciousness is always in connection with the higher consciousness. Similarly, it is in an open state to the centres. That is, it is in connection with centres. So, it receives the influences coming from the surroundings. In summary, in the awakened state, consciousness is in communication on the one hand with the being and on the other hand with its surroundings, that is, with world life. By this means, it receives influences both from above, from the superconsciousness and from below, from the world. And by this, it prevails over the whole nervous system and through it, over the organism. That is, it governs the body in accordance with the necessities coming from the superconsciousness. We previously stated that actually the consciousness centre directly governs the body. The being utilises the body by using this centre.

During sleep, some centres' connections to the outer realm cease. These centres, besides the consciousness, connect to the unconscious. These centres are now related to the superconsciousness, not to the world. And we call this introversion of the centres. And such introversion of the centres which are not sensitive to the outer realm at that time brings about the state we call the sleep state. Therefore, these centres are passive and motionless towards the outer realm but in contrast, very active and mobile towards the superconsciousness. At that moment, because the consciousness and related centres are free of their connection to the outer realm, in order to transfer the results of their daily acquisitions to the unconscious, they render their first accounting regarding the conscience by the knowledge of comparison in the unconscious with ease. These results will stay there, in the unconscious. Since they are not compared yet with essence-knowledge by the essence-being, there are discrepancies between these and essence-knowledge. Because of this, this knowledge cannot be included with the essence-knowledge synthesis in the subconscious. It remains in the unconscious, at the field of the being which is near to the consciousness. Its accumulation here, as previously said, continues until the moment of death.

Therefore, centres appearing immobile and passive towards the surroundings during sleep achieve important deeds within. However, their activities are not extrovert but introvert. And all of their preoccupation consists only in the procedure of passing on daily events to the unconscious. For the soundness of this procedure, they must cease their connections to the surroundings and withdraw into a rest in relation to daily life; that is, the state we call sleep must occur.

*
* *

Explaining the mechanism of dreams becomes easy in that state. Dreams occur in two ways, that is, by the intervention of two influence sources: one of these is the influences coming from below, from surroundings; the other is the influences coming from the superconsciousness.

First of all, let us study the influences coming from the surroundings. When a sleeping person's foot is touched by a feather slightly – but not too strongly to disturb his sleep – vibrations coming out of here will not wake the centre pertaining to the foot but will disturb it because it is busy with its own deeds at that time, it does not want to be busy with this influence coming from surroundings. Because of this, as if shrugging off this influence coming from the foot, it conveys this to the subconscious via the channel of unconscious which it is connected to at that time. In effect, for this centre which is motionless towards surroundings to convey an influence coming from there in this way is a motion. However, it can make a small motion to do this in the face of this influence coming from outside, which is not too strong to wake it. Nevertheless, if the influence becomes a little intense, these motions increase; and the increase of motion frequencies of the centre towards the surroundings obliges it to turn from within to outward, that is, to wake up.

Now, let us continue assuming that it is not awoken. When the influence coming from the foot enters the subconscious, it grabs the suitable ones among the endless impressions existing there and activates them. By this means, an application of imagination occurs in the subconscious automatically, without control. Reflection of every motion occurring in the brain to the consciousness centre either directly or via other channels is a rule. However, these reflected influences are sometimes too weak to invoke impressions in the consciousness. In that case, the consciousness centre does its duty without comprehending.

Here, the images occurring in the subconscious reflect to the consciousness via the channel of unconscious. If these reflected impressions are strong enough to activate consciousness, frequency of the consciousness sufficiently increases to receive these images belonging to the surroundings and comprehends the images and wakes up at the same time. And at that moment, the dream is on. If the vibrations coming from the subconscious do not evoke enough motions in the molecules of the centre constituting consciousness field, the consciousness centre continues with its preoccupation and is not busy with these images and no dream will come.

Let us say that the images reflected to the consciousness from the subconscious are comprehended by the consciousness in ways suitable to its material structure, that is, to its world reality as much as possible. Therefore, the dream is not something seen. It is a kind of imagination. Because of the occurrence of an event, that is, all exchanges between consciousness and superconsciousness starting from the awakening in the foot happen in milliseconds, dream is momentary. Every man tickled by a feather does not necessarily have a dream. For example, the centre connected to the foot is so preoccupied with its deeds that influences coming from the foot do not activate it. Similarly, vibrations coming from the subconscious may not be intense enough to activate the consciousness ... Then, no dream comes.

*
* *

Let us come to the mechanism of dreams whose reason is connected to the higher places, higher consciousness. When a being wants a man to have a dream for some purpose, it sends vibrations pertaining to the dream which it will show him to the higher consciousness field of the being which that man is subject to. These influences sent to the higher consciousness pass to the consciousness via the channel of the unconscious and increase the frequencies of the molecules of the centre expressing consciousness. This state brings about the comprehensions of the impressions pertaining to the incoming vibrations in the consciousness. And this happens as follows: at that time, consciousness is actually turned towards the unconscious.

Because the influences coming from above are purposeful, each of these comes down as adjusted in order to evoke a required impression which exists in the unconscious. And these adjusted influences descending to the consciousness, which is actually in connection with the unconscious, results in consciousness's receiving the required impressions from the unconscious. And comprehension of images coming from the unconscious occurs in the consciousness.

So, the being that wants to show the dream, by sending adjusted influences according to qualities of innumerable materials in the unconscious, ensures the taking out of materials it wants from among these towards the consciousness field.

Thus, this kind of dreams occurs as well through imagination. Dreams coming from above or below can easily be discerned by more or less experienced mankind. The ones coming from below are rather disarrayed, vague and dim. The ones coming from the higher consciousness are ordered, vivid and deeply impressive.

*

* *

As is seen in this mechanism, in the latter group, that is, in dreams connected to the influences coming from above, there are purposeful devices addressing rather the consciousness. These aim to teach man certain things. These dreams are shown for various reasons such as revealing some stages of future events that need to be known for essential reasons: giving warnings in the face of some situations or delivering intuitions of some necessary knowledge.

Nonetheless, there are no stirrings in the universe that can be outside the control and directive of the unitary. Starting from a single motion to all motions of universe, every stirring is subject to the directives of the unitary. Therefore, upon seeing that we use terms like random, unconnected for the dream coming from below, it should not be think that we mean by this that they are futile and unnecessary. There is no motion or occurrence in universe that is unnecessary, meaningless or futile. Our usage of the terms above for the dreams coming from below is relative to the dreams which are connected to the influences coming from higher consciousness. They, as well, have their own particular ways of execution. They, as well, occur in another devised and calculated way. Thusly, as they are pondered upon, many things are learned and gained.

So, in the dreams seen by the influences coming from above, materials in the unconscious are used as images. In the ones coming from the surroundings, images are constituted by the materials taken from the subconscious. Nonetheless, if the being wanting to show the dream sees it necessary to put into effect its purpose, it utilises not only knowledge pertaining to this world life in the unconscious but also some knowledge from the subconscious, belonging to past lives. Naturally, images taken from the subconscious in this way are rather devised and proper, not like the flimsy images taken from the influences coming from surroundings. After giving this knowledge, explaining the mechanism of mediumship becomes easier.

*
* *

Mediumship occurs through influencing, that is, exchanges of vibrations. So, it is necessary for the vibrations coming from the beings to be fitting to the nature of mediums.

It is natural that in each world existing in the universe, matter conditions are different. The embodied are always states of formations in grades of the matter conditions of the sphere they exist on. And each of them has their own particular magnetic fields. Because of this, since the incoming vibrations are obliged to find the matter forms which are closest to each state and condition, it is necessary for the vibrations to harmonise with the particular nature of the medium in the world to be adjusted according to their magnetic fields.

Around our world, there are many fields of influence extending from density to fluidity. They surround the world almost like concentric circles. Each is a field of influence belonging to the beings in duty. The densest region of influence is the region which is closest to the surface of the world. And this belongs to rather backward beings. Nevertheless, these regions should not be considered concentric, by subjecting these to the spatial world. Here, we remind you of the example we previously gave about the functions in the hydrogen mass. So, there are milieus of influence around the world, starting from the dense and extending away to the subtle.

*
* *

Any influence to descend from a higher than planetary source to a man in the world is in a different subtlety in ratio to the structure of that man. In this state, there is no sympathy between them.

Therefore, that influence cannot descend to that man as it is. It is necessary for it to soften, to discard some part of its intensity, to become acceptable and digestible for mankind until it reaches that man. Because of this, it needs go through some transformations, be filtered through some filters, to become cruder. And these are done in the milieus we have just mentioned. So, each field of influence that will ensure this is a transformation station, that is, a transformer for the incoming influence.

*

* *

The farther the being that will send influence to a man is from that man – that is, the greater the difference is in evolution between them – the more the numbers of the transformative fields or transformer stations that influence will go through until it reaches where that man is. On the other hand, the closer the being that will send influence and the man, that is the medium, that will receive that influence are in regard the fluidity, the smaller the numbers of transformer stations in between are. More or less evolved beings that are closest to the world can make connection with some mediums they can contact, without going through transformer stations directly. This is because magnetic fields of these are close enough to be able to contact each other without transforming.

For example, when some people need to go under the possession of these kinds of simple beings because they need to be tried and tested, then beings in duty stick such simple beings to those people. In this way, obsessions occur and the simple being who is the obsessor can send its influences to that man directly, without needing the way stations. Actually, such simple beings or obsessors do not have the power to be able to use some transformers. For, this is an issue of evolution as well. Their comprehension is not suitable for this. They automatically stick to suitable people they encounter. Sometimes, these obsessors may be a crude milieu of transformation which is very close to the world, and are used as a station by higher beings.

*

* *

First of all, we will explain the communication mechanism constituting the most sublime form of mediumship which is of a sublime being in duty with a medium in duty.

An influence, departing from the being in duty and consisting of vibrations that can evoke certain meanings and impressions in the medium, starts to advance towards the medium chosen for this deed. As we have said, after going through a great number of transformer stations, it communicates with the higher consciousness of the being of that medium. After all, we had previously mentioned that only higher consciousness fields of the beings with other beings and with their spirits are open and they may contact this field. These influences landing at higher consciousness are immediately sent via the channel of unconscious to the medium's centre governing the function or capability which is needed to be utilised.

It is a rule that influences arriving in the brain increase the motions of molecules constituting the brain centres. They increase their accustomed frequency of vibrations, which means that their capabilities and powers increase accordingly. For example, if here the medium needs to convey the incoming vibrations to surroundings by speaking, then influences in the higher consciousness immediately arrive at the centres related to speaking via the channel of unconscious and activate them. These influences are adjusted in accordance with the impressions to be evoked in them. Since every influence entering the brain must be reflected directly or via other ways surely to the consciousness centre; during the coming of influence from the higher consciousness to the speaking centre, this influence passes to the consciousness centre as well. Influences passing to the consciousness lead this centre to activity according to the purposes inherent in these influences, by increasing the vibrational frequencies of molecules in the centre expressing the consciousness. Consciousness receiving influences in this way sends them back to the higher consciousness via the channel of unconscious. Here, the purpose of sending the influences to the higher consciousness is to inspect if they arrived exactly at the centre or not. Being inspects this. Actually, inspection is done by the being in duty, but it appears as if this is done by the being of the medium.

In consequence of the inspection, after the state of the influence entering the centre of speaking is judged as correct or wrong, this judgement again comes to the consciousness via the channel of the unconscious. Consciousness commands the centre under its governance to do or not to do it in accordance with the correctness or wrongness of the judgement. And the centre acts only after receiving this command and if it has received the command to do it, it makes the medium speak by influencing the required organs. At that time, as the medium translates the meanings contained in the incoming influence into words, takes necessary words and images from the knowledge and impressions belonging to that life in the unconscious. It is not necessary to involve the subconscious for this immediately. However, if it is necessary to take some impressions from the past lives according to the quality of the communiqué to be given, then the centre for speaking via the channel of unconscious again takes this knowledge from the materials in the subconscious.

Since the influence cannot be spoken unless it again goes through the inspection of the being after it arrived at the centre for speaking from the higher consciousness, this centre should not act before the result of the inspection. Although, the centre for speaking appears as if it waits for it, actually here there is no waiting. This is because the completion of the necessary applications for the influence's passing from the centre for speaking to organs for speaking takes a few seconds, whereas the influence's going from the consciousness to the higher consciousness via the channel of unconscious and going through the inspection and then going back to the consciousness via the channel of subconscious and, from there, the command's going to the centre for speaking, is completed in milliseconds of time. Therefore, the centre for speaking does not need to wait for the result of the inspection for a long time. For, at the time the influence is arriving just at the centre for speaking, its inspection has been done and completed by the ways we mentioned above. As is seen in this mechanism, there is not much difference between the mechanism of dreams seen by the sublime influences we have just explained and the mechanism of such sublime communications. However, the difference is the process here is more vivid and has gone through the inspection mechanism.

Here, the being who gives the communiqué, as we have said above, can also use, if necessary, the materials in the subconscious, by appealing to it. These materials in the subconscious, as translated into words in the related centre, begin to be spoken by the medium. The impressions belonging to them may not be evoked in the consciousness. These impressions, because they belong to past lives, actually do not exist in the consciousness. As advancing towards related centres via the channel of unconscious and coming by the consciousness, if they continue without activating the cells of comprehension there, comprehension of the consciousness centre pertaining to the impressions of these does not wake up and man does not know them. In this case, this is automatic transfer.

In the inspected communication, there may be communiqués whose meanings do not need to be reflected to the comprehension of the medium for various reasons. Although these communiqués are reflected from the consciousness centre to the higher consciousness to be inspected as well, comprehension does not occur in the consciousness; and this happens in this way: The consciousness centre is very complicated. It is constituted by molecules combined with atom combinations that have various frequencies. Some parts of these molecule groups are particular to the comprehension and other parts do not pertain to the comprehension of man but only to the governing vibrations of the consciousness centre over other centres, that is, to its vibrations activating them. And in the deeds the consciousness having the centres to do, if comprehension belonging to these deeds is not required to occur in the medium, then the frequency of incoming influences to the consciousness centre does not have the quality to alert the parts of consciousness pertaining to the comprehension but a quality to alert the molecules pertaining to administrative deeds.

Then, the consciousness centre acts in a way to have the related centres activated in accordance only with the meanings of vibrations arriving at the related centres but because the comprehension centre is not active, that man cannot have the comprehension of that deed. And in this case, automatic communiqué and automatic activity are in question. If all the groups of comprehension molecules in the consciousness centre are activated then consciousness both renders the act of governance, and man, naturally, becomes aware of what he does. In this case, the aware communications are in question.

In controlled communications, if the being giving the communiqué does not want to reflect the meaning of the communiqué to human comprehension it then sends vibrations in such quality and value that these cannot be in a state to activate the molecules groups of comprehension in the consciousness centre. They only activate the molecule groups of the consciousness centre and ensure the constitution of the meanings belonging to the communiqués given through it at those centres. In the mean time, as the consciousness centre gives this command to the centres, the comprehension in the state of human is not aware of these deeds. For, molecules belonging to that part of the centre are not in activity. However, the governing molecules of the consciousness bear upon the meanings of those vibrations which are reflected to the centre and sent up for inspection. So, in this way, a non-comprehending control has been established via the channel we mentioned above. Therefore, the difference between the comprehending and non-comprehending controls is, in the case with the former, impressions activate the comprehension molecule groups in the consciousness; and with the latter, they do not alert these groups.

*
* *

Besides the mediums in great duty, the case here with the ordinary communications of mediums with average beings for the individual and small communal evolutions is actually similar to the previous one. The difference is that there is no control mechanism here. That is, the being does not inspect if the vibration it sent to the medium was transmitted correctly or not. It only suffices with sending its influences to the higher consciousness of the medium. It is not interested with how the medium receives or conveys these. However, the being giving the communiqué is controlled by superior beings.

Influences coming from that being to the higher consciousness of the medium, as subjected to the mechanism of initiator, guiding and propulsive influences which we previously explained in the topic of influences, are filtered through a few stations according to its distance to the medium and land in the higher consciousness field of the medium and communicates to it. Influences, from the higher consciousness via the channel of the unconscious, go to the centre to which the organs to convey these influences to the surroundings are subject, that is, to the centre for speaking. At the same time, they are reflected to the consciousness centre as well. If the impressions belonging to the images wished to be evoked and required to come from the subconscious are not in a state to be reflected to the comprehension as they are taken from the subconscious via the channel of the unconscious, these vibrations are not of a quality to activate the cells belonging to the comprehension molecules of the consciousness. Then man cannot comprehend them.

In this case, again, automatic communication is in question. However, since each centre is always under the command and management of the consciousness centre, no centre can be activated without commands from it. The consciousness centre receives these influences which do not alert comprehension molecules in it and sends the necessary commands to the required centres according to these influences. Sometimes, incoming influences are of a quality to evoke the images belonging to the meanings they carry at comprehension cells of the consciousness; that is, they are in a state suitable to the vibrations of comprehension molecules of the consciousness centre in order to activate them. Then, the medium goes into action by knowing the deed he does. Nevertheless, in most of the communiqués, this activity occurs with comprehension.

As it is seen here, the consciousness centre, unlike the previous group, is not subject to an inspection mechanism to give 'do' command to the execution centre. Meanings coming from the being are executed by the centre without inspecting their correctness. Because of this, in this kind of communications, situations besides mixing of impressions taken from the unconscious in between the communiqués as well as impressions taken from the subconscious and not subjecting them to inspection may sometimes result in alteration in the meaning of the communiqués, their degeneration or conveying the opposite meaning the being wishes to express. Frequent or rare occurrences of such situations depend on the capabilities of the mediums, degree of power of the being sending the communiqué, and the conditions of the structure and the milieu. For, it should be remembered that during the communiqué, comprehending or automatic thoughts, wishes of the sitters or assistants in the session influence the mediums – even in spite of those assistants.

And this happens as such: This influence can never go to the higher consciousness field of the medium and cannot alter the communiqués but by utilising the channel of unconscious which is open to the consciousness at that time it can easily influence the consciousness field and may bring about more or less indistinctness. This indistinctness, which emerges in the consciousness according to the intensity and variety of these influences coming from the surroundings, may hinder the flux of influences coming from the higher consciousness. For, the contact field of the unconscious that carries the influences coming from the higher consciousness and of the consciousness becomes more or less occupied by the influences coming from the surroundings. In this case, centres begin to make the medium say strange words by these mixed and confusing influences they receive from, on the one hand, the subconscious and on the other, from indistinct consciousness.

All of these states are not purposeless and in vain but are states arranged by the beings in duty for the increase of refining experiences of the mediums and others around them. Here, there are innumerable factors such as development of capabilities and attention of the assistants and the mediums; testing their good or ill intentions and measuring their degrees of courage, resolution and perseverance through their behaviours in the face of the consequent misapprehensions.

*
* *

For the automatic communication to be understood well, we see it as useful to summarily repeat its mechanism. Every vibration arriving at the brain must certainly be reflected to the consciousness centre either directly or via other channels. For, because the being is connected to the human body via the consciousness centre, the

160

centre governing the brain, nervous system and consequently the whole body is the consciousness centre. Therefore, without its approval, nothing can be done in the organism. Otherwise, that is, if every incoming influence attempts to use the centres directly, without appealing to the consciousness, this situation not only attacks against the freedom of the being but also disturbs the wholeness of the organism; and a situation emerges such as disintegration of this wholeness, which is not in accordance with the necessities and the order is disturbed. There is no power mighty enough in universe to disturb the divine order. Therefore, every external influence that wishes to do this or that activity must definitely act without disturbing the wholeness of the organism. For this, every influence entering there must go through the approval of the consciousness. So, influences sent from outside and executed by the organism, whether comprehended or not, must definitely go through the approval of the consciousness centre.

However, influences arriving at mediums at high, average and low levels, although they are reflected to the consciousness, are sometimes not of a quality to activate the comprehension molecules belonging to the meanings they carry – as we have said – in the consciousness. Influences of this character end up only having the related centres to do necessary deeds via the consciousness centre, without human comprehension involved. That is, the consciousness centre – without human comprehension involved – gives positive or negative commands to the required execution centres about the putting into effect of that deed, under the influences arriving at it. Those centres, according to this command, reflect the influences that are arriving at them from above and that have acquired their meanings by going through various channels to the surroundings by translating them into their communiqué tools.

And this happens as such: As we said above, consciousness is seven-eighths of the being which is connected to the brain. Therefore, consciousness is also contained within the whole of the being. It only occupies the molecule ensembles in a certain part of the brain cells pertaining to human life. These molecules exist in groups. As some of these groups constitute human comprehension, some other parts do the deeds belonging to the conduction of the

161

brain centres according to commands from the being. Therefore, the comprehension mentioned here only belongs to the human brain, or more correctly, a comprehension belonging to the human. This should not be mistaken for the comprehension occurring in the essence-being.

So, comprehension not occurring in the comprehension cells of the consciousness centre does not mean that influences arriving at the consciousness centre will not be comprehended in the essence-being, either. Because of this, an event which is automatic, which remains unknown by the comprehension molecules in the consciousness centre and consequently by mankind has been comprehended by the essence-being. Such is the automatic character; influences from outside arriving at the brain and waiting certainly for the commands of the consciousness centre in order to be executed by the executing centres either interest or do not interest the comprehension cells of the molecule groups constituting the consciousness centre; and this depends on necessities. If they interest them, consciousness centre does its activity upon other centres with comprehension, that is, it knows the deeds it does while it is in its human state. If the incoming influences do not interest the comprehension molecules, consciousness centre renders its administrator duty as usual but its human state is not aware of the deeds it does, whereas higher consciousness of the being is aware of those deeds with its own comprehension and it governs the consciousness centre with this comprehension of its. So, here, from another angle we fortify the meaning of the knowledge we previously gave about that human comprehension is not same with the comprehension of the essence-being.

There are various reasons for the bestowing of automatic communiqués. For example, a sublime being wants to hide from the medium some of the meanings of the communiqué it wishes to convey. Therefore, it sends its influences to the consciousness centre without touching the comprehension cells in the consciousness centre. Then, the consciousness centre approves it automatically, without knowing its meaning, and commands the centre for speaking to act accordingly. It should be remembered that impressions in the consciousness actually comes from knowledge in the unconscious. However, because the consciousness is always in connection with

162

the unconscious, especially in the trance state; not evoking impressions in the consciousness means that the knowledge to be consigned from the unconscious to centres has not activated the quantitative values of the consciousness up to a degree to cause its awakening. If these values are sent to the comprehension molecules in the consciousness to a sufficient degree, through the motions occurred in it, impressions begin to be evoked and the consciousness begins to act with comprehension.

Likewise, as happens in some backward communications – regardless of the state of the being – a simple being, as completely free of the condition of whether these impressions are evoked or not in the consciousness centre, also acts automatically and only expects the consciousness to put into effect the required influence in the centres. Therefore, impressions belonging to the meanings expressed by those influences are again not evoked in the consciousness; and the consciousness acts automatically.

Sometimes, the nature of the medium and state of the consciousness centre are not suitable for impressions to be evoked in the consciousness centre by incoming influences. The consciousness centre commands the related centres upon only the impression evoked in the consciousness about the execution of the required deed. It has them to do these deeds. And sometimes, incoming influences are not in a state to evoke these impressions. In short, because of various similar reasons, without evoking impressions belonging to the meanings of the incoming influences in the consciousness, the consciousness centre works only with impressions about the execution of those. In that case, the character of automatic mediumship emerges. We repeat that all of these situations occur under the control of sublime beings and in accordance with sublime necessities and imperatives. There is nothing arbitrary and random at all.

*
* *

Now, let us take the obsession mechanism which is the crudest of the communications. Here also the technique is similar to the previous ones. However, here, as the necessity of the character of a backward communication, during the communication, freedom of the being who is obsessed has been abolished – in quantities less and more in accordance with the degree of obsession's intensity. Even, in some intense degrees of obsession, man enters into a state of not knowing himself any more. He becomes a toy in the hand of a simple being that is called an obsessor. Obsession occurs under such a mechanism.

First of all, the being that will obsess should be quite backward and closest to the dense layers of humanity of the world. Because of countless reasons such as evolution, increase of refining experiences of a man, his going through the knowledge of comparison; a simple being with a very narrow comprehension, excess desires, thoroughly selfish starts to send its crude influences to the higher consciousness of a man by the approval and consent of sublime necessities. For this, as we previously said, there is neither a possibility nor a necessity for it to pass through transformer milieus. It sends its influence directly to the higher consciousness. At first, it does not prevail over the higher consciousness. However, its crude and dense influence, when passed to the field of consciousness from the higher consciousness via the channel of unconscious, occupies that field. And then, it completely prevails over the consciousness.

When this prevalence advances a little bit more, it goes up to the higher consciousness and eventually, the obsessor being covers the whole field of higher consciousness and takes it over. Then, influences coming from the essence-being of man cease almost completely and instead of the essence-being, influences begin to come from the obsessor being. In this way, because of the lessened relation with the higher consciousness, consciousness turns towards the subconscious. It starts to receive all commands from the obsessor which has taken over the higher consciousness. And because the obsessor occupies the whole field of higher consciousness at that moment, the man who is obsessed starts to comprehend the obsessor as his own being.

The obsessor, starting to influence the consciousness centre in this way, connects the consciousness centre to the subconscious as well. This is a situation similar to the dreams that occur with influences coming from the surroundings, whose mechanism we previously talked about. That is, the obsessed man begins to live a peculiar life constituted out of the irrelevant and disconnected imaginations taken randomly from the knowledge of his subconscious by the obsessing being in accordance with its whims. And he sees himself in the identity of another being. This means that consciousness is only face to face with images constituted in the subconscious, as well as the influences coming from the higher consciousness which are of the obsessor and filled with desirous, ignorant and selfish meanings suitable to its simple nature; and the obsessed man loses his own identity within these confused states, that is, he feels himself in other states.

In the mean time, because the obsessor has been using both the consciousness and subconscious of that man as it wishes, it gathers these images according to its whims and capacity; and brings about the impressions in the consciousness that are suitable to its inclinations. Here, because the consciousness centre takes the impressions all the time from the obsessor, its perceptual identity comes as well via the channel of the obsessor. Therefore, man sees everything from the viewpoint of the obsessor and cannot have a comprehension pertaining to his own being. If the obsessor does not reflect these impressions to his consciousness at all, then he does not know anything and acts as an automat. Nevertheless, through the mechanism we talked about above, he leaves his will completely to the obsessor and the obsessor uses and directs his consciousness as it wishes, without reflecting anything to his comprehension.

*
* *

Now, we will also say a few things about the scheme of influence that a hypnotist uses on his subject; and which is more or less fitting to the obsession mechanism.

No matter how powerful a man is, as long as he is within the narrow possibilities of his body, he cannot directly govern the higher consciousness of a man, unlike an obsessor on the outside who is in a more or less free state. However, without knowing its mechanism, hypnotists stop the connection of the unconscious to the higher consciousness of the subject by the influences they send out in various ways. When the influences that are supposed to come from the higher consciousness cease, hypnotists starts to send their own influences to the consciousness. Here, foreign influences, unlike in obsession, do not arrive from the higher consciousness but directly from hypnotists to the consciousness via the channel of the unconscious. As you see, there is not much difference between two of these in regard to the technique. Once this mechanism is established, the subject begins to act with the influences of the hypnotist. If the hypnotists do not send influences to evoke impressions on the subject's field of consciousness then he acts automatically, completely without comprehension. Nevertheless, since these influences, that is, the meanings in the suggestions of the hypnotists already exist in the unconscious, these meanings or impressions can be reflected to the consciousness, when necessary.

*
* *

We see it as helpful to talk a little as well about some communications that are called inspiration and which put into effect the manifestations that mankind call genius, creativity in the life of sciences, arts and ideas. These are influences which are not connected to great plans of duty and which depend on the ordinary and average mechanism of communication we mentioned above, and are sent by mediator beings in duty, such as guarding and assisting beings who want to help with individual and some communal states of mankind. Here, trance is not needed either. For, trance is a state put into effect with the purpose of decelerating the motions of the brain centres in response to the surroundings in a state akin to sleep so influences coming from the surroundings can be removed during the flux of a long communiqué. However, in inspirations, there is no such sending of influences for long durations. These come intermittently and in short periods which can be deemed as a moment.

*
* *

Knowledge given to the world by the beings in duty through mediums put into effect very major movements which are generally related to communal plans. From time to time, in some extremely

166

exceptional situations, sublime beings of the plan of duty ascend to the world as themselves and act both as ruler and as guides to the right path in order to evoke a major movement among mankind and to have them acquiring mass breakthroughs; to give cultivating knowledge related to general and communal orders, regulations and methods; in short, to ensure their fast evolution in the world. These powerful beings have caused great and mass revolutions in the world with the institutions of religion they established to disseminate among mankind the higher knowledge they receive from the sublime plan of duty to which they are always connected.

Great religions, which were established in this way and displayed strong influences within the communal plans, have ensured that consciences reach higher levels through their strong and orderly sanctions. Religions, with this side of them, are of the vehicles for preparing mankind to the plans of duty. Religions have put into effect the current high and evolved state of the world, and have ensured the initial communal preparations of the next great transition cycle; and each of them, within their own constitution, have shown to mankind the most appropriate ways of preparing for the plan of duty, by responding to the various and differing needs, imperatives and necessities of their own times.

Each religion, by saving mankind from the darkness of ignorance, has led them to the great divine path with the profound intuitions they have given within the directives, examples, symbols and knowledge in accordance with the time and necessities. All religions have helped mankind in elevating the level of reality equilibrium line of their conscience mechanisms to the uppermost levels of their possibilities of comprehension which are within the allowance of the necessities particular to that moment.

As we have just mentioned, in order to enunciate and teach the necessities of an established religion and to ensure the initial adaptation of mankind to these teachings; a being in duty from the sublime plan of duty came in the midst of mankind by embodiment in the world, and mankind has called these embodied beings in duty prophets or saviours.

Mankind, who came into the world in order to prepare for the plan of duty, are not left unattended. If this was the case, mankind could not have come so far in their evolved states. Therefore, communal states arise, as individuals do, always under the supervision and observation of the sublime plan of duty. In the universe, there are great beings in duty, who are charged with this duty.

Mankind has begun, especially as their comprehension expands, to overflow the narrow physicochemical rules of crude matter they have lived within; and have always struggled strenuously with the need to learn the reasons for their existence because of the intuitions and instincts filtered through their essence-knowledge into their consciousness about the possible existence of some laws and orders based on more encompassing, wider comprehensions. The initial question preoccupying them was: Who made the things and especially, themselves that they see in their surroundings and who governs their fate? Therefore, the concept of God is the first powerful reflection of a need that emerged in their comprehensions; and which originates from their essence-beings, with the help of superior vibrations.

From the moment their comprehension started to develop, mankind has begun to look for a god. However, previously, this need of theirs was in a simple state in accordance with their comprehension which was yet too weak in regard to value. Therefore, man could not afford more than to search for his god within the limited possibilities of his five sense organs. The intuitions sent by the assisting beings that tried to respond to this need of theirs could only be possible through symbols that could address only the five sense organs of mankind. Mankind had not reached the levels of comprehension enabling them to understand the meanings those symbols actually indicated. Therefore, intuitions of divine concepts gave them only ways of symbolising these with the things they knew as most powerful in their surroundings.

For example, initially, the symbol of sun represented the god; a great river giving life to a country was again such a symbol. These symbols were sufficient only for a while for the simple comprehensions of early times. However, comprehensions were increasingly valued, and human comprehensions which increased in value with high sublime matter combinations were entering a state of dissatisfaction with these symbols. As a consequence of all these states, in order to introduce divine knowledge to mankind, from the plan of duty, beings in duty ascended into the world and established the religions of the book. Each of these religions completed some missing aspects of human communities. In this way, the paths of carrying mankind to a state of further advancement, which are delineated in accordance with the great plan of destiny, have been shown to mankind.

Each religion has taught the things that have needed to be known by mankind up to the highest possible levels of intuition their comprehensions could reach within the uppermost possibilities of the realities they lived in; and has accomplished its duty perfectly.

First, it introduced mankind to automatically preparing states of the discipline of the application of the intuition of duty through various forms of worship and obligations. And by teaching mankind to love each other, it also showed the directions belonging to the great preparation of advancement towards duty, with direct directives. It instilled in them all kinds of deeds that are necessary for orientating always to the higher realities of their consciences, by showing them various ways of virtue; and with various sanctions, it ensured the ways of delivering mankind to the illumined possibilities of the preparation to the intuition of duty.

In short, religions made mankind converge on the threshold of the great transition cycle of the world which is near to happening today. If religions were absent, mankind would be much more backward than its present level. In this way, the beings in duty to ensure the preparation of mankind for the plan of duty accomplished their duty perfectly.

However, although mankind has passed from early times to the middle times, they were not yet properly endowed in regard to comprehension during the times religions were established. Because of this, religions which came from the same source, that is from the plan of duty and followed the traces of great truths in the same degree, could only give these truths to mankind at particular times and only in the forms they were able to understand. Thus, prophets and saviours could only disseminate the truths that needed to be disseminated among mankind by using symbols.

Therefore, all great books of religion are full of powerful symbols carrying the intuition of truths, a piece of which was arranged and calculated in accordance with their respective times.

For example, judgement day is one of these symbols and it expresses the world's nearing cycle of transition or the closing of this world cycle, which is a great truth. Likewise, in order to give intuitions enough for comprehensions about some truths that have deeper meanings, the concepts of heaven and hell are symbols, a piece of which is bestowed upon the world by the beings in duty, in accordance with sublime necessities. Each way of worship has been imposed on mankind through exact calculation in accordance with the necessities of the times, life conditions, developmental states and equilibrium states of their consciences; and thus, by an automatic layout, preparations have been made for enabling mankind to orientate to the higher components of conscience and consequently to become convenient for the higher plan on which today they are converging.

In the meantime, innumerable virtues commanded by the religions – such as love, compassion, solidarity, forgiveness, tolerance, sacrifice, resignation, benevolence, honesty, sincerity, some obligations toward their fellow human beings and even towards the ones other than their fellow human beings – likewise, on the contrary innumerable vices forbidden by the religions – such as selfishness, begrudging, enmity, envy, revenge, malice, dishonesty, hypocrisy, usurpation, stealing, homicide – have prepared mankind for higher comprehension plans, sometimes automatically and sometimes within a semi-comprehending illumination.

Nevertheless, in time, development of these comprehensions towards a higher plan has increased so much that the need to understand and interpret the intuitions given by the religions through symbols emerged intensely in mankind. This should also be deemed as the total success of the religions. Today, mankind vehemently wish for the utmost clear knowledge of the sublime intuitions evoked in them by these symbols. Nonetheless, only two – or at the most – three per cent of mankind can succeed in extracting these meanings from the powerful symbols which are successfully established by the books of religion.

However, sublime beings in duty who always receive their directives from the divine plan have observed mankind's present longing and higher needs. And this book is a gift to the world from the part of the plan of duty which is engaged for the world. It contains the knowledge for mankind who are thirsty in their need to continue to seek and expect their evolution. Intuitions of the great truths have been given by the books of religions within symbols powerful enough for mankind in accordance with the times and necessities; and in this book, clear knowledge of the truths that will conclude the world revolution – of which premonitions were previously given – and the intuitions of the coming super-world cosmos are written that these will be the last reality of today's world which is on the brink of a great revolution.

*
* *

Interventions of the beings in duty which grew clear in the world towards current times and put into effect great religious institutions and many other communal situations have not been seen as so clear and encompassing in the world's initial cycle of mankind. For, in initial cycles, within their still developing comprehension, mankind was not in need of such major communal evolution. Mankind, whose comprehension was still at the stage of automatic intuition, was mostly leading individual lives. And some small communities that occurred in the mean time were completely different from the great communal concepts as currently understood. Transitory communities of those times occurred under the needs arising out of a few very simple instinctual intuitions such as worry over starvation, the instinct of fear, sexual needs etc.

In these simple developmental stages, the comprehensive communal lives of mankind were not established yet. And this was a consequence of lacking the enabling power of their comprehension to put into effect such a situation. That is, powers of gathering, establishing and administering – which are necessary in sufficient degrees to gather individuals and to establish common activities towards a certain goal and to conduct them – had not yet occurred in their comprehensions. Because of this, these first humans whose level of equilibrium of their conscience duality was always set on the plane of the earthly cravings were confined to the lower realities for most of the time. For, the first humans who had just started to separate from the automatic advance in the stages of subhuman did not yet possess the possibilities of direct intervention to their bodies with their comprehension which they would acquire in future through a wider scope of freedom.

If the case had continued like this, it would not have been possible for them to rise to higher stages of developmental equilibrium levels by themselves. Because of this, in order to ensure their ability to elevate the equilibrium levels of initial developments, the necessity and imperativeness of the individual interventions coming from outside into the comprehension of mankind had to continue for a while. Naturally, as comprehension developed, that is, as they widened their scopes through refining experiences in the human state; external interventions rather headed towards the side of increasing the possibilities of comprehension for their intervening developmental mechanisms by themselves.

*
* *

We have already mentioned that self-intervention of comprehension at the beginning of the human life could only be possible through external interventions and assistance. In these initial cycles, everything is automatic and without comprehension. Because of this, mankind called this instinct. In early times, higher communal plans had always intervened over mankind. Here, however, expression of intervention should not be misunderstood. What is meant by intervention is giving a direction, organising and programming. Interventions that have more extreme meanings than those are not for the stage of humanity. So, in early times, classical expression of these external vibrations in comprehension was via the instincts. These instincts should be considered separate from the heavier and cruder automatism existing in animals. For, between these two automatisms there is a wide difference in disposition. Likewise, such differences also exist between the automatism in animals and in plants.

As comprehension is refined, these instincts become richer in characters and enter into forms and states which mankind calls intuition.

The start of the cycle of intuition in the world has occurred more or less in equality in regard to general value. Voids and deficiencies that could not be filled by instincts have started to be filled gradually with the birth of intuitions; and the communal life in the world, which is the symmetry and preparation of communal plans in the higher realms, has thus been established. And during this establishment, parallel to the development of comprehension and also as the results of this development the need for secession of the whole into parts, fragmentations, organisings and organiser has emerged. Because of this, as the dispositions, necessities and imperatives increase, similarities between bodies and similarities of instincts caused by the lack of content in comprehension – which is particular to the early cycles – have ceased to be; and different states put into effect by evolution have manifested in the bodies not as previous slight differences but as wide value differences.

From this social formations moment onward, individual and communal gatherings – again, in the most automatic sense in regard to human life – have started; some individuals have led these communities in regard to various value measurements: such as selfish leadership, leadership at a stage of conscience, and leadership at cycles of major and general development that have arrived at certain times.

It is this imperative that has made some of mankind acquire abilities of sensitive communication; because of this, strong mediums have come; some certain transitional stages occurred; and the plans of emotional preparation for duty have started through the intuitions of some knowledge, grasping and reaching towards the higher paths of the universe; and finally, towards the recent times of the past, these plans have taken their most developed states and intuitions have manifested in communities in the form of more powerful symbols and reforms.

In summarising comprehension's development – as the lot of the world – briefly and generally, we have also given general knowledge on how and in what way the communities were constituted.

*
* *

Each of the communities in the world has occurred because of imperatives raised by preparation for the great plan of duty. It has
been previously said that a man, as a single individual, could not
make this preparation completely on his own. The knowledge we
have just given has also taught that comprehension, when remaining alone, could not ensure intended developments. Mankind can
never develop by living alone throughout the world.

Races, nations, communities, societies, families that exist in the
world are the consequences of the imperatives and needs explained
above. Of these, first, let us take the races.

*
* *

According to the world's social, natural and geographical conditions, certain differentiations and groupings in human structures
and comprehensions have occurred through the approval and influence of sublime beings in duty, in accordance with necessities
that have come filtered through the unitary. And in the main areas
of the various formations, transformations and deformations made
by the comprehensions over their bodies, some common qualities
and characteristics particular to certain groups were distinguished.
Comprehensions gathered within such groups carry the somatic
and psychic (both are one and the same, but are concepts belonging
to various manifestations of the body) peculiarities of that group
and they lead to the phenomenon of race.

This knowledge indicates that mankind's separation into races is
the consequence of their comprehension's indirect influence over
their bodies. That is, differences in races are not comprehension's
direct efficacy over the body through the influences it receives from
the being but rather states raised out of the occurrence of changes
over the body by influences coming from the surroundings and
events in the surroundings. So, different races are the result of
mankind's imperative – in accordance with their developmental
needs – in having come down the world in this or that condition
and in having utilised those conditions this or that way. As two
men from white and black races who came into the world with certain evolutionary needs display different characteristics with their

skin colour; likewise, they display, among the same people – again, according to the same necessities – more or less different psychic actions and reactions depending on their bodies.

In short, white or black, yellow or red; all mankind aspire towards the same goal, shoulder to shoulder at the same path, by overcoming the same obstacles with the same difficulties. And this journey is for all. Monopoly or privilege for anyone is out of the question. Whatever kind of advance is necessary for the development of each being, it is an obligation for that being to follow that advancement. Today, the paths to be travelled are painted white; when necessary, they can be painted yellow; and again if necessary, they can be painted black or red. Therefore, skin colour and any characteristics accompanying these colours which cause racial segregation of mankind do not have any value that may justify such segregation. These are simple materials in part of the transitory developmental vehicles that need to be used on the paths to be travelled; and the necessities of the imperative of the mass advancement on the path of preparing for the duty.

*
* *

By this imperative, more comprehending and systematic communities occur as a consequence of these developments. And at the head of these comes the community of the nation or the state.

We have previously mentioned that certain duties and deeds in the universe are done by beings in duty, who are in groups and cadres, and that these groups are interconnected by various aspects and in this way, a system of organisations has been established up to the unitary. These systems that ensure the execution of plans of duty in accordance with the principles of the universe take very important roles in the developmental and evolutionary plans of all beings.

*
* *

The life of mankind is the last stage – starting from below – which is the symmetry of the system of organisations that prepares the intuitions of them. Therefore, completion of the preparations belonging to the intuitions and more or less the knowledge of the

175

plan of duty in the life of mankind is an imperative. The first and last duty of mankind in the world is to fulfil the preparatory necessities to the plan of duty. After all, mankind necessarily obeys these necessities through the interventions of higher assisting influences in all stages of evolution that have passed from their most non-comprehending initial stages up to the highest comprehension: comprehension of intuition of the duty. This obedience occurs through mechanisms either of a completely automatic character or within more or less illumined intuition. These semi-comprehending or non-comprehending automatisms have various technical possibilities which will ensure mankind prepares for the plans of duty. And one of these technical possibilities is the communal living of mankind within the community of nation or state.

*
* *

Nation or state, above all, is a large community that is established among mankind. This big crowd of mankind who gathered together with mutual purposes is subject to an orderly, programmed, coordinated working mechanism oriented to certain goals. This mechanism advances in accordance with the great order and in complete harmony with the advance of the world.

The nation community is constituted of a great number of secondary communities. These secondary institutions are directly and indirectly connected to each other. For example, at the head there is a ruling leader. In a hierarchical sequence, there are other ruling mechanisms that are connected to him. Within these mechanisms, the rulers and the ruled advance in successive order, connected to each other. All activities of this mechanism – apparently oriented to material purposes – are actually for the preparation of mankind to ever higher plans which are the symmetry of this community; and this preparation is the preparation of the intuition of duty. Therefore, within the deeds done in this community, it is possible to find the drafts of the preparations belonging to the plan of duty. In a community of nation or of a state, what mankind calls duty – according to their own comprehension – is only in fact the preparatory materials of the intuition of duty. As a necessity of this preparation, mankind will attain the real knowledge of duty through these materials and by strenuous efforts.

In short, nation or state are social constitutions established in the world under the supervision of the governing sublime beings in duty in order to prepare mankind for the great plan of duty.

*
* *

No nation on the world is alone and isolated. Each of them is directly or indirectly connected to each other in the path of the same purpose. These constitutions lead mankind to the points intended by the super-world plan of duty and are conducted by the same hand in a great harmony. Beings execute this deed with complete comprehension of their responsibilities. And these beings in duty work to ensure the execution of the deeds of other communities, organisations, families, individuals who exist in the structure of the nation and state organisation properly and honestly through various means. Contradictory activities that have emerged in any part or individual constituting this community, depending on its location and significance, may cause more or less intense shocks in the whole community. So, the groups that have evolved within the community constitute communities separate from those communities. As parts of the big community disintegrate as such by evolving constitute the other states which are more evolved, the coordination and cooperation among individuals who have stayed in the big community have disrupted. Individuals can no longer follow the mutual goals and necessities of that community. The structure of that nation or state starts to collapse or degenerate; and individuals aspire to work not for the community but for themselves. Eventually, the big community disintegrates and leaves its place to a more advanced mutual community, that is, to a nation or state. This situation is the necessity of the evolution and harmony of the order of the world.

*
* *

Within a nation, there are various activities preparing individuals for the intuition of duty. Although some of them are done under easier and more comfortable conditions, most of them are realised under strenuous, tiring, harrowing conditions. For example, as someone may be living his life in abundance without much effort, another tries to earn his living by in extremely hard jobs, such as working down in a coalmine. As one person considers himself almost free of feelings of responsibility, another may feels the pressure of heavy responsibility. Some become rulers; others drift among the ruled. All of these are but different kinds of lifestyles, existing among the natural functions of a state or nation organisation and preparing mankind for the intuition of duty from a different angle and through various applications. Among them are school life, business life, office life, army life, social life, public service life, political life, family life etc.

However, beyond their apparently material goals and worries, such a great mutual purpose is inherent that it prepares all individuals within the community one by one, through these complicated and hard ways, to a superior intuition, to an intuition of knowledge of duty. Therefore, the community of nations expects without exception from each of its individuals to do his duty – which is his lot – with total devotion and goodwill by reconciling his actions with his duties for the great community of mankind without falling into earthly cravings. As the individuals of that nation do this they benefit from the great blessings of the purposes aimed by the community. And they converge on the illumined, beneficial paths of the next plan of duty with strength and speed. On the other hand, if the individuals of nation fall into selfishness and aim only for their personal interests and work selfishly on the expense of others, they miss the opportunity of acquiring higher gains, above all, of embodying within that nation. And because of this, they come face to face with the imperative of leaving the world in frustration, needing some new and suffering embodiments because they have connected with their earthly cravings and remain at the lower levels of their equilibrium of conscience. The reason for this is that with their states connected to the lower levels of conscience it is impossible for them to converge on the plans of duty.

We repeat: the establishment of nations that appears orientated to some material necessities of the world actually aims for preparatory paths that will continue within a different and sublime comprehension of time, which will transcend the borders of the world. That is, these establishments have superior and more encompassing roles than their apparent purpose in the world. Therefore, neglecting the real goal by aligning with these material sides that appear as necessities of worldly life decelerates the tempo of advance of the conscience mechanism and delays overall development.

*
* *

Attaining the true intuition of orientating among nations towards the same goal means joining the meritorious journey of that goal. After comprehension attains such degrees of development – similar to the small organisations' unifying and turning into larger organisations as they rise up within the plan of duty – it becomes necessary for small nations to unify under the light of evolution in order to make up larger communities and thus to do wider and more encompassing deeds and to advance faster in the path of mutual goals; hence, the great community of the world, which is constituted by small communities that have acquired a high and strong comprehension of mankind, gains the merit of becoming a more suitable symmetry of the plans of duty. And this can be considered as strong steps of mankind who have comprehended their true duties towards the wider communal plans.

*
* *

The activities of nations on the path of development accompany the activities of many disembodied beings in duty, whether these be automatic, semi-comprehending or comprehending. Each of these organs of service are the organs of a superior organisation engaged with duty over the activities of individuals, groups of whom constitute the community we call nation or state in the world. Therefore, the discipline of functioning and the unswerving order and conducting of the duty within a nation comes from a super-world system to which that nation or state is connected. And this, of course, is graded to the degree of merit acquired by that nation with all of its individuals.

179

As nations seek to rise without losing their true goals of establishments and make efforts on the path of this wish, these grades go higher and in ratio, their evolutionary automatism is elevated as well. In short, systems to which nations are connected are small components, part of the more encompassing, interconnected great organisations of duty in universe. And these components take various forms according to the developmental necessities of any nation or state in the world. Here, the purpose is – as it is with every vehicle in the world – to prepare mankind en masse for the intuitions of the plan of duty; as automatically, semi-comprehendingly and comprehendingly. A nation or state that complies in every sense with this preparation is to accomplish its duty and to cultivate in mankind the super-world plan of duty with merit.

*
* *

All communities are for the development of individuals. However, it is not correct to separate individuals from the communities as if cutting them with a knife. For, communities in the world are initial preliminary exercises for the great organisation systems. The purpose of organisation systems is to advance towards the oneness, the unity. Therefore, in this regard, individuals cannot be separated from the concept of community. In order to explain it further, we need to elaborate on reciprocal functions of the individual and communal plans.

What is the individual plan? A body is the evolution singular of the being. According to the principle of destiny, it has one plan. There is a plan dedicated, prepared, regulated in accordance with evolutionary necessities for each body. A plan is not a crude and narrow framework. It always has wide fields of movement in accordance with possible requirements. Therefore, it has the quality and disposition to give space for tests and trials, and consequently for freedom. The principle of this plan depends on the evolution of the spirit to which the body is subject; on its degree of evolution; on the cadres, conditions, possibilities on the path of evolution; in short on all necessities of the evolution.

What is the communal plan? The universe is not a field of materials where individuals evolve unattended. It is the whole of the

180

devices, regulations, necessities in an extremely profound and sublime mechanism operating on sublime principles of which we can and will barely intuit their comprehension; that is, the unitary itself. The universe is an expression of the divine order. Therefore, although every individual, every singular body has an individual plan; it is always related to and regulated by the states of the other singulars, that is, other bodies in relation to its own plan. Evolution always advances within the communal plan. Otherwise, order and harmony are out of the question.

*
* *

Bodies are always encountering each other's states in certain milieus or certain spheres of certain cosmoses. This encounter also indicates the management of individual plans, which are regulated by sublime principles, in another mechanical way. All of these deeds, devices and conducts are executed within the organisational systems of the sublime plans of duty, by the labour of those beings in duty.

Besides, in the life of tests and trials, there are many topics where bodies associate with each other; and this situation is an expression of the preparation to the super-world, to the plan of duty. In short, over the individual plan is the communal plan. The communal plan is, besides having been orientated to a purpose, a complicated plan which regulates the individual plans through a secondary mechanism.

These regulations occur under the influence and supervision of the plan of duty, in accordance with directives coming from the unitary. That is, individuals find their own fields of tests and trials, of development within the endless combination of life which is prepared by the innumerable influences flowing from the various levels of the plan of duty into the communal plan they live in. As the charges of influences on the individuals increase, as development accelerates, as comprehension matures; communal states are regulated pertaining to the individual's plan.

Here, the point to consider is: the communal state is prepared not for a single individual but for every individual of the communal cadre. Let us take a communal plan for 100 individuals, although this is a crude example. From these individuals, for (a), the state of 99 individuals is in question. However, from the same 100 persons, for (b), the state of another 99 persons, including (a), is in question. Likewise, for (c); the state of the 99 persons, including (a) and (b), is regulated. That is, 99 persons are not utilised for one individual. Beings in duty assign these 100 persons with duty to each other through extremely subtle layouts. However, the degrees of evolution for these 100 persons are certainly not the same.

The need and evolutionary necessity of everyone changes through, again, the same subtle mechanism. (a)'s state in relation to the 99 persons is not the same as (b)'s state. Similarly, within this communal plan, the state in regard to the matter also changes for each individual. All of these occur with quantitative changes in the matter combinations and bodies, which are brought out with the influences sent by the beings in duty by virtue of their position. Individuals, unaware of the mechanisms here, think they are tumbling around within some mysterious events which they cannot understand.

On the one hand, someone may be poor according to the quantitative changes combination realised in accordance with necessities within the plan, while another is middle class because of the regulated quantities up to a certain degree; on the other hand, another is rich; one is cultured, another ignorant; one is a musician, another a street sweeper; one is happy, another unhappy; one is good, another bad; one is diseased, another healthy; good natured or ill-tempered; selfish or altruistic – and all other states occur through the individual and communal quantitative changes technique via the channel of influences coming filtered from the unitary, in order to fulfil the necessities of developments – in accordance with the original principle – within time and space cadres; and quantitative changes of matter which is subject to the same mechanism are regulated in accordance with the above states, as well. As the scope of this knowledge between influences and beings widens, it is possible to attain higher intuitions. So, these are the hidden goals beyond the apparent goals of the communities seen by mankind.

*
* *

We have said that within the society of nations there are a great number of such mutual plans, that is, communities. We also stated that apparently interconnected – and necessarily to appear as such – states of these communities are actually subject to functioning of the duty organisations. According to this knowledge, we also need to study the small community of family that is established – again, with the same necessities – within a nation or a big community under this light.

Family is, in the real sense, an orderly and regular part of community – which makes the whole of the community of mankind – preparing the richest materials for the applications of beings that came down to world for their development and constituting a robust ground for this application. Family is the most perfect vehicle, preparing mankind for the plan of duty. Great meanings aimed at the mankind community can be summarised by the richness of all developmental materials within a small family community. This truth indicates what significant roles a family constitution executes in the preparation of mankind towards the plan of duty.

As a matter of fact, no lower or higher component or preparative in the world can be outside the scope and necessities of family knowledge. After all, the structure of a family is built in ways and forms to gather all richness of evolutionary material. Certainly, everybody has passed through a hearth and home and benefited from the blessings of it.

*
* *

The most primitive and simple preparations of a family community begin with animals and even plants. And the most primitive form of this preparation is sex. Sex is the crux of many mechanisms. And one of these cruxes is the family constitution. Likewise, sex is also the crux of many bitter sweet events, of happiness, of disasters, of sufferings in the world; briefly, of the developmental components. In short, sex is a factor activating developmental mechanisms in the world from various sides. Sex reality affects the conscience mechanism which orientates both to duty and to earthly cravings in varying ways. As sex can lead to many virtuous, elevating possibilities, it can also open the door to disasters, sufferings, woes, mental institutions and death as well. The first powerful preparatory component of family life is sex automatism. That is why the key to a great number of tests and trials is hidden in it. A family establishment which has been opened by the key of sex prepares mankind for the responsibility and intuitions of duty with all of its necessities and imperatives – even though in automatic ways – this preparation becomes for mankind a perfect advance of the evolutionary path.

*
* *

What are the developmental materials provided by the hearth, which is such a powerful vehicle in the mechanism of preparation of duty? It is possible to pick the answer of this question from the knowledge about the communal plan we have just given. As understood from this knowledge, developmental components prepared by the family institution – as some may think – are not necessarily to be pleasing or gladdening mankind or gratifying their earthly cravings. On the contrary, most of them display characters like suffering, difficulty, trouble, torment and even torture; and actually the most powerful and beneficial side of the family institution is constituted by this tough, stern and regular facade of it. By carefully observing the events that have occurred from the first moment to the current days of a family that has been established, one will acquire profound insights and knowledge in this topic. Even the events occurred that have just before the establishment of the family start to provide the expected results from the working of the family mechanism.

On the topic of two persons of either sex coming together, although at first there seems to be some easiness belonging to both, a great number of hardships and even impossibilities – which need to be overcome separately by each of the candidates – may emerge. And each of these becomes an issue of test and trials and observation for both parties. For example, during that time huffiness, resentments, quarrels, fights and even murders may occur. These are suffering but powerful evolutionary materials that are deemed as negative ways, still at the beginning of the family.

After the establishment of the family a great number of problems emerge like cost of living, disagreements of the couple, adaptation to married life etc. These ascribe separate burdens, duties, tasks both to the man and woman. They come out from these struggles either victorious or defeated; and in either case, they encounter a great number of consequences which are bitter or sweet, depending on the apparently successful or failed states of the tests and trials; and accordingly, they gather speed on the path of the intuition of duty. Eventually, children are born. Nurturing them and seeing them grow up, their illnesses and health, their deaths, accidents and pains etc. provide for the mother and father observations which sometimes take the path of joy and sometimes sorrow. In the mean time, the peacefulness they will feel when they have attained the comprehensions of passing successfully through these experiences will elevate them through positive and joyful paths; the frustrations and pains they will feel at the end of the unsuccessful, inapt tests and trials they deem as negative will also cause them to advance on another path.

Afterwards, countless consequences of the feelings of responsibility because of the problems like training and education of the children, their good or bad upbringing; likewise, grown-up children's behaviours against their parents and other members of the family will line up as endless issues of tests and trials, of refining experiences. All events of family life that appear as sources of suffering or joy in different ways actually give mankind the intuitions of the great plan of duty.

In summary, an apparently happy family, an apparently unhappy family, a family leading a life full of disasters, a calm or noisy family; in short, all families that are subject to various conditions of life, are only powerful elevation vehicles regulated according to the needs and orientated to development of individuals. This valuable vehicle – with all of its happiness, pains, disasters – becomes a perfect ground for the application of preparing necessary intuitions for the plan of duty which is the goal of mankind, and provides all kinds of possibilities of this application. There the loves are born, the loves are lost; births, deaths, partings, reunions follow each other. All of these become rich developmental materials, each with the joys and sorrows they cause.

Just as a mother is elevated so high when she feels happy for her newborn baby, the mother that cries for her dead child gets ahead that much in her state. However, we will remind you of this point again: all these states of the family, its progress in the path of development, its advances or pauses, are completely subject to the assistance and supervision of the beings in duty.

The family allows the simplest and automatic exercises of the path of preparation to the concept of unity which expresses the complete form of the evolution towards the end of universe. As seen most of the time, facial and personality similarities between the partners is an expression of a synthesis constituted between the magnetic fields of the bodies – as of the necessities of the family community; and it indicates that beings are converging on each other. The better this magnetic fields synthesis is constituted, the more perfect the cohesion is within the family; and the closer the family comes to its true goal.

*
* *

We have said that descent of beings to the world is to encounter materials which they need among the world matter and to utilise them.

Earth, among the spheres of our solar system, is the one which has the most abundant developmental materials. These materials should be devised and arranged according to the miscellaneous needs, and to render them useful for the deeds of mankind. Beings of the plans of duty which have taken on these acts do their duties within various duty organisations assigned to the world, in accordance with their merit and power. Of course, it should be remembered that this must be in accordance with the directives coming from above.

With these assistances, a great number of devices, orders and constitutions are put into effect which are beneficial for the developments of world beings and at the same time, of mankind who have more encompassing states. For example, occurrence of natural disasters within an order; all global states pertaining to politics, economics and sciences; and in the middle of those, all nations, states, tribes, communities that have been established with all of their secondary

186

constitutions are always conducted by the organs that serve within great organisations under the directive of the unitary.

Therefore, conducting all communities in the world such as nations, states and families is connected to the above. And the purpose of these connections is to help the beings, that is, mankind – who came down to the world with the need to prepare for the intuition of the plan of duty and attaining merit for this plan – to attain their goal. Thus, every man benefits endlessly from the infinite possibilities of these establishments, most often automatically and semi-comprehendingly by direct or indirect ways, that is, both by living within the necessities of them and by observing the others living within those necessities. Here, the meaning of automatic, we have previously explained.

Mankind's benefiting from these communities does not always occur by seeing their true purposes. Almost always, mankind joins in these communities – according to their world realities and values – eagerly and willingly, only for their personal interests and through this wish they work with heart and soul in these communities. And the kinds of wishes vary, depending on the quality and quantity of the earthly craving components of each person. These qualities and quantities sometimes descend to the levels of selfishness which are very low. For example, a big gang of bandits can be established. However, with equilibria adapted to the higher levels of the conscience mechanism, these wishes can display very noble and high manifestations, as well. For example, with a pure instinct of love, all burdens of a family can be shouldered. However, apparently no one wants to see or think the original great values of all these constitutions that will lead mankind to the superior and real benefits through paths which are sometimes very sweet and sometimes too bitter and demanding.

*
* *

As everything else that exists in the world, constitutions of nation, state and family are not the end but the means. True ends of these means are not the apparent material gains and realities of the world which are very transitory and cannot be taken even as a

187

speck to beyond the world, but to acquire essence-knowledge which will emerge after many bitter and sweet events – which mankind will encounter as they say let me live in this or that reality or run after this or that gain – go through applications in the conscience mechanism.

And at this point, we state once again the relation between the conscience mechanism and enrichment of essence-knowledge. Now, we will repeat this knowledge as a summary so in the comprehension, there may be no dark and vague aspects regarding it.

*

* *

Conscience realities that are evaluated with world comprehension are not the essence-knowledge of the being. These are appearances of the matter states – according to the necessities of the being's embodiments in crude matter – that display various forms within the duty–earthly craving duality. These realities do not necessarily follow the same sequence in everybody; they line up according to necessities and needs. And knowledge of comparison to be collected from the events that will arise as a result of the collision of these opposite components will increase the values of the being's essence-knowledge and these values will reflect to the spirit as its degree of evolution within comprehension formations.

This situation briefly indicates the gist of the states of the ever-changing realities in the world at the conscience mechanism; and of the roles of all these mechanisms that enrich the essence-knowledge; and finally, of the services the being renders for the evolution of the spirit. Likewise, these realities operate the conscience mechanism, as on the one hand they increase essence-knowledge, and on the other hand they can shift towards the higher realities by taking strength and speed from essence-knowledge. That is, as the realities connected to the brain enrich the complexity of subtle matter combinations belonging to the comprehension in the essence-being, illumined lights reflected to the brain from the essence-being convey the equilibria of conscience to the higher levels, as well. Thus, as essence-knowledge increases, tugs of conscience on the path of knowledge of duty increase the level of earthly cravings as well.

188

And there comes a moment when the distance between duty and earthly cravings shortens close to the plan of duty. And it becomes easier for comprehension to orientate to the duty front. And when the plan of duty is reached, from that moment onwards, conscience duality is no more. Instead, another duality of evolution, that of a different quality and which advances with deeds of great duty begins. And this duality follows the being up to the unitary.

*

* *

Mankind which constitutes the most intense moments of this tug – especially at the middle stages of humanity – lives continuously in shifts of ease and uneasiness. These states correspond to the equilibrium and imbalanced states of the conscience components that emerged distinctly. The ease puts the man into a state of satisfaction in accordance with his comprehension. So he sees himself in resolved problems. However, at the moment the equilibrium line of conscience starts to be disturbed at higher or lower levels – in accordance with the necessities and emerging needs of the essence-being – he is annoyed. The feeling of his old reality is about to collapse in the face of a new reality that irritates him. This suffering increases with the degree of equilibrium's disruption.

This situation takes on various contents and forms according to each cycle and level. Sometimes –especially at the less advanced stages – it manifests as real pangs of conscience. These types of pangs are seen more at equilibria's shifting downwards. In the advanced developmental stages of being, it is not these pangs but various states and forms of confusion that occur and these are not least significant as uneasiness. All of these states of uneasiness or suffering conclude the equivalence of conscience realities at far higher levels and consequently, the increase in essence-knowledge; and convergence of mankind towards the destined plans of duty.

Therefore, man needs to reach the higher realities by trying to get over the confusions following the digested, fully functioned realities of the level he exists in as soon as possible, so that acquired merits can start to function timely and consequently, the normal progress of the essence-knowledge on the path of development can continue without cessation. So, when a man encounters any un-easiness or confusion or pangs and when his conscience starts to burn with the sparks of any pangs; that man needs immediately to pull himself together and have his comprehension browse among the components of his conscience, to orientate to the higher com-ponent of his conscience which he has neglected so far, to start sending values to it through his wishes and on the other hand, to put his wishes, habits, desires belonging to the lower reality in the background and not to feed them with values, and above all, to make the very necessary efforts to do this.

As he does this, conscience equilibrium begins to be set gradu-ally at higher levels. And when this happens, the joy of much greater ease and happiness to be born will sweep away all troubles and hardships of the past. Nevertheless, their knowledge in the es-sence-being, as a rich charge of development, converges man closer to the sublime plans of evolution; and the increase of ease in man is actually the result of this state.

*
* *

Mankind may think of questions like why this component of earthly cravings was necessary or more correctly, would it not be possible to attain higher realities and to increase the essence-knowledge and consequently, to fulfil the preparation for duty without the distinct duality of earthly cravings in human life? An-swers to these questions have already been given in previous knowledge. Let us make them clear here.

We have said that knowledge to be useful for the spirit's evolu-tion has to become essence-knowledge, that is, has to be the being's own property. And this is, as we have said, a quality that can be acquired only by the being's becoming moulded by the events and making huge efforts. That is, the being will have some conclusions after the applications it will have through the body by struggling with world events in regard to their positive and negative aspects; and these conclusions will provide essence-knowledge. Actually, repeated embodiments of mankind are for them to encounter the infinite manifestations of events, both bitter and sweet. The reason for this is to increase essence-knowledge.

However, here another imperative emerges as well. If the factors aiming the possibilities and opportunities of struggling with the events and getting moulded by them do not exist there would be no need for emergence of such demanding and effort activating events. And if mankind could be made to advance on the evolutionary path with undeserved processes, then they could be imprisoned and dragged uncomprehendingly. However, the knowledge we previously gave indicates that such an evolutionary process cannot be possible. For, such kinds of advancements which works like a complete machine irrelevant to the comprehension and freedom of beings can only be subject to the principle of mechanical evolution – as we have previously explained – which has passed within the dark and infinitely long imprisonment at the initial stage of universe when beings were yet devoid of comprehension and power. And the greatest result evolution under this principle provides for the beings, again as we explained, cannot go beyond the hydrogen atom's state of merit, which has not yet had comprehension and gained the powers to free themselves from imprisonment and has been merely forced to adapt to mechanical motions.

When the beings are put into events they have not deserved, they cannot gain benefits that are worthy for the stage of humanity. For, in this case, at the manifestation of those events of which they cannot designate and appreciate the causes and effects, it will be impossible for them to be able to enter their knowledge of comprehension; and when there is no knowledge of comprehension, essence-knowledge cannot be; and the evolution expected from humanity cannot be realised. Whatever the events may be, when their causes and effects are unknown to mankind they remain vain and purposeless. Only the conclusions arrived at coming out victorious or defeated after being moulded among the deserved bitter and sweet events, by the help of the knowledge of comparison on the face of the causality principle, can put into effect essence-knowledge – which is the evolutionary factor.

Therefore, mankind needs to be entitled to events which are regulated to their evolutionary needs so, by comprehending this entitlement, they can find the knowledge of comparison which will take them to the conclusion while they struggle with those events

191

and they can attain the possibility of making an accounting of these. A child beaten, if he does not know the reason for this beating, cannot properly benefit from it. And when he cannot benefit from it, since he does not appreciate the degree of the situation, he cannot make efforts to improve his behaviours.

In order for him to benefit from this beating, his comprehension needs to be awakened; for this, he needs to be informed about why and because of which weak sides of him he deserved this beating. And this can be possible by activating his weak sides that lie in wait and making these obvious. Moreover, this effort mechanism has a role in the application of the plan of fate – which we will explain later. This knowledge explains why some earthly craving parts – which will bring about some hard and harsh consequences – stand against the duty components and why the beings in duty cause such situations.

So, the mechanism of the duty–earthly craving struggle is needed. And because of this, the earthly craving is a valuable factor on the path of development.

*
* *

In the developmental mechanism, the earthly cravings' standing against the duty component is not vain and unnecessary. The earthly craving is a perfect and fundamental vehicle, set in place for leading man to the knowledge of comparison, as we just have said, by whipping up the efforts with its whole and parts. Evolutionary mechanism will gain its ever-increasing speed across lives from the apparently negative powers of the components of earthly cravings.

If the wood to be cut were not resistant, there would be no need to use an axe. The earthly craving is like the resistance of the axe. And the axe symbolises the efforts belonging to the struggles to be done for overcoming this earthly craving. Therefore, if the earthly craving does not exist, there is no need for struggles and efforts. And when it happens, unmerited evolutions are expected to come one day, spontaneously; and as we have just explained, such a thing is impossible. Therefore, the earthly craving must exist so the efforts to be able to pass to higher components may find the field of realisation. These efforts are fundamental processes that allow knowledge of further stages and their becoming the property of the essence-being.

*
* *

Now, we will provide knowledge pertaining to these earthly craving parts and the state of a man who bustles and endeavours within the struggle of preparation for duty in comparison with the realm he lives in as an individual.

Man is a whole of combinations constituted with matter-parts assigned to the being which is the vehicle and expression of a spirit's evolution in universe. Therefore, the body is a vehicle assigned to service in the world for a being which can use it according to its developmental imperatives. The being influences the world matter through the body – which is under its governance and at its service – by utilising its crude material state. These events occur in accordance with the superficial time reality to which the body is subject. On the other hand, influences coming from matter are reflected to the spirit via the channel of the being, by gaining in value from spherical time comprehension. In this way, the evolutionary needs of the spirit are fulfilled.

The being uses the body for its test and trials, experiences, observations; in short, for all its needs which are the necessities of its plan; and millions of assisting influences arrive at this body from outside, and of course, only via the channel of that being. These influences may come – as from the very high, from plans at various levels and stages of evolution as well – in order to put into effect results at various levels of intensity and power.

All of these influences descending to the body in order to fulfil the necessities of the delineated plan of destiny belonging to the being's bodily life in the world are always under the control and supervision of higher plans. Therefore, none of these influences, from the smallest to the greatest, is in vain and unnecessary. Each of these displays states pertaining to the conscience mechanism that we previously talked about and is regulated in the organism. This regulation occurs in harmony with the necessities and imperatives of the being's plan for the world.

*
* *

The body is an organism. Therefore, there are cells, organs, systems which constitute it. All of these parts make up the whole of the body organism by becoming subject to each other and becoming systemised; and its organiser is the brain which governs that body. However, this brain is connected to the essence-being. Therefore, smaller organisms that constitute the body organism also have their own beings, that is, organisers which are much simpler than of the man; and they, in their own right, serve the evolutions of relatively much simpler spirits. So, the being who governs this body is responsible for all these states of the human body.

Beings, after they use – that is, benefit from – the bodies as much as possible, by relinquishing their usage over those bodies, they severe their connection with the brain which conducts them; and we call it death.

*

* *

A being builds a body with the help of superior beings; uses it as long as it benefits from it; and for this, it has control over all parts of that body through the brain and in this way, obtains its material needs via the channel of that body.

In this respect, there is not much difference between a being – who is yet in a state of ability to use a human body – using this body and a being – who is governing a huge solar system constituted with ensembles of matter and beings – conducting this system. There are differences between these only in evolution, width of scope and complexity. Therefore, whatever the meanings of a human being's influences over a body are, the influences of a being in duty over a solar system are the same but more encompassing and complex.

*

* *

When a man is born, his being has a state that reached a certain level of development. Likewise, he will have certain deeds to do in the world in accordance with this certain state of development. So, execution of these deeds is his duty belonging to his world life. That man's living in the world is to realise the world application plan which is prepared before he descends to the world, by his being with other beings in duty. Therefore, that being, before he came into the world, designed and ventured the deeds he needs to do and promised to do them. Now that he promised this and his descent to the world is for executing his promise, then it is necessary for him to keep his promise and pay his due, that is, to execute the designed plan after he descends to the world. For, it is imperative to execute the deeds determined by the approval of the plan of duty. By this way, determined deeds are executed in harmony with the equilibrium of the conscience mechanism.

*
* *

A being who owns a body because of certain needs begins to live in the world at a level of conscience equilibrium that is suitable to his developmental state and takes place in various communal situations according to his plan. None of these descents and placements is arbitrary or random.

The making of an individual plan is not a simple task either. As we previously said, a man has innumerable connections with the communal plans in which he lives. These are taken into consideration. For example, according to whichever nation, religion, community – with certain mores – family and individuals – with certain inclinations, merits, wants, powers and level of development – that being needs to come into and to make communal plans with them according to whichever mutual needs, all of these are minutely calculated, regulated, mutually determined and planned beforehand and naturally with the help of beings in duty in accordance with his developmental imperatives. This is the plan that needs to be executed in the world. The being gets prepared to descend into his surroundings in the world, which is regulated with this plan. During this regulation; the beings of the bodies who will be parents of that being are consulted; their decisions are taken. And according to these decisions, if some improvements and alterations need to be done in the bodies of the to-be parents' either individual or communal and even economical states, these are regulated as well. That is, their situation – according to the newcomer into their midst – is also straightened out by the beings in duty. Shortly, everything is arranged.

In the descent of a being to the world, numerous beings are working in their service. Bodies in the world who are related to that being generally participate in these preparations automatically. Parents, relatives, midwife, doctor, hospital, nursery, orphanage, school, community, state – in short, near and far a great number of bodies are unknowingly taking on duties in various ways for the current and future life of the being who will descend to the world. And they most often do their duties automatically. So, mankind work for attaining the intuitions of the great plan of duty within the establishments and communities we have mentioned before, by making automatic efforts in order to fulfil these automatic duties.

*
* *

A being, who owns a body built around a plan prepared with such minute calculations and by the activities and labours of numerous beings in duty will certainly be in debt to the individuals of the communal plan to which he is connected. And he has shouldered these debts even before he come into the world. In spite of this, if a day comes and he forgets the promise he gave on the face of the preparers and the helpers and compromises, denies his debts, slackens his execution of his plan and, moreover, if he attempts suicide, he will be doing such a distant and contradictory act. Such a contradictory act against the intuition of duty is the lowest level of the earthly cravings in that life; and his responsibility is heavy, albeit automatic. Automatism of this heavy responsibility manifests very intense sufferings and tormenting reactions. Only the knowledge of comparison – which is very demanding – of this heavy automatism can push such a man further within semi-comprehending states.

The body serves a being and becomes a symbol of that being in the crude world matter. It is similar to the symbol of the spirit, which is the being, in the deeper sense. Therefore, this relationship of body-being-spirit, which is different from each other but extends from the body to the spirit, evokes in mankind in the world an assumption that there is spirit in the body.

*
* *

196

To trace the individual evolution of a being who came into the world as a man, let us start from a much earlier time and take a stage where no evolution and development exist in universe. Here, to be able to give the intuition about the factors the development progresses by, we will use a symbolic scheme of a projector. We would like to repeat that the scheme we will use here is only to give some an impression about these truths.

Previously, we talked about the sublime principle – of which we cannot say anything about its true nature – which governs spirits as well as universes. From among the forces of this principle orientated to infinite universes and spirits, we will give the intuition of the one orientated to our universe by merely this symbol of a projector. However, this projector will not be the original principle governing universes and spirits. It is only a force of it, pertaining to our universe, that is, to the relation of matter universe and spirits. This can only be expressed that much.

The original principle's state or aspect pertaining to our universe – which we symbolise with the word force – certainly does not fit into the ordinary meaning of such a word. For, not only this word but no other motion, word, meaning or image exists in our universe to sufficiently express this state. Since we are helpless, we express the aspect of the original principle orientated to our universe and the spirits that will render their applications there (even these expressions are symbols incapable of expressing the originals) with the word force.

Therefore, according to this expression which we will – again – symbolically explain with this symbol; the force is the whole of the necessities of the original principle which are intended for the cohesion of all the matter possibilities with the evolutionary needs of the spirits pertaining to our universe. Let us elaborate on this: in this force of the original principle are inherent the states related solely to our universe – which we symbolise with the concept of evolution – from the needs of the spirits pertaining to infinite universes, as well as, all of the matter possibilities of our universe which are the counterparts of these needs. So, realisation of the purpose of this force – which contains the needs of the spirits and all possibilities of universe matter – of the original principle, which is to make a unity by

197

unifying the spiritual needs and matter possibilities, gives the ultimate and most sublime implication of the meaning we express with the word evolution. This intuition is about the need of spirits pertaining to our matter-universe of the infinite universes. Here, there is no word uttered about the other universes.

*
* *

We start to trace the evolutionary progress in the universe, with the concept of a projector which is a powerful symbol. The lights of this projector represent the force or the necessities of the original principle we have mentioned. The source of this light is not the original principle itself but the force of it which is merely orientated to the universe. On this topic, it should be needed to suffice with so much intuition and not to attempt to go further. Otherwise, mankind can gain nothing but falling into vast and inconclusive confusion from which they cannot pull through.

So, this light, coming out of the source – which we gave an intuition about above as a cone – descends at the universe-substance, the primary matter that waits at that moment as inert, amorphous and passive. The tip of the light is in that force and its base is in the primary matter. It should be remembered that in this light are inherent both the needs of the spirits and the possibilities that will manifest in matter in the face of these needs. And these needs and possibilities will be unified only within this light and the evolution will be executed. So, we call these executor forces of the light as necessities. Therefore, the necessity has a distinct aspect and state according to each universe; and its aspect belonging to our universe is the force of the original principle which is directed at finalisation of the unity of the needs of the spirits with the matter possibilities.

The first place which this projector light lands on in our universe is the amorphous state of primary matter. These expressions should be intuited, without thinking in terms of spatial concepts in the world, because there is neither a place nor a distance. These images are mentioned only about the aspect of this great truth which addresses mankind, to be able to give intuitions.

The zone where the cone of light first lands the amorphous matter is immediately illuminated. This illumination at the base of the cone of light, which is in the primary matter, expresses the needs of the initial spirits which to start application have encountered the matter possibilities at that zone of contact. Here, the base is yet dimly illuminated and too distant from the tip. This is why we call this zone an obscured stage. This is what occurs in this zone: on the face of the needs of spirits which are inherent at the end part of the light, that is, at the base of the cone which connects to matter, inert matter has started to move and with this motion, the principle of the mechanical evolution of the spirits has started to work.

After this state occurs, that is, after the initial possibilities manifested in the amorphous matter; the zone illuminated by the projector light, that is, the base of the cone of light, begins to become more illuminated. At the same time, the base gradually rises towards the top and the distance between the cone's tip and base begins to shorten. However, this distance should not be considered a distance that can be measured in kilometres; and it should be remembered that these are each symbols.

As matter's possibilities to manifest increases, the base of the cone becomes more illuminated and continues to get closer to the top. This indicates that possibilities of matter increasingly manifest and the needs of the spirits causing this manifestation are fulfilled in a wider scope, the developments increase and the zones become illuminated.

In this way, the initial mechanical principle of evolution in the universe, that is, the sub-hydrogen stage, which we previously described as a long and dark zone, matures.

*

* *

The base of the cone of light rises up to the starting field of the hydrogen stage. From there on – as we previously explained – spirits are connected with matter. The initial applications of the spirits start at this stage to adapt passively and mechanically to the motions of matter which are monotonous, mechanical but to be complicated with a very gradual tempo within a very long time. In this regard, we also call this stage the passive adaptations stage of the evolution. At this stage, spirits will be made accustomed to the motion of matter, by being dragged passively within an imprisonment during a time that continues almost infinitely. Here, the base of the

199

cone of light has been illuminated a little more and has drawn nearer to the summit.

*
* *

The base of the cone of light, by continuing to be illuminated, rises up to the hydrogen atom's stage of being. From there onwards, with the initial simple active behaviours of the spirits, starts the principle of development in matter. Here, there is both the primitive activity of the spirits and the principle of automatism which strictly controls and supports this activity. Afterwards, the cone of light, as it continues to rise, reaches up to the stage of building of plant bodies – which are preparing the beings to the intuitions that are the first sparks of comprehension. In plants, the exercises start for the transition to initial primitive intuitions. At this stage, boundaries of freedom – although still very limited – are a little wider and automatism of intuition has appeared. As the base of the cone rises, these automatisms of intuition will increase in scope and turn into intuitions in animals. Development in animals is slightly faster than development in plants. As the base of the cone rises from the stage of animality to the stage of humanity; the initial preparations of some features of comprehension in mankind start to emerge as well in animals.

*
* *

The base of the cone of light continues its illumination by rising further and reaches the hydrogen's stage of humanity where comprehension begins. From there onwards, a semi-comprehending and subjective stage of evolution is the preparation for the plan of duty and the zone here is in a quite illuminated state. As the base of the cone of light gets closer to its tip in this way, comprehension brightens, preparations progress towards the stage which will start from the plan of duty; and finally, the base of the cone rises up to the stage of the plan of duty which is the super-human and beyond the hydrogen cosmos. When the base of the cone of light reaches this stage, the zone is thoroughly illuminated.

From there onwards, necessities manifest openly. This situation allows comprehension to adapt swiftly to necessities. From there

200

onwards, the behaviours of the spirits will start to unite with the necessities. Up to this point, the beings could follow the base of the cone of light as if they were pushed and dragged by various mechanisms. From then on, by means of comprehension's merit in unifying with the necessities, the beings actively start to go towards the top with their own comprehension by working hard to climb the light beams of the cone of light. And this occurs quickly as much as comprehension is able to adapt to the necessities, that is, to enter the state of unity with them. That is why we call this progress also the active adaptations stage of evolution. At this stage, evolution has a rather subjective character, relative to the previous stage. The intuition of this concept will be received better as we later explain the topic of time.

*
* *

From the plan of duty onwards, the distance to be traversed by those beings who started to climb from the base to the tip of the cone of light with an increasing abundance of possibilities of power is still very long. For, although relative to the distance from the base to the tip of the cone of light that descended to the primary matter at the initial stage, its distance from the plan of duty to the top has been considerably shortened; there is still an almost infinitely long distance between its base in the initial stages of the plan of duty and its tip.

However, the base of the cone of light which is thoroughly illuminated at the plan of duty will increase its illumination quite swiftly and its speed of rising to the top will accelerate in a degree beyond comparison to the previous ones. This stage is a true stage of evolution. As we said, as the illuminated zones of the cone of light which increases from this stage onwards rise towards the top, they will give speed to the adaptation of the necessities belonging to the universe with the behaviours and comprehension of the spirits. And as it gets closer to the top, the field of unity will widen accordingly.

As the fields of unity of the spirits' comprehensions with the necessities advance by getting wider and wider, the base of the cone of light reaches such a point that there, the whole of the necessities

201

and all the spirits' behaviours and comprehension related to this universe enters a state of complete unity and the base of the cone, reaching the top, completes its journey at that singular illuminated point. This singular illuminated point where all behaviours, comprehensions, possibilities, influences, in short, necessities unify is the unity of comprehension which we call the unitary. This is the whole universe. It has only a singular magnetic field which is the singular magnetic field of universe. At this point, there is no separation. Everything is unified there. There, a singular comprehension, a singular behaviour, a singular necessity, in short, a singular universe is the key point. And this point expresses the realisation of evolution in the universe.

*

* *

Here, in order to prevent the possibility of a major misunderstanding, we need to point out the following: the tip of the cone of light, as we have said before, is not the original principle itself. It is a force of it, not particular to all universes but to our universe only. Likewise, the behaviours of spirits are not the spirits themselves. They are the manifestation of their needs, not pertaining to all universes but to the matter-universe only. Therefore, here, considering the unitary as a state where the original principle, matter and spirits unify is the greatest of all mistakes. We had previously explained the reason for this. All states here are only opened and closed by the spiritual behaviours and necessities that gathered around the concept of matter-universe. However, beyond them unending events continue onwards.

*

* *

So, here it is clearly explained that the cone of light is the universe itself. And the universe exists only with this cone of light, with the original necessities. A single point of the universe which is deprived of the beams of that cone immediately declines to darkness, into an amorphous state, that is, condemned into a state of extinction, in the sense mankind understands. So, there is no speck of universe that exists outside the scope and encompassment of the original influences coming filtered from the unitary. The ones who receive this knowledge will more powerfully gain the intuition of the truth that each stirring in the universe can be possible only by the approval and control of the unitary.

*
* *

After talking about how the universe develops – as it is subject to the original cone of force light – within general and symbolic outlines, it is necessary to explain the evolution of an individual in a wider context, starting from the beginning of humanity.

Humanity is an intermediary plan, which allows subjective and semi-comprehending preparations between the more or less passive developmental stages that have been passed and forthcoming active and true evolutionary plans. And its significance in regard to this preparatory state is very great. Subsequent to humanity, the next is the stage of duty. Since comprehension in mankind is not yet illuminated with the knowledge of duty, active adaptations pertaining to the plan of duty do not begin in human life. For, at the stage of humanity, none of the behaviours of spirits has yet been powerful enough to constitute a unity with any necessities at all. Mankind has not reached the state of ability to climb up the cone of light by its own power, unlike in the higher plan. Nevertheless, mankind has now reached the threshold of the stage of duty where the comprehending elevations start and has started direct preparations for that stage. Therefore, it is time to elaborate here on the necessary problems pertaining to the development of mankind.

*
* *

Later, as we will explain while elaborating on the topic of time and space, the life of mankind –despite innumerable embodiments – should be considered a single life from beginning to end. In this duration, there will be a great number of individual developmental stages of man. Boundaries of each stage are limited with certain realities. Therefore, in the life of each man, there are separate realities particular to himself, his own stages. Differences in reality for mankind at various stages of reality are less in mankind at developmental

stages which are close to each other. The more the distance is between stages, the larger the differences are accordingly.

*
* *

Let us take the initial human being as an example: the distinct
thing about him is – compared to other stages of development –
that an automatism seems to prevail in him, raised out of the lack
of comprehension. He most often cannot afford more than a state of
doing his deed with semi-comprehension or none at all. And this
state can continue on like this in many cases up until the quite advanced stages of humanity. And yet again, throughout the whole
of humanity, complete comprehension may not be established. We
have already said that the purpose of all these automatisms is to
prepare mankind for the knowledge and comprehension of duty.

*
* *

The beings using human bodies live within innumerable events –
which are subject to conditions – by utilising the possibilities and
conditions of the milieus they use the bodies of. For, these events
will prepare mankind for the intuition of duty. Natural and accustomed discipline of the plan of duty will be learned by the innumerable applications to be done on the face of the stern and ada-
mant countenances of these events. Therefore, for the beneficial
events to occur, mankind needs other beings, that is, communal
situations. However, these communal situations do not only cover
mankind. Animals and even plants are included. And this situation
is an imperative; in other words, a necessity of the imperativeness
of gradual preparation of cultivating each other within a massive
cadre of beings in the world. The most objective example of this is
body cells. Mankind lives with these primitive beings in each
other's embrace and as destined to each other within a vast communal plan. The cells constituting the heart of a man, for example,
need the body of that man for their development just as that body
needs those cells in order to live. As the illness of either of the two
affects the other, the health of both ensures mutual well-being.
Therefore, communal lives that exist among all these beings are not
in vain and purposeless.

*
* *

The communal plan is a synthesis of individual plans which advance side by side, unknowingly getting strength from and standing by each other in order to fulfil the developmental necessities within their own possibilities; and this is an imperative of the developmental automatism in the life of mankind.

Besides the communal plans mankind make with beings that are much smaller than them, there are more significant plans they make with comprehension with their fellowmen, even with some disembodied beings. All of these plans are the imperativeness of development. For, as we have said, the development of man becomes possible by his engagement with the preliminary applications of the intuition of duty belonging to the plan of duty. However, in the great plan of duty, before everything else, there is coordination and cooperation in the true sense. That is, there, there is a complete unity among them, an inseparable cooperation in all of their activities relative to the organisation groups in that plan. This situation is an unfailing basic of that plan. On the contrary, when working in separate ways, it is not possible to be able to do application of such a tight coordination and cooperation. And when this is the case, no preparation can be done towards the plan of duty which advances within a collective activity.

*
* *

As we previously said on the topics of nation, family and communal plan, big or small, all communities in the world are made up of human beings who are unified around mutual aims. Although complete cooperation – which is natural in the plan of duty and considered ideal or even unknown for the world – that is, a unity with comprehension which is put into effect at certain points does not exist in the world communities; the effort of unknowingly preparing and getting dragged towards that ideal exists in mankind; and this is the imperative of the need that is called evolution at that stage. This state flows on automatically.

Actually, there is almost no community in the world that is constituted with a true comprehension of duty and by individuals who could display the power to advance for the sake of any goal as a single individual. Nevertheless, all of these communities – by their completely different automatisms with qualities in general which are activating various earthly cravings – allow the appetite, desire and striving of mankind to cooperate with heart and soul; and the real but hidden goal here is the preparation of mankind for intuiting the meaning of the obligation of cooperation within a complete unity and with the real comprehension and knowledge of duty; and their doing the exercises of this with the help of these automatisms.

Individuals in a family; children learning in a school; workers working in a factory; soldiers drilling in a barracks; public officers working in a public department; diplomats reaching a decision in a meeting; patients getting treated and doctors caring in a hospital; citizens constituting a nation; in short, the innumerable communities of mankind are powerful and entraining vehicles ensuring the sublime intuitions of the great plan of duty with their automatic qualities.

*
* *

Every man is under the service of one or several of the communal plans. This serving is sometimes optional but most often mandatory. These mandatory propulsions are still orientated to sublime purposes. Actually, mankind is willing to propel itself forward out of anxiety to survive. Some spend their lifetime in a mental institution as a result of self-indulgence; some are imprisoned; some remain buried in gruelling conditions in the depths of mines for a lifetime to earn their daily bread... All of these are for attaining the intuition of the knowledge of duty, that is, for reaching states that enable mankind to adapt the comprehension of divine necessity and to harmonise with it. The more a man makes efforts to do it and be successful, the closer he gets to the plan of duty with fast and sure steps; and the sooner he gets over the suffering, heavy stages of world life. If he cannot do this and is continuously defeated by his earthly craving; if he does not make efforts to pull through and complies with the backward feelings and simple thoughts; if he sees the world as a means for satisfaction of his earthly cravings but not a means for the application of his world plan and if he acts in this way and violates the necessities of his plan, then things go awry.

In this case, his communal plans, preparations and life conditions which have been advancing automatically are directed into a path for improvement of his actions. This is done by the beings in duty. That man observes the stern look of his life conditions, without comprehending the reason for them as he starts to fall into hardship; his affairs turns bad, material or emotional problems and pains start to follow one another. He is still not aware of the origins of these and his life feels grim. He attempts to put the blame on fate, luck, society, mankind etc. However, the developmental mechanism which is unfailing in accordance with his plan regulated by his states and behaviours continues to work without paying any attention to his fuss. If he still does not behave and try to improve his comprehension, things will continue to get dimmer, his troubles increase and he struggles to the point of rebellion.

However, this rebellion directs him to a dead end and leads him to a prison, a hospital, a mental institution or to a grave; or any other similar life conditions which are heavy and compelling. All of these are the events that occur out of the execution of decisions made by the plan of duty through beings in duty in order to have him do the deeds which are necessary for his evolution particular to that moment but which he cannot with his own comprehension.

*
* *

Therefore, what mankind needs to do in order to be able to leave this intermediary milieu, this suffering and arduous world soon and successfully, is to work to digest the realities of their conscience mechanisms which are connected to altruism and love of duty and to rescue themselves from the strong bonds of their selfish desires and appetites which they do not want to leave out of the pressure of their earthly cravings, with comprehension. And the success in this depends only on the efforts done by resignation, self-sacrifice and love of duty.

We give a worldwide criterion which ensures the safety and success of the directions of the efforts that must be done in this struggle. This knowledge will make easier the distinction between the concepts of good and bad. Good and bad are concepts pertaining to the higher and lower realities of conscience respectively. If these concepts can be discerned well from each other, it becomes easier for comprehensions to regulate the advance of conscience. Each deed to be done should harm neither the higher nor the lower. This is the criteria. For example, while intending good for the lower, harming the higher is bad. Likewise, while doing good to the higher, harming the lower is again bad and in either case entails the responsibility at the scales of conscience.

Actually, if the ones who have more or less advanced comprehensions take the deeds to do into consideration within this context they will see that if the good to be done either for the higher or the lower is true goodness it will beneficial for the other as well and will not harm it. However, if a deed done for the one side harms the other side then that deed will not be a true goodness for either side. For example, a man who rescues a child from a beating – for simply doing good for the child – by a father who is responsible for that child's upbringing – who does this for deterring the child from his stealing habits – and encourages the child's bad whims by doing so, may look doing good for the lower from the superficial outlook but harms it by disrupting the duty of the higher. Therefore, as a matter of fact this deed is bad for the father as well as for the child.

If the man acts with such attention and succeeds in avoiding bad, how nice! He will arise by a swift path. If he cannot succeed, the possibilities and regulations which should ensure this success by enforcing him through automatic ways will be waylaid on his path by the help of beings in duty.

*
* *

In this way, through getting used in various ways in a life of fits and starts, the means of the body are exhausted. Eventually the body gets sick, aged and becomes obsolete. The being is obliged to continue its development in milieus that have possibilities beyond the limit of that body's sufficiency. In this case, again with the help of the beings in duty, the old body is abandoned. The being is elevated to the circumstances of the higher stage. For this, the being leaves the world by the event of death. From that moment on, that is, at the initial moments of his transition to the spatium; all secondary influences coming from his surroundings are ceased, except for the influences coming from its own spirit. That being is left completely alone in an isolated state within its own being.

This situation is akin to the state of a man who has been put into a room and left there after all of his senses have been removed, so that he is even senseless to his own body. We say akin because spatium life expresses a much more profound and internal loneliness. Therefore, spatium life is not a space for the beings. At that moment, their space is only their beings. Because of this, at the being's initial transition there, it is not possible for it to contact, speak and meet the world, the super-world or the beings around him who are similar to him. All connections to his surroundings are severed. This is for natural reasons arising out of the being's state of heavy selfishness, as well as imperatives on which we will elaborate below. This state, after it continues as long as needed, is abolished by the influences that start to come from the surroundings and the being begins to recognise his surroundings, identity and needs with his awakened comprehension by means of these influences.

*
* *

After death, the being naturally becomes free but if it cannot yet complete all preparatory application of the plan of duty in the world, it is not deemed as having completed the stage of humanity. Because of this, although it has left the body, that being is still at the stage of human. For, no matter what, it has to return to the world in order to finish its unfinished business. And until he completes the preparatory applications there, its habitat will be the world; in the communal plan, mankind!

So, the human being who has passed there, that is, who is isolated from all influences when it dies, has to spend some time in the spatium. There is a significant reason for this. A being, after rendering the application of its plan pertaining to the world life, needs to make an accounting of its assets, to completely absorb and appropriate them. For this, it needs to retreat for a while, to turn to its essence-knowledge, that is, to do an accounting of them by comparing the knowledge it acquired in the last world life with its former knowledge.

We previously said that mankind accumulates their assets in the world in their unconscious while they sleep. And, following death, the being's entering into a state of isolation by severing its connections to the surroundings allows it to do the necessary applications for comfortably digesting all of this knowledge. Therefore, the spatium life is a profound and fundamental moment for contemplation and accounting for the being. And one of the reasons for inserting intervals called death into the human life that continues across a whole world cycle is to ensure this possibility.

Here, the most perfect application of the knowledge of comparison is done. For, during that time the being is not disturbed by the realities coming from the surroundings and the conscience mechanism which works freely finds the opportunity and possibility of making bitter and sweet comparisons of all the accumulated knowledge and appropriating their conclusions to the essence-being.

So, in order to assist this application, all outside influences are ceased at the moments following death. There is no influence which can occupy and pull out its comprehension. The beings in duty prevent this. Nevertheless, it is still under the complete control of the plan of duty. If the coming of some influences to it from below is seen as necessary for its accounting and contemplation, this can be done only under the approval and control of the beings in duty. That is, the deceased (X) cannot get in touch whenever he wishes with his friend (A) who stayed in the world. This act is either permitted or not, in accordance with the very minute calculations pertaining to the contemplation and accounting of (X) during that time. When not permitted, then no power can allow its contacting mankind.

A being who passed to the spatium cannot communicate with other beings like itself for an initial period of time as well. This is due to permission with the above-mentioned rules. For, there is no arbitrary thing over there. Everything is accrued under the very carefully planned control of the plan of duty. In the same way as the minutest needs and imperatives have been calculated when it was alive, the necessities of the deeds following death are done in the same way. When the being who passed to the spatium does not receive influences from the world and its surroundings, it is compulsorily left alone with the impressions of images existing in itself and starts to live within them. This state is like a very deep and powerful dream. However, this living is not for pleasure or suffering. Even if there are pleasures and sufferings during that time, the real purpose is the being's appropriating the acquisitions that have been gained in the world – by the knowledge of comparison.

And there, the completely free working of the developmental mechanism under the control of the plan of duty drags the being to the compulsory synthesis and analysis which are done most often by suffering knowledge of comparison. In the mean time, because there are no mitigating influences of surroundings, painful emotions arising out of the comparison and increased thousands of times more than in the world put the being into tribulation. And knowledge can only become digested as essence-knowledge after such an intense settling of accounts.

Thus, all results are received. During this settling of accounts, since some very surprising situations for the being may occur, we call this the being's state of confusion. As we have said, this contemplation and accounting do not always, even most often, pass at ease and calm. Especially at the initial periods of the transition it occurs generally together with states of uneasiness, intense suffering, torment, heavy confusion and bewilderment. Depending on the imperatives and necessities of the contemplation and accounting, more or less easy states may also occur. Sometimes, it may be turbulent to the extent of hellish torment.

*
* *

After the being has gone through so many confusions and the accounting of its acquisitions and has digested its knowledge; the assisting influences from above start to reach it again. It also receives influences from the surroundings. Thanks to all of these it starts to get free of the confusion and bewilderment and recognises itself and its surroundings and starts to think about its future with its expanded comprehension. It appreciates the degree of its gains and losses; and starts to feel the need of returning to the world for

211

completing his deficiencies. If this need is necessary to be fulfilled, the beings in duty who appreciate this immediately get ready to assist it by the directives coming from above. And they start out to arrange and regulate the most necessary and beneficial individual and communal plan for it.

It is willingly bonded to this plan. For, it appreciates that his salvation will be ensured only by the application of this plan. Therefore, it promises to be faithful to this plan in the world and upon this promise, it embodies in the world as we previously explained. When embodied, since it will again be under the rule of the superficial time; all riches in it that belong to the comprehension of the spherical time are erased. And all of these are cast away to the subconscious. The comprehension subjecting to superficial time begins to live in the world within new circumstances. And besides the impressions remaining from the spatium, the help of the beings in duty will support it in the world and guide it in the application of this plan.

In this way, lives will follow each other; and with each coming of the man as his essence-knowledge and comprehension increases, his possibilities and imperatives for shifting to the higher parts of the realities at the conscience mechanism increase as well. Since the conscience equilibrium will start to be set on the higher levels from now on, the bitter sides of the accounting in the spatium after death gradually decrease. There is a rule here. The more comprehension is expanded, the shorter the period of the isolation state in the spatium, because the faster the accounting needed to be done there is completed.

*
* *

A man that lives in the world should know, above else, what his duty is; about what he prepares for; from where he comes and where he goes to; and especially how to behave according to the concepts of good and evil in the sense we have just described. And unless he knows these, there will be neither a necessity nor possibility to rise upwards, to the plan of duty. For, as long as he stays in this state, there is no deed for him to do in the plan of duty. For this, he needs to be prepared for the necessities of the higher plan and to return many times to the world within various links of the chain of embodiments.

It is impossible to accept that a man whose comprehension works merely in automatic ways while doing even the simplest deeds could immediately attain the power to grasp the relations of the universal events and matter combinations on the face of the causality principle and sublime necessities, and could reach the scope of capability to conduct the sublime deeds of the vast realms by comprehending all responsibilities of them at the end of a world incarnation of 50–60 years. Seeing that even the comprehension of the most hard-working man develops throughout the whole life with the speed of an ant, it is a mistake to think that attaining such a universal comprehension is possible within a few world lives. Therefore, the being's attaining the merit of a complete knowledge of duty is possible only after completion of the rings of the chain of lives which are passed on in the human body for tens of thousands of years in the world.

*
* *

After this knowledge, it is easily understood that for mankind in the world there is no question of obligation of duty. For, the order of the universe which is based on immutable truths cannot be executed by the realities connected to the superficial time comprehension in the world. In order to attain the honour of meddling with such great deeds, mankind need to go through the stages of preparations we explained above; and here the most perfect mechanism which helps them is the conscience mechanism.

The shifting of the conscience mechanism towards the higher parts means that its levels of equilibrium are getting increasingly established at levels which get closer to attaining the necessary qualities for these great obligations. That is, it means the setting up of the equilibria between them in the fields increasingly closer to the plan of duty; and the making up of the opposite components out of the materials closer to the necessities of duty. Therefore, the oppositeness here is seen not in forms of tugs which have schisms

213

in between – as it is in lower levels – but as a harmonious advance whose intention is supporting each other and reconciliation.

After all, another meaning of the completion of the human cycle is the abolishment of the opposition between components of the conscience duality. For example, while in the conscience mechanism at the lower level there is an opposition between the emotions of forgiving or hanging a man who killed his father; at the higher level, it displays a duality in the form of preferring this or that way of easing the pangs the same killer will feel anyway because of this bad deed; and for a man, this is rather a more or less sweet activity of a comprehending preparation for the knowledge of duty than an exhausting opposition.

*
* *

This initial conscientious flux of the preparation to the plan of duty has been explained by the religious and moral institutions and they bonded these with some several disciplined sanctions. These initial flux of conscience have been taken by these institutions within the duality of virtues and vices; and these sanctions have led mankind automatically towards the virtues that make up the higher opposite of the conscience. Most powerful and to the point sanctions of this automatism are the symbols of the heaven which is promised to the good ones and the hell which is particular to the bad ones. We have said that symbols of heaven and hell are up to the point. Indeed, all advances in the lower levels where the line of equilibrium of the conscience is established and that belong to the badness we call selfishness carry along all kinds of torture and suffering which cannot even be expressed by the concept of hell. On the other hand, levels of equilibrium of conscience duality that are set in the higher parts contain the feeling of happiness of self-sacrifice, altruism, love and, especially, of the love of duty which the symbol of heaven attempts to express.

*
* *

Higher levels of conscience are together with resignation and self-sacrifice. Therefore, one cannot pass into there with the desires of

214

the lower levels. Higher levels are the closest steps to the knowledge of duty which has no relevance, even in the slightest degree, with those kinds of selfishness. So, the concept of payment that is expected against a deed at the lower levels leaves its place to the reality of volunteering that is based on the love of duty at the higher levels. Even the personal interest that has been ambitiously run after at the lower levels may be a source of suffering for the ones at the higher levels. In this way, a being who attained the power of ability to do his deeds with heart and soul and with the purpose of serving others around by distancing away from the state of obtaining his material interests and even making it an end for himself has now matured enough to leap from the uppermost levels of the world boundary to the fields of duty. And when he reaches this degree, after completing the suitable duty given to him by the plan of duty, he passes directly into the plan of duty.

However, there is an intermediary plan which those of mankind who have completed the world school but have not yet taken on duty will pass through; and we call it the semi-subtle realm. And after passing over this intermediary plan, the beings will reach the initial stages of the great plan of duty and begin their true evolutions.

*
* *

The numbers of lives a human comprehension has to live in order to reach the uppermost boundary line belonging to the humanity – although it cannot be stated certainly because of the great number of freedoms and tests and trials – it is a fact that this is limited to 500–700 embodiments on average. It is quite natural that this number is not certain. As a matter of fact, although even one life of man is regulated and planned, it is not possible to express the duration of it with certainty because of the imperatives of destiny. Again, for the same reasons, it is impossible to presuppose which developmental stages mankind will reach at what time as they apply their plans. For, this impossibility is caused by the ever changeability of the results of that being's efforts – as a consequence of some freedoms recognised to him – which will be appreciated by the plan of destiny.

*
* *

We have said that the measurement of time beyond the world and higher plans does not fit world time and there are great differences between them. Indeed, time measurement and comprehension of the plan engaged with the administration of the world cannot be compared with the simple comprehension of time in the world. For example, all the long-term deeds which ages do not suffice in the world can fit into a second – in our measurements – of the time measurement of the super-world. Although it is very simple and coarse, an example of this which can give an intuition to mankind is dreams. Likewise, it is similar to the way drowning people are reported to see their whole life in every detail during their last second.

Nevertheless, this point should be remembered that time comprehension particular to the world is not lacking, deficient or insufficient for the world. The value of world time is exact and perfect for the world. That is, comprehension of time particular to the world is the true measurement of the development of world matter for the world. And as mankind learns about the techniques and mechanisms belonging to the world, it is unnecessary and even harmful to compare the comprehension of time particular to the world with universal time forms. For, the immense difference in between makes it impossible to understand the simple architecture of the world which is such a small, even negligible part within the tremendous mechanism of universe; and wipes away the world realities.

Therefore, while studying the factors and mechanisms which have given developmental direction to the world, taking the comprehension of time particular to the world into consideration is more beneficial in regard to the objectivity and clarity of world knowledge. And also, it is an imperative of the developmental necessities of the world.

*
* *

It should always be remembered that widening of the concepts of time advances head to head with the development of comprehension. That is, establishment of the high comprehension of time becomes possible by going beyond certain stages of development. In higher realms, there are states of time which address the comprehensions of those realms.

*
* *

One of the significant qualities of time suitable to world comprehension is the imperative of its limitation with a beginning point
and an ending point. That is, despite the ideas of infinity which are
sometimes talked about in world life, world comprehension needs
relativities of beginning and ending points in its cultivation and
evolution through applications; and this need is suitable also to the
time form which is valid in the world and addresses world comprehension. Therefore, every reality's beginning at a certain point
and ending at a certain point is a time expression which is only
valid in the world and moulded into the world comprehension.

With this knowledge what we intend to mean is: actually such
beginning and ending states do not exist. Occurrences and advances
of all realms flux uninterrupted, continuously towards the purposes
determined by the necessities. These fluxes become only a ground
for manifestation in accordance with the comprehension of the
stages they go through and with time measurements valued by these
comprehensions. That is, conceptions of time such as those that have
started here and will end there or have ended are based only on the
measurements moulded according to the world comprehension.

For higher comprehensions, the meaning of such beginnings and
endings do not carry the value mankind think of. They contain completely different meanings regarding the possibilities of the time of
high comprehension. Therefore, it is impossible to understand the
events of the higher realms with world comprehension. World time
measurement which is abundantly sufficient for world realities is
very simple compared to the comprehensions of time in the higher
realms. Because of this, realities bonded by world time remain in a
quite barren state relative to the truths in the higher realms.

*
* *

As to the reason for the barrenness of world time: we have said that
time is related to comprehension. The more the scope of comprehensions expands, the more comprehensive the time system they
are subject to becomes. However, the expansion in the scope of
comprehension means their gaining more values, an increase in

their values. Since the comprehension of the human realm is almost within the same cadres of values, the time it is subject to is a simple system. The simplicity of this system is because of the imperative that it has to have a focus, a definite beginning and states of past, present and future. This situation is the imperative of the simplicity of the world matter and of the comprehension which is subject to it.

There is a limit in the comprehension of world time. In world time, there is the imperative that certain points should follow each other at certain intervals as cycles. Likewise, every reality has a beginning point and an ending point. However, high comprehension of time displays great differences on this regard. And these differences are certainly the consequence and necessity of the richness and encompassment of the comprehension values belonging to this time, relative to the values of the simple time. This comprehension possesses such subtle matter combinations that vibrations emanating from these attain a time measurement, qualified with a great speed and scope which is incomparable with simpler comprehension. According to this comprehension, the states of past, present and future in the flow of time do not have to follow each other in one direction, unlike simple comprehension. In higher comprehension, all of these states of past, present and future connect into a single occurrence as a total. However, this single occurrence display forms with infinite aspects. That is, within that single occurrence which means a moment, infinite concepts of time are gathered, orientated to every direction.

*
* *

This needs to be explained more objectively. For some problems to be well understood, it is necessary to intuit the time reality as powerfully as possible. To make it easier, we will explain the topic of time with diagrams and graphics.

We call simple time which is subject to the understanding of three dimensions superficial time. For, the flow of this time, as shown in Figure 2, advances in one direction like a spiral circles drawn upon a surface.

Let us point out that this diagram is simply a graphic drawn to explain the concept of time and to ensure the objective comprehension of simple time.

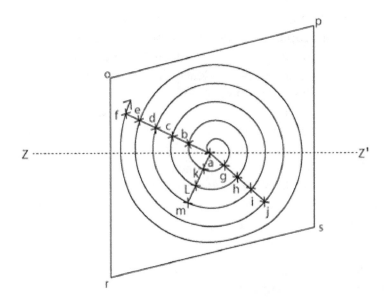

Figure 2

As seen in the diagram, superficial time does not advance in a straight line. Around a point of a long line, upon a surface that is vertical to that line, it revolves spirally by cycles. In this diagram, there is a surface (o–p–s–r) where a straight line (Z–Z') pierces it vertically at a point (a). This surface is exactly vertical to the line (Z–Z'). And upon this surface, there is a spiral drawn starting from the point (a). As this spiral is drawn, because it advances vertically to the line (Z–Z'), no matter how long this spiral is, it does not travel any distance on the line (Z–Z') but merely draws cycles around the point (a). So, this is the progress of the superficial time comprehension. And the line (Z–Z') is the original time which encompasses universe. And let us point that this original time is not the spherical time particular to the higher cosmos which we will mention later. This is the manifestation of the super-universe time principle in universe which encompasses all realities of time and traverses throughout our universe. We do not talk about it for now.

Upon the progress of this spiral, let us define point (a) as the moment a man is born and point (f) as the moment he dies. Let us take one of his states which continues its development from his birth to his death, let's say a capability of him. As seen in the diagram, as this capability goes from point (a) to point (f), it has passed through each of the spiral circles that came along from points (b, c, d, e, f). As seen clearly in the diagram, each of these points constitutes a period on the flow of the spiral. For example, a circle is completed between (a) and (b). However, following at once, there is a second and wider circle (b–c) and a third circle (c–d) follows it. In this way, circles run after each other, getting wider until the final circle (e–f). And each of these constitutes a period, that is, cycles a piece throughout the lifetime. And these periods come after another by following an order. Here, the concept of past period, present period and future period exist as fundamental; and this is an imperative of the superficial time comprehension.

In life, some capabilities have continued to develop as this line (a–f). However, all capabilities do not. For example, as seen in the diagram, the development of capability (a–j) has continued for four periods of life and stopped there. Likewise, development of the capability (a–m) has been shorter and continued only for three periods. There are shorter developments of capabilities as well, for example only for one period. Therefore, in the life of a man, all of his capabilities do not develop to the same degree.

*
* *

Now, we will explain sublime time comprehension. Although we will talk about it on the diagram as well, in order to intuit as much as possible such a comprehension which does not exist in the world, intuitions should be forced while studying the diagram. Here, imagination should be used and the concepts intended to be explained should be tried to intuit by visualisation; and if contemplated with patience, very precious intuitions will be gained.

We call the sublime time comprehension spherical time comprehension or perceptual time. Sublime time comprehension is not a simple system, unlike the previous one, which revolves upon a surface as spirals in one direction. This is a time complex which advances by flowing in all directions within the whole of a sphere. Here, the concept of time flow in question has infinite directions advancing from the source of the sphere towards each of the infinite points of the circle and infinite scope which is in accordance with these directions. Figure 3 is the cross-section of a sphere.

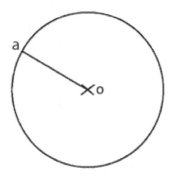

Figure 3

That is, it is like a cut half seen after a solid sphere; for example, a ball is cut in two equal halves with a knife cutting through its centre; and as seen in the diagram, this is only a surface consisting a circle. The line (o–a) is the radius of this circle. Now, upon this surface, it is possible and natural that a superficial time flow comprehension exists as spirals revolving around the former (o) centre. Therefore, on one cross-section of this ball there is a superficial time comprehension. This is a value sufficient to contain all realities of a man's life in the world. However, this cross-section should be imagined not on the ball or on paper but in the imagination. Without changing its position, other cross-sections can be made from other parts of the ball, providing it always crosses from the centre.

And in this way, infinite imaginary cross-sections can be obtained. We can divide this ball in two halves from separate directions as much as we can, depending on how sharp our knife is, how perfect our technique is and how wide our imagination is. In the mean time, because the position of the ball will stay fixed, directions of spirals displaying the simple time upon these infinite surfaces do not fit each other and superficial time spirals in infinite directions occur. So, within a sphere, there are – we could say in almost infinite numbers – distinct possibilities of superficial time. And the moment we join all these distinct time comprehensions and imagine connecting them into a single occurrence, we may then visualise spherical time comprehension. We also call it perceptual time for short. If a man who lives in the world can use his comprehension at a moment in time's progress upon only one surface, a being that lives in a super-world plan can use its comprehension – which is almost the infinite multitude of this comprehension – at the same moment in perceptual time. This situation, naturally, can only be intuited in the world by visualisation.

This knowledge teaches that perceptual time has a richer scope which cannot be compared with superficial time. According to this, with superficial time comprehension a man can only move in one direction at a given moment. For, he has to follow a single sequence within the concepts of past, present and future as obeying the imperatives of superficial time with all of his comprehension, acts and behaviours. And he will certainly participate in the sequenced periods of a spiral. For, his material state is not suitable for his getting out of it. However, a being obeying perceptual time has the possibility of living the concepts of past, present and future in infinite directions at the same moment by joining them into a single occurrence. For, the subtle matter milieu which it exists in permits it to live upon all surfaces of a sphere at the same moment.

*
* *

In order to conclude the knowledge about the superficial and perceptual time, we need to explain these two time comprehensions by comparing them relative to the original time in universe. We will give this knowledge upon diagrams as well.

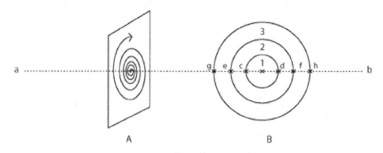

Figure 4

In Figure 4 the line (a–b) is the original time which traverses universe. The drawing (A) shows the flow of superficial time on original time; and the drawing (B) shows spherical time. Superficial time, as seen in the drawing, revolves around a point (x) of the flow of the original time and draws a spiral with its periods. Regardless of the numbers of periods, this spiral does not abandon the point (x) on the original time; it extends while it remains at its place. Therefore, in the time reality (A) which shows the duration of a lifetime, there is no advance and flow on the original time. However, there is the application of the realities of a single point (x) on original time; and as we have shown in the previous diagrams, this can continue at a few or all periods of superficial time.

On the other hand, when the drawing (B) is studied, the cross-section of three concentric circles are seen, indicated by the numbers 1, 2 and 3. These spheres should not be considered three separate circles within each other. This shows the three stages of the first sphere's growth, that is, the smallest one at the centre, by expanding in all directions. For, the development of the spherical time occurs not in the form of a spiral's extending and contracting in one direction upon a surface but of the sphere's growth, that is, expanding from its centre towards all directions at the same time.

For example, here the sphere numbered (1) shows a stage of its smallest states. The sphere numbered (2) is one of its further, widened stages; and the sphere numbered (3) is its widest stage. So, perceptual time develops in this way. When this development is compared to superficial time on the flow of original time (a–b), it is seen here that while perceptual time, that is, spherical time, as has been in the state of the first sphere, takes the part (c–d) on the flow of original time into its scope. When this sphere takes its size numbered (2) as its comprehension develops, advances on the flow of original time and occupies the part (e–f), when it gets wider and enters the state of the sphere numbered (3), it traverses the part (g–h) on the flow of original time.

Therefore, although the development of superficial time comprehension does not progress at all and remains at one point on the flow of original time, each developmental moment of spherical time comprehension is together with the advance on the flow of original time. Because of this, the real evolution starts from the super-world plan of duty where perceptual time prevails. Indeed, millions times of a result which could hardly be attained by spending enormous efforts as a necessity of world life can be attained in exchange for the smallest effort in the super-world realms.

*
* *

As we can more or less easily explain time in diagrams, we need to elaborate as well on space which depends on it. For, when space does not exist, the presence of time, that is, its manifestation in universes, cannot be possible. For the flow of original time in the universe to manifest in cosmoses, the concept of space is needed, which is suitable to the structures of those cosmoses. In other words, the explanation of the mechanism of time needs the material milieu and variations of matter. Therefore, unless the concepts of time and space are not joined, neither time nor space can manifest in cosmoses. We will explain this truth later in detail. So, since superficial and perceptual times are distinct from another with great differences, as we explained above, then spaces belonging to the world and to the super-world which rigidly depend on time comprehensions should be as much as different from another.

*
* *

Now, let us explain the space belonging to spherical time. Space is an expression of the imperative of matter to localise its various components. Let us explain this expression according to both time realities. First of all, let us point that if the explanations here are not to be applied on any object but to be imagined as described, understanding the topic of space becomes easier.

Let us explain first the space in superficial time. For the periods to occur in superficial time three conditions must occur. First, a material milieu (this milieu is not the space) in order to establish the passing of flow of time and periods; second, the motion for the constitution of these periods and for the flow of time; and third, binding of the motion to that milieu in order to appreciate the occurrence of motion and establishment of the periods. So, this is the space for superficial time.

Therefore, after gathering the above conditions together, it is necessary to define and accept superficial time space as such: in order to establish and appreciate the flow direction of a motion to occur in a spiral direction and the beginning and ending points of certain periods; the binding of a material milieu to that motion puts into effect superficial time space. Here, the term of milieu is not a space; it only expresses the non-localised matter components. That is, there are matter components but not their localisation – in other words, not their positions, which can be relative to each other. The effectuation of this localisation, the constitution of the space entails the binding of those components to a motion, as we have said above. Therefore, time and space are inseparable. This is such an occurrence that, as we will explain further, the manifestations of two great principles – which are connected to the original principle – manifest according to the various cosmoses of universe and adapt those cosmoses – with all of their events, realities and comprehensions – to themselves.

In comparison with a body, we express superficial time space as such: the connection of the motions of the body with matter and the value of matter in these connections brings about the whole of space. We will make clear this apparently vague expression with an example. Imagine a stone thrown in the air. First of all, here there is the motion of stone and there is the period character that can be expressed by the beginning and ending points of this motion: this is the first condition. Afterwards, there is the need for the milieu in the air, which allows the establishment and appreciation of the motion and the period points: this is the second condition. Finally, there is the comparison or relation of this motion and of the period points to the milieu: this is the third condition. Thus, the stone's motion in the air which manifests through these three conditions puts into effect the space particular to superficial time comprehension.

Therefore, on the face of a body's comprehension, a milieu that establishes the periods of motions, that is, their beginning and ending points by binding to the motions of that body, is a space. All matter is included in this milieu. On the face of a body, which we accept as a matter localisation, the space is a whole localisation with all of its stones, soil, horses, cars, planes and humans. Space is graded in infinitely minute nuances such as a metre square soil an individual stands on, the space he looks at by raising his head up, the city, the homeland, the continent and the world. Here, there are infinite space possibilities.

*
* *

Let alone grasping the space belonging to perceptual time, which has infinite possibilities when compared to the space of superficial time comprehension, even to intuit it with the most powerful imaginations would not be that easy for mankind. Nevertheless, we will give an intuition of this, as well. However, here it is necessary to use the imagination and try to advance with intuitions.

Before everything else, let us state this that there is no such reality of space according to world comprehension. Therefore, we should not try to visualise things that will be told here upon world matter. As we said, the intuitions of this can only be conceived in the imagination. However, let us also express this that power of imagining, that is, imagination is a very subtle matter milieu as well. Therefore, the space kept live in the imagination is a true and genuine value.

First of all, visualise an imaginary sphere. As we said previously, on a single surface of this sphere, visualise again imaginary superficial time and the space that exists together with this time; let these be imagined. This is a simple time and space, and it has a certain single direction. After visualising this imaginary simple time and space, visualise a similar imaginary second simple time and space but with a different direction. In this way, providing that they have different directions, let imaginary third, fifth, hundredth, thousandth, millionth and infinite simple times and space be visualised separately. As these are to be visualised in the mind's eye one by one, all of them still remain only as superficial time and space. Their synthesis should be done only by a powerful intuitive activity.

For this, let all of these infinite flows of time at infinite directions and all of these infinite milieus establishing and binding these flows be thought of as a single time and a single space. In this case, a single time – which flows to infinite directions at the same moment – and a single space – out of the concept of infinite milieu, which establishes those flows by comparing them to these infinite directions – emerge, and this is the spherical space. This is because this space ensures the flow of time within the sphere. Here, the milieu is the imagination itself. As a matter of fact, only a milieu which is composed of the very subtle matter of the imagination can bind the flows of motions which express such infinite directions and period characters. Otherwise, this cannot be done with the coarse matter of the world.

Therefore, the whole of the imagination – itself included, together with all these motions and milieus – which binds the infinite milieus in the imagination into one occurrence by these milieus' establishing the infinite motions in a sphere by comparing them to the flows at infinite directions and periods puts into effect perceptual or spherical space.

Performing this imagining entails hard work and thinking. Nevertheless, powerful intuitions can be gained here with more or less effort. This sublime time and space mechanism which is impossible to realise for mankind who live in the world, in a coarse milieu may be possible to realise only up to a degree, as we said, with the very subtle materials of the imagination for much of mankind. However, for beings in the higher realms, who are subtler than the subtle milieus in the human imagination, living in this reality of sublime perceptual time and space is a natural, even obligatory situation.

*
* *

We have said that superficial time does not traverse any distance in original time, and that the perceptual time always advances on the original time. Now, we will explain – by benefiting the value of this knowledge – what it means in the evolution of beings by elaborating on the jogtrot development of a man who lives in superficial time comprehension and on the evolution of a being who advances in original time, and the emergence of their results in the developmental mechanism.

Even though the knowledge given above about time and space explain superficial and the perceptual times and spaces in detail, further explanations are needed to extract the solutions of the problems we have just mentioned from this knowledge. If the diagrams below are studied carefully, it would be possible to understand this significant point with ease.

In the whole life of humanity, there is a field of development that a being has to go through with all its endless aspects. And this field of development is determined and limited. For, it has a beginning and an ending within its reality. We show this field by the distance between the parallel lines (A and B) (Figure 5).

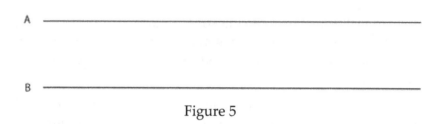

Figure 5

Here, this field of development, which is the imperative of the superficial time comprehension has a beginning point and an ending point. Let the beginning be the line (c–d) in the zone between the parallel lines (A, B) and the ending be the line (g–f) which crosses the point (e) (Figure 6).

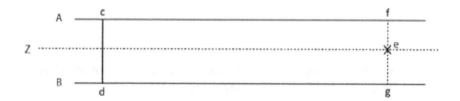

Figure 6

So, all capabilities and states of the humanity which needs to be developed for mankind to prepare to the higher plan, that is, to the plan of duty where perceptual time prevails; and which begins at the border (c–d) and is completed at the border (f–g) fills the zone (c–d–g–f). This indicates the whole stage of the world life, which passes through from the first life the man started in the world and after innumerable embodiments to the last life when he completes the world. The line (Z) here is the original time. And the point (e) is a given moment in this time. Therefore, this given moment in the original time contains the total of the all preparatory capabilities of a man, which are needed to be developed and matured throughout the whole life of humanity. The preparation of a man throughout the whole stage of humanity in the world will mature at this moment on the flow of the original time.

Naturally, the surface (c–d–g–f) should be imagined in the mind's eye as vertical to the line (Z) and as traversing that line only at the point (e). This point (e), is a point at a certain moment of the original time where the human being begins his development and will reach again, after maturing his inherent powers which need to be developed. That is, the evolution of the being in the state of human beings starts from this point on the original time and ends, again at this point. And until this stage is completed, there is no advancement on the original time. Because of this, we had termed the evolution in the stage of humanity as the subjective evolutionary cycle. For, unless the field (c–d–g–f) which constitutes the developmental stage of the whole mankind is traversed, the point (e) has no flow on the original time (Z). Here, mankind is withdrawn to its own powers and only preoccupied with their preparation for a higher plan. For mankind to be capable of going out of this field and of entering an objective evolutionary principle is possible only by fulfilling all necessities of the stage (c–d–g–f).

Thus, from the beginning to the end, many embodiments, uncountable life circumstances and evolutionary materials that mankind will go through will occur and end within this field (c–d–g–f). However, in the mean time, this field will be gradually filled, starting from the border (c–d) which is the furthest from the point (e) and constitutes the most primitive stages of humanity up to the border (g–f); this filling will occur through various embodiments. By accepting each embodiment as a symbolically expressed triangle, we will explain how this field is filled with triangles and how a man comes from the backward stages to the border (g–f) which is his last stage (Figure 7).

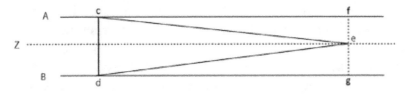

Figure 7

The base of the triangle on the parallel (A, B) will cover this field by starting first from the line (c–d) and getting closer to the point (e), that is, to its tip. And this will occur through periodical addition of other triangles whose tips are always at the point (e). Each of these triangles expresses a single life in its embodiment. So, the line (c–d), by advancing on the parallel (A, B) cycle by cycle in each embodiment, will converge on the line (g–f) and eventually the line (c–d) will adapt on the line (g–f). The meaning of this is: a man has developed all his capabilities which need to be developed belonging to the stage of humanity and by completing all his preparations, he has reached a state to advance on the original time, starting from the point (e). Let us elaborate on this knowledge with a diagram.

Now that the whole life of mankind occurs at the point (e) which is a moment of the flow of the original time, then all lifecycles of man, that is, his births and deaths will occur at this point. However, there are imperatives which depend on this point, on the necessities of that moment and which fills the field of development of the stage of mankind; and they are the aspects of mankind which are needed to be prepared for mankind to be able to make advances on the original time, starting from the point (e). And it is shown symbolically with the field (c–d–g–f). This field has near or far imperatives in respect to the moment (e).

The coarsest, most primitive states of these imperatives are the far-flung border (c–d) from the point (e) which is the ending of the development. As this border gets closer to the point (e) the field narrows, the preparations mature and the necessities of the point (e) are fulfilled. That is, the state of completion of the required deeds for the man to begin to move advances starting from the point (e). Eventually, when the line (c–d) exactly overlaps with the line (g–f), that is, the line which is supposed to be the base of the last triangle adapts on the point (e) on the original time, all necessities are rendered and the field is thoroughly traversed and cleared. Thus, in this diagram which we show as the graph of the life of humanity, we explain how the line (c–d) shifts on the parallel (A, B) and converges on the line (g–f) with the each flow of the life of humanity by cycles, lifetimes, stages or leaps – which are all same – and consequently, how the necessities of the stage of humanity are fulfilled.

First of all, let us draw the diagram of the first man of the world. This man is a being whose capabilities and talents are in a most primitive state. Therefore, his states which need to be developed will be found at the furthest place – which is the border (c–d) – from the line (g–f) which is the ideal point of the field of development. This man is still preoccupied with developing initial mankind capabilities. Therefore, his life will begin from the line (c–d). In order to complete the diagram, let us join the point (c) and (d) with the point (e), by drawing lines. The resulting (c–d–e) triangle is the graph of the first embodiment of the first simple human.

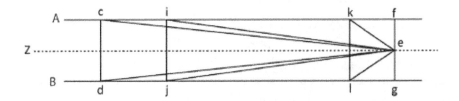

Figure 8

Now, let us move to the second life of this man (Figure 8). Its line of development will start on the parallel (A, B), at the side of (e) of the line (c–d) and from the points which are closest to this line. In order to make it more obvious in the diagram, we show these points by distancing them, with the line (i–j).

In this way, as the graph of the second life, the triangle (i–j–e) occurs. As the bases of the triangles which will occur in the 3rd, 5th, 10th, 50th etc. lives of the man gradually converge on the line (f–g) and eventually reach the points (k–l). Then, the parts (c–d–l–k) of the field (c–d–g–f) have been completely lived, the preparations at these sections have been completed but the fields (k–e–f) and (l–g–e) have not been completed yet. And finally pertaining to the stage of humanity, in this case, the base of the triangle completely adapts to the line (f–g) and the lives of the man in the world are finished. Such a moment comes that all necessities of the point (e) for this man on the flow of the original time belonging to humanity are realised, that is, that being develops all his capabilities and completes the preparations.

If studied carefully, in this diagram, the line (c–d) which is the initial primitive border of development at the field (c–d–g–f) which shows the whole stage of development of humanity, shifts on the parallel (A, B) and as it shifts, the parts of this field which have been lived and completed their development grow and the parts which still have not developed reduce; and finally, when the development in the whole field is completed, the line (c–d) which is the beginning border of the field adapts to the line (f–g) which is on the original time point at the border of the last stage. And in this way, all necessities belonging to the stage of humanity of the point (e) – which is a moment of the original time – are realised.

When the development of mankind reaches this point, the realities of superficial time comprehension will end; true evolution will continue on the higher plans of duty which are the perceptual space; and human beings will get free of the subjective evolutionary process and enter into an objective evolutionary flow advancing on original time.

We state some significant points, which can easily be understood by the diagram of superficial time development. In superficial time development, the developmental parallel does not change throughout the stage of humanity. This stage is a field of development belonging to the preparation of the being, which is limited with the necessities of the point (e), which is a moment in the flow of time. Therefore, it is a subjective evolutionary stage. Each cycle of embodiment in this field is added upon another like a series of leaps. However, these leaps cannot violate the developmental parallel at any point at all. Let us express this according to the diagram: each newcomer triangle adds on to the previous triangle and accrues some amount of preparations that need to be completed in the field of development into the previous one. In that case, there are no interruptions in the development. Cycles silently add on each other.

So, on the original time, whereas the withdrawal of a man into his cadre of preparation and his preoccupation with his own preparations throughout the whole of humanity expresses his subjective evolution; so the great number of embodiment states which are aimed only at the completion of the stage of humanity entail the taking all of these bodily lives as a single life in total. That is, embodiments of a developmental cycle which to occur throughout the whole of humanity are actually nothing but the imperatives of a single life. And this imperative is to fulfil the necessities of the point (e), which is a moment in original time.

*
* *

Now, we will explain the progress of evolution in perceptual time using another diagram. Here, the most obvious feature is that each evolutionary flow of the being accompanies its ever progressing on the original time. It has, now out of its own cosmos, entered into an objective and active evolutionary state within the organisation systems by acquiring the merit of obeying the necessities of the flow of the original time.

Previously, we had said that time develops in the spherical time by expanding in all directions. Differences in expansion which occur, starting from the beginning of perceptual time's development, make advances on the original time as well, as they follow a fast and unlimited progress of development. That is, the lines of development here do not continue on in parallel but extend and widen by continuously distancing from each other.

In order to explain it with a diagram, let us take four concentric spheres in various sizes (Figure 9).

When these four concentric spheres are cut in two halves, provided that they are cut from the exact centre, and one of the cross-section is studied, four distinct cross-sections are seen, as in the

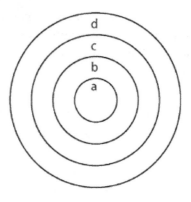

Figure 9

diagram. These cross-sections put into effect the centrifugal state (a, b, c, d). Each of these are the four distinct stages the smallest sphere at the centre takes on by increasingly expanding. That is, out of the expansion of the sphere at the centre with size (a), the sizes (b, c, d) have occurred. So, the sphere (a), as increasingly growing, has reached the size (d). Now, in order to compare these cross-sections to each other within the expansion of the sphere, let us pull the cross-section (d) away like a folding hood of a camera from the smallest cross-section (a) by keeping it fixed. Here, a cone occurs. Naturally, the base of this cone is the cross-section of the sphere (d) which is the largest and outermost. At its tip, that is, in its narrow side, is the smallest sphere (a) (Figure 10). And the layers (b, c) in between are made up of the cross-sections of concentric circles in various sizes.

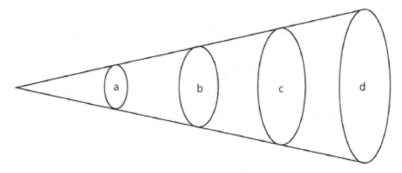

Figure 10

Here, the differences in width of the cross-sections (a, b, c, d) of the cone show the developmental values of the perceptual time relative to each other. For we have said that each cross-section here actually shows the differences in expansion of a sphere which grows on top of another. So, the difference of a cross-section relative to the previous cross-section shows the width of the sphere's development particular to that moment. In this way, the diagram below expresses the developmental width of each cross-section which belongs to its own capacity (Figure 11). The difference in width here also indicates the advancement made on the original time during the development.

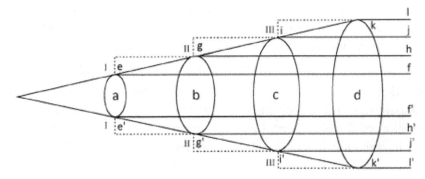

Figure 11

For example, the parallel (e–f) and (e'–f') shows the developmental degree particular to the sphere (a). The following parallel (g–h) and (g'–h') shows the developmental degree of the sphere (b). The distance (I) between these two parallels indicates the difference in development between two developmental stages and also the traversed distance on the original time.

Similarly, it is easy to see in the diagram the expansion of the fields of development (i–j) and (i'– j') with (k–l) and (k'–l') belonging to the increasingly expanding spheres (c) and (d); and the occurrence of their differences (II) and (III) pertaining to the development and flow of time between them.

The term of developmental difference here means: Previously we had talked about the comprehensions start to adapt to the necessities starting from the beginning of the plan of duty and so, by the adaptation of comprehensions to the necessities of the original principle pertaining to all spirit and universe relations a unity is reached and finally, the unitary is attained. And because of this, the evolutionary stage which begins from the plan of duty has been called as the field of active adaptations. So, now we show this truth as well in the schematic explanation of spherical time. For this difference, which is seen in between the two developmental stages of the spheres and which is called the progress on original time, is only the expansion of this field of adaptation. However, this sphere development certainly has an ending, which is the ending of the universe. After all, the increase of these developments is accompanied by the expansion of the field of true adaptation in universe. And the expansion of the field of adaptation means the realisation of the unity of comprehension which we call the unitary.

We remind you that in the continuation of the superficial time realities there is not such a development, that is, the progress on the original time which means advancing towards the unitary. Expansion of developmental lines at every moment – as it is here – is not in question in the development of superficial time. There, only the preparations of rendering all necessities of a moment on the original time within a certain field are done.

*
* *

Both diagrams regarding superficial and spherical times show that in spherical time, unlike in superficial time, there is no developmental mode which continues on uninterrupted by the adding of the leaps on each other as staying within a certain field. Here, again unlike in the former, there are no separate cycles. On the contrary, there are new and ever expanding fields of development. In other words, here, there are no periodical movements of advance which are in a limited field, imprisoned within a single moment of the original time but the fields of expansion, progression and development within an infinity that reaches to the boundaries of universe. And this progression comes to an end at the unitary. So, by saying this, we explain in detail the meaning of the phrase said previously that true evolution begins with spherical time comprehension.

236

*
* *

Now it is time to explain a very significant problem. This problem is the quality of the space which puts into effect the time forms by ensuring the adaptations and connections of the states of the original time – which advances in universe in accordance with the original necessities – pertaining to cosmoses to the matter milieus in those cosmoses. On the one hand there are motions which put into effect the time forms and on the other, there is the matter milieu which needs to be bound with those motions for the occurrence of the time comprehension. However, unless the third condition we listed in the relations of time and space, that is, the binding of this milieu with the time motions, is ensured, space cannot be built and the manifestation of the time form cannot be possible. Therefore, here there is a major factor which plays a fundamental role in the universe mechanism.

So, in order to constitute space and to establish the time form particular to a universe, the factor which binds the existing matter milieu with the motions belonging to the time form is the sublime principle of destiny, and its necessities which manifest in the universe as the mechanism of destiny permeate the universe as filtered from the unitary, together with the original necessities and the original time. Therefore, in short, space is the manifestation of destiny in cosmoses and in the universe. That is, the space in a cosmos which results from the binding of the motions belonging to time with the matter milieus is the manifestation of destiny in that cosmos.

Therefore, destiny is the flow of the principle of destiny in universe which puts into effect the time and space forms particular to that cosmos by binding and establishing time in cosmoses with matter milieus and works under the directives of the original necessities and obeys it. Destiny manifests in cosmoses in accordance with the possibilities of those cosmoses. For example, the superficial time space in the hydrogen cosmos is the manifestation of the destiny which is particular to this cosmos.

Thus, the destiny which permeates the whole universe from the unitary by carrying the original necessities puts into effect all formations, deformations and transformations of cosmoses by utilising time which depends on the original necessities again. So, we now explain in more details that all formations, deformations and trans-formations the beings put into effect in matter occur only through the assistance, intervention and controls of the beings in duty in the cadres of original principle, principles of destiny and time in accordance with the directives filtered from the unitary.

This knowledge gives the intuition to mankind about the true roles of destiny and time in the universe. If destiny and time coming from the unitary did not exist; in accordance with the necessities of the original principle, the technical activity of the states of the universe parts which pertain to their endless formations and transformations which are necessary on the face of the momentary behaviours and merits of spirits would lose its focus. The factor which appreciates the degrees of merit of spirits on the face of the necessities determined by the original principle pertaining to the evolutions of spirits is destiny. That is, the technical component of the original necessities in the universe is destiny. Destiny renders this function with the assistance of time and uses it as a measurement. We make this mechanism a little bit clearer by explaining it with a coarse example.

A school has certain classes and a high seat of proxy which appreciates the ordering of lessons in accordance with classes and placement of students in certain classes in accordance with certain merits. Now, if a student starts from the first class and automatically misses out all other classes without becoming subject to any control whatsoever and goes out of the school gate, he is not deemed as having graduated. Therefore, this student should be examined, tried and going through strict supervisions termed as test and trials once a year or even a few times a year by the officers authorised through the proxy; in short, what is necessary to be given to him as considered particular to that moment from that school and if he acquired merit to what is necessary to be given to him should be examined.

If the child, as the result of this test and trial, has learned the rightful lessons of the class he is in and has earned the right of them, then he has succeeded in the examination and acquired the merit to pass to higher classes, to finish the school. Otherwise, he is left in the class which is most suitable to his degree of merit and knowledge and to be subjected to education and teachings accordingly. That is, there is no rule in this school that students will remain in this or that class for such and such a period of time and when this time is over, they will automatically miss out the classes and finish the school.

Life is similar to this. The original principle, which we call the highest and most authorised seat, has regulated the schedule of the world school. Even a slight digression from this is not allowed. However, again in accordance with this schedule, students – that is, mankind – should work and make effort to move up to the classes there; and in proportion with these effort of theirs, they should acquire merit for the grades and classes which need to be reserved for them and should prove it as well. As mankind do this, they move up to the classes they are merited for; on the other hand, the ones who cannot acquire the merit of the state they are in because of laziness or inaptitude are subject to treatments according to their degrees of merit. And this entails two conditions. One of these is the freedom of efforts necessary for mankind to prove their merit; and the other is the existence of a factor which appreciates this merit, and which measures its degree of accordance with the original necessities, and which regulates and prepares the most worthy and suitable matter states and circumstances for mankind regarding those necessities.

So, this technical factor which ensures the proper application of the original necessities and evaluates by appreciating the degrees and measures of reconciliation between the beings and the original necessities is the mechanism of destiny in the universe.

Thus, manifestations of the principle of destiny – which depends on the original principle that exists in the super-universe – that work in the universe as the mechanism of destiny puts into effect the manifestations of destiny in cosmoses in accordance with the possibilities of those cosmoses; and its manifestation in cosmoses are the infinite states and circumstance of space. Therefore, the mechanism of destiny which appreciates beings' degrees and measures of merit regarding the original necessities and which regulates beings' material possibilities in the flow of the universe according to this merit is the manifestation of the sublime principle of destiny in universe. To define the manifestational ways of destiny in other cosmoses – which manifest in our cosmos within certain space forms – with the comprehension and views of this cosmos is certainly not possible. However, we only state that these manifestations, as they arise from the plans of duty towards the unitary, certainly change their function which is valid in our cosmos in accordance with their scope. When reached at the unitary, it expresses a state of unity which is unified with all necessities, comprehensions, possibilities and states.

*
* *

Here, there is a point that needs to be explained. The mechanism of destiny, as it performs its functions in the universe, advances together with the principle of time which is subject to the original principle. The state of the principle of time in the universe is original time. And as it passes through various cosmoses, original time has manifestations according to those cosmoses. We have just explained one of these as superficial time comprehension particular to the world and the other as perceptual time particular to the super-world cosmoses. So, the mechanism of destiny can render its function in the world only with original time. That is, the mechanism of destiny, as it does the accounting and technical expression of the original principle, utilises time as the measure.

The mechanism of time is both very necessary and imperative. It is very necessary because in the realisation of what the original principle determines as the boundary and the essence, time is the criteria and measure of the principle of destiny. If time does not exist, the principle of destiny remains measureless and cannot render its technical function.

It is imperative because if the appreciative quality of the mechanism of time does not exist, there is no harmony in the mechanism of destiny, and consequently, no connection between the original principle and the plans of duty and evolution, and no reconciliation between these principles, plans and the order of occurrences and flows of the cosmoses; and finally, determination and evaluation of the value differentiations become impossible; and therefore, the quantity and then the quality remains without order; and in this case, all applications lose their focus.

*
*   *

We have called the manifestation of the flow of original time in the world superficial time. On the other hand, we have said that manifestation of destiny which flows across the universe and displays manifestations particular to every cosmos is the space forms in the world. So, the space which does not separate from time and finds its measure of value and grade by time is the result of the principle of destiny's function in the world. With this knowledge, we have explained the manifestation of destiny in the world which manifests as the state of space together with time. And we clearly stated that all realities that exist with time and space are the imperatives of the degrees which mankind needs to be worthy of or to acquire by efforts based on freedom; and again, which are measured and calculated by time and space, that is, appreciated by the beings in duty in the cadres of time and space.

For this is a truth, that the applications of the original necessities and of all mechanisms connected to these necessities in the universe are the obligatory sanctions to be done by the beings of duty, working at the organisations in the cadres of original necessity, of original time and of the mechanism of destiny. And the influences belonging to the mechanisms of destiny and time which are filtered from the unitary and permeate into the universe with original influences find the grounds of application with the universal activities of the great plans of duty which are engaged within the cadres executing these mechanisms. And all staff of these cadres are powerful beings who are firmly placed at their posts and duly comprehend their duties.

*
*   *

After this knowledge given about time and space, this is well understood: in the world, declaring that such is the destiny of this or that man in any issue means that the gathering and binding of all

241

matter combinations depending on certain times which put into effect the events that man is in the midst of about that issue have manifested in this form at that moment; and the ones who have well grasped the definition of space comprehend that this means that around a man, spaces according to him are built.

Likewise, a phrase such as 'he is not destined' means that matter combinations belonging to an issue about him have not occurred in the expected way but in other forms; and again, this means a space which is built around that issue out of other matter forms and states than the expected ones. In short, every state and form expressing space, every state of events is a manifestation of destiny. The milieu which becomes the ground for the motion of a man moving his hand is space and manifestation of destiny.

For a walking man, the places he steps on are space; for a man looking at the sky, sky is space with its stars, clouds, colours, with its whole appearance and state; and is manifestation of destiny. For a man who turned his attention to some point of his body, that point is space and manifestation of destiny. For a man thinking, the imagination is space; the comprehension making connections among events is space and manifestation of destiny. In short, everything seen in the universe, every being, the man itself, is a space and all of these are manifestation of destiny in their own cosmoses. For, formations of all of these, their connecting to each other in various ways, their subjection to analysis and synthesis in the form of innumerable combinations, that is, occurrence of all events and matter states are the various variations of space; and they advance within the function of mechanism of destiny.

*

* *

The beings are continuously in tests and trials because of the freedom they have. Behaviours, positive or negative reactions on the face of these tests and trials, in short, successes and failures, are concluded by the occurrence of matter combinations appreciated and determined by destiny, that is, infinite states and circumstances of spaces; and the beings live in various states of these events in accordance with their degrees of merit. So, each of all events and all matter combinations which put them into effect are only the spaces which are the manifestations of the mechanism of destiny. In short, the minute measurement and calculation of the degrees of the beings according to their acts and behaviours so these can be bonded to the forms after going through applications of accounting in order to be adapted to the states in the original necessities means the effectuation of various matter and event forms and devices, which is done by the mechanism of destiny through using original time, under original necessities.

After this knowledge, it is not right to talk in certain terms about the futures of world mankind who are not yet into the plan of duty and whose states are subjected to tests and trials even down to their smallest movement, by stating names and times. For, mankind concludes the advance of their surroundings and spaces, that is, in one word, of their destiny by themselves in accordance with the directions they use their freedom at. Words about future can be uttered, under some conditions, only at the plans of duty for which the truths are realised. Strict judgements about the future in the world would mean rejecting the authorities of freedom of all mankind. Even an ant which you set free after some point to go to another point either reaches that point by walking on the path at some speed, or makes it longer by spending time around or turning right or left; or it turns back and changes the path completely. All of these determine the forms of the results it will have, that is, its destinies. The knowledge given above up to this point is sufficient to state that among the forces of the original necessities which we accept as descended to the universe symbolically with the light of a projector and which encompass spirits and matter, there are also the mechanism of destiny and original time; and that they play important roles concerning the realisation of the original necessities.

*
* *

Now, we will give you some knowledge about the advance after entering the stage of duty.

The plan of duty is a stage in which evolution can be started and continued on with open comprehension. The automatic and semi-comprehending developments which have reached up to the plan of duty have entered here a complete comprehending stage. And the clear meaning of this is: comprehension of the beings have started to adapt by their own powers to the beams of the cone of light which we said that they climb up in this plan. Because of this, we call the stage of duty as the stage where active adaptations start. As advanced at this stage, comprehension's fields of adaptation to the necessities widen as well, that is, comprehension of the original time that flows as it evolves, adapt in wider scopes to the divine necessities belonging to the spirit and universe relations.

In other words, all comprehension unifies with these necessities and consequently, with each other; and we call this a state of unity, that is, the unitary. Nevertheless, the unity at these initial stages of the plan of duty is yet a long way off from being complete but it has started to occur. For example, now that we accept the infinite necessities of the original principle like an infinite value as (n) which belongs to the relations of the needs of spirits and the possibilities of the universe-substance, the comprehension of the beings at this stage has yet adapted in a very small scale at the initial stages of duty. And with whichever necessities comprehension has entered into harmony, that is, the state of unity, there it becomes truth. And that being makes up a part of the harmony there. So, this is participation in harmony, to become part of the harmony. This knowledge also explains the meaning of the statement that the plan of duty is a plan of realisation. So, in tandem with the start of this plan, comprehension proceeds to penetrate into the universe truths with greater power. That is, within the harmony of these truths its scope increases.

Similarly, this knowledge explains another great truth as well. Various beings who have reached a state of reconciliation upon the same necessities have become a unity with each other as well. Therefore, in the various stages of the plan of duty, there are various duty groups which have unified upon certain necessities, becoming a unity. Among them, unlike in the world, there are no differences in realities. For, they are actually in harmony with the truths. There, there are not realities but truths. Nevertheless, we repeat that this harmony has not immediately contained the whole of the plan of duty. The complete and total harmony is only possible at the unitary; and this is still at a distance which can be deemed as infinity relative to the initial stages of the plan of duty.

*
* *

At the unitary, there are no realities any more. The original necessities which are the original principle's flux in universe, the mechanism of destiny and the original time which are the flux of the principles of destiny and time in the universe put into effect the unity by joining with the comprehensions there. That place is the truth itself. It is the last boundary of the universe and the expression of the realisation of evolution. The whole administration of the universe is possible only with the permeating influences filtrating from here.

*
* *

Traversing the paths which seem endless, starting from the initial stages of the plan of duty up to the unitary occurs also through very complicated mechanisms. In order to give knowledge about this topic, let us go back to the moment when the base of the cone of light in the symbolic projector was at the initial stages of the plan of duty. The beings started to climb up towards the top of this cone of light. We have mentioned about the comprehensions here which become partners on certain necessities and that they entered into a state of a single being.

Such a state does not exist in the realm below the plan of duty, for example, in the world. Since it is not possible for mankind to reach any truth at all, mankind lives only in the relativities of the truth, that is, in the realities. Because of this, whatever the number of comprehensions in the world is, there are the same number of realities. This is because, in the world there is not the truth itself but relative and miscellaneous manifestations of truths which vary in accordance with various capacities of the comprehensions. The things which can be valued in accordance with each comprehension's own capacity will certainly be different from each other. Because of this, in the world complete agreement and unity of comprehension upon any point is not possible. This can only start from the plan of duty.

These reconciliations which start at the plan of duty load some deeds and duties on the beings and subject them to some obligations – in accordance with the width of their fields of adaptation. And they widen their fields of adaptation more according to the degree of merit they will acquire while rendering their obligations; and they climb up the higher steps of the stages of plan of duty which arises towards the unitary.

However, these obligations of beings, as it may come up to mind in the lower plans, are not things that are given or taken. For after all, entering into a state of reconciliation with truth means unifying with it; and the true meaning of what we call obligation emerges from this unity. Therefore, as the beings rise up at the stages of duty, their obligations increase automatically under the mechanism of destiny. No one charges the beings in the plan of duty with obligations, as long as they increase the merit of their obligations regarding the mechanism of destiny. So, in this case, the beings in there are not completely free of the tests and trials either.

*
* *

Now, let us state the way of occurrence of the merits of these obligations. We have said that the beings' first step into their unity of comprehensions in the universe, under the necessities of the mechanism of destiny, begins at the plan of duty; and we have said that this is the comprehensions' attainment or realisation of the necessities, truths. So, the imperative which results in the beings' obligation of duty is because of this realisation. These realisations advance together with perceptual time mechanism. And the beings in duty are already subject to the conditions of perceptual time and space.

It is because the realisation – which we symbolised with the symbolic projector – means the adaptation of comprehensions to the original necessities; initial realisations start at the initial stages of the plan of duty and by gradually rising, reach its final scope at the unitary. Therefore, the beings' rising by climbing up the beam of the original principle light which ascends to the universe means the adaptation of comprehensions to all necessities that exist within the scope of those light beams, their entering into its harmony and increasingly merging into that harmony in wider scope.

When this climbing reaches the last boundary of possibility of the universe which we call the unitary, then that being's comprehension has adapted to all necessities contained by this beam of light, has become complete in harmony and consequently, attained a state of prevalence over the parts and the whole of universe. That is, it has merged into that great harmony as if it has became the universe itself. Thus, starting from the first stage of the plan of duty as the beings gradually climb up the original principle light, they enter states of prevalence over the universe parts at degrees of their harmony with the points they are in; and this prevalence is completed within the unitary.

*
* *

As to the manifestational way of these obligations, the realised obligations, with this realisation, have already entered into applications of these truths. And each of these applications is an obligation as well. In this way, the application of certain truths imperatively results in the cooperation of certain comprehensions. And from that point on, the imperativeness of some cadres and organisation systems emerges. Because of this, here, we need to talk about the cadres. This is a truth that no possible state in the universe is thinkable outside the necessity, imperativeness of evolution and the mechanism of destiny. There is nothing like arbitrariness.

This principle is valid and unchangeable for all groups, all connections, and all cadres. Therefore, the cadres are the imperative results of the organisation systems that need to be engaged in the universal mechanisms depending on the sublime necessities which are determinant in the execution of completions and fluxes in universe. Every organisation system, in whichever cadre it should work, is built and performs according to it. So, establishment of the cadres should be in accordance with the basic principles, main mechanisms. For example, the performance of the mechanism of destiny which we talked about is regulated with the activities of organisation systems which are established within certain cadres.

*
* *

247

There are three main cadres in the universe, in accordance with the necessities which are filtrating from the unitary.

1. Cadre, plan and techniques of the beings in duty in the cadre of the original principle.

2. Cadres and techniques of the beings which are included in the cadre of mechanisms of destiny.

3. Plans and techniques of the beings which are included in the cadre of the mechanism of original time; and the issues providing their entire realities particular to themselves.

So, there are innumerable organisations – connected to these three main cadres – which execute the necessities belonging to the evolutions of spirits in universe with all details and the great organisation systems which are made out of these organisations which are interconnected through hierarchical orders. All of these are made up of beings in duty on behalf of others or on their own account in accomplishing the uncountable deeds to be done in universe, starting from the initial stages of the plan of duty up to the unitary; and these beings in duty execute their duties within their organisations without even deviating a hair's breadth, under the principles and directives of the above-mentioned three main and coordinated cadres of duty which descend from the unitary.

These duties are the innumerable deeds belonging to various realms. For example, there are duties executed by innumerable and interconnected organisations such as the time stations particular to the world, the stations managing the coarse kinetic motions, the stations managing the individual and the small communal evolutionary plans; and finally, the stations with ever-expanding scopes conducting and executing the general evolutionary leaps, plans and related matter transformations of the masses with wider scope. Among these duties are the deeds of a great organisation which is from the sublime plan of duty and engaged in the great revolutionary activities of today's world, including as well the activities for putting this book into effect.

So, in this way, the beings engaged in the universe deeds with ever-increasing scope take a stand proper to the merit of duty in accordance with duty, within a system organisation and a principle of coordination and cooperation and an order of hierarchy. This procession, as it evolves in this way, continues within an order, sequence and harmony onwards to the unitary where the evolution – that can be intuited by its expression in our universe – is realised.

*
* *

We have stated that organisation systems are established starting with the plan of duty. Similarly, we have said that the initial organisation has started at the initial stages of the plan of duty. Now, it is necessary to give the necessary knowledge about the initial establishment of the organisations.

Previously, it has been mentioned that mankind, having completed their time in the world, cannot directly pass to the plan of duty and will remain in a semi-subtle realm for a while. For, before mankind passes to the plan of duty, they need to regulate some aspects of their life which they cannot yet complete in the world in accordance with the necessities of the world, which are, for example, the current circumstances of the world; and it is only possible for them to live for a while in this semi-subtle realm.

As to the semi-subtle realm, there, all of the world realities and conditions have ended but the new states of that place are preparatory to the duty and complementary for the deficient sides of mankind. And this deficient side is the true aspect of love that will manifest there, which mankind intuited but could not recognise while in the world. That place is a plan of love.

In this plan, the comprehension of duty in the plan of duty has not yet begun but within the applications and obligations of the love in there – in qualities unknown by mankind – there are components which gradually constitute the merits of comprehension of duty. Of course, these preparations in there are subject to perceptual time technique which is beyond simple time comprehension.

So, after the beings who have passed into the semi-subtle spend some time in there and did sufficient preparations, they gradually start, in groups of three or five, to do initial preparations belonging to the necessities of the plan of duty. The only point which can be intuited by mankind about the communications in these groupings is the concept that love has various variations which shift towards the duty. However, mankind can understand neither this love nor its variations in the true sense.

So, these beings who render the last preparations of entering the plan of duty with their small constituted groups, during their applications pass to the initial stages of the plan of duty by shifting with a silent, undetected and extremely sweet flow; and they are immediately assigned with deeds belonging to the initial stages of the plan of duty. They now become the beings in duty in carrying out the plan of duty, working as individuals while preserving their small group in there because of the mechanism of adaptation which we explained above in detail. Since, in there, there are no transitions such as death and rebirth, unlike in the world, this transition occurs, as we have said, as an awakening and with very sweet impressions. In the semi-subtle realm, there is no death. For, the subtlety of matter in there does not entail such intense transitions. These states are only imperatives which are valid in the coarse matter cosmos belonging to our world.

*

* *

In the plan of duty, there is no question of uniqueness, that is, any activity as a single individual. In there, only groups work. However, each group is considered a single individual. That is, every individual of that group is the group itself and the group is the one individual. Therefore, assignment of a being in duty in the plan of duty, for example with a deed, means the assignment of the whole group to which that being in duty is subject. This is because all of the comprehensions in that group congregate upon that duty as a single comprehension. Therefore, here there is no question of separate identities. And this is one of the characters – which is unknown and impossible to apply in the world – of the wholeness in the plan of duty. For example, in very rare cases, a single embodied being in duty who has taken on the duty of creating a worldwide movement and come down to the world with a great duty is single and separated from his plan, while in the world. However, he is not a single being who is a member of his plan which supports him but the organs of the organisation in a state of unity to which the whole of that being is subject.

*
* *

We have said that the plan of duty is the plan of adaptation to the necessities. Therefore, it becomes an imperative for the comprehensions which have adapted to necessities, to harmonise with each other and to constitute a unity. In this way, a duty group or a single organism, made up of three or five persons who have passed to the plan of duty, begins to do its first duty within a complete cooperation. This first duty is deeds belonging to the lowermost stages of the plan of duty. For, starting from this stage, on the path to unity there are infinite stages more to go through in order to reach the purpose, that is, to adapt the whole of the original necessities and to merge completely with the harmony. Between the unitary and these initial stages of duty, there are innumerable activities, deeds, duties and states.

However, even at these initial and relatively simple stages there are very great deeds and duties in world measurement. For example, they are assigned with the evolution of a man in the world; a part of the beings in duty and who support the more or less small and large groups such as guardian spirits, guardian angels, helpers, teachers of the classical spiritualists, occultists and mystic schools are generally the beings who belong to this stage of the plan of duty. At the same time, they can be used – even as semi-comprehending – in other greater deeds by more superior organisations than them.

*
* *

Let us name the initial stage of the plan of duty (A). Here, as the duty groups works, of course, they are always under the control and even directives of the influences coming from above. Actually, this situation is valid and imperative at all stages of the plan of duty up to the unitary. The symbol of the cone of light descending from the unitary – which we previously gave – always explains this imperative. As a duty group works at plan (A) under the supervision of a higher group of duty at plan (B) we call the higher group (B) as the organiser and the group at plan (A) the organ.

So, the groups at stage (A) swiftly take distances on the flow of the original time by rendering duties with the perceptual time technique and because of these activities, they widen their fields of adaptation. In the mean time, their deeds, duties and obligations increase and widen their scope accordingly. In this way, they pass to the higher plan, that is, plan (B). Now it is easily understood that passing these groups to plan (B) means the expansion of their fields of adaptation accordingly. That is, as these groups pass to stage (B), as a result of the joining their comprehension with the comprehension of some other groups, larger groups occur which have an increased number of individuals and consequently have increased comprehension; and of course, comprehension also widens accordingly.

This means that, rising from the lower stages to the higher stages, at the higher stages numbers of groups decrease as individuals of groups increase. And the scope of the comprehension level in the group which joined the contribution of the comprehension of the individuals in the other group swiftly widens; and this is a natural result of the imperativeness of adaptations. As the fields of adaptation widen, groups unify and the number of groups decrease. This situation continues onwards up to the unitary; relatively small organisations of the previous plans which unified within the much wider organisations as they rise to the higher stages, when they reach the unitary, congregate as a single organisation.

Here, all comprehension enters into a state of singular comprehension. That immense comprehension becomes a force which can be intuited by no man. Now, it cannot be named as an organisation or a plan. It is, as becoming one and single, everything within the wholeness of the force belonging to the universe with all possibilities, necessities, comprehensions and the whole of the universe. And we can only express this as the comprehension of unity which we call the unitary.

*
* *

Here, we will state a point which we previously mentioned, for the last time. It should not be thought that with the above expressions a theory of pantheism has been meant which is valid in the world. What has been said here are only necessities and truths belonging to the matter-universe. In the book it has been repeated over and over that the matter-universe is but a means, as well. The end of these means is the realisation of the part of the needs of the spirits belonging to our universe which we can name as evolution; and this is expressed by the unitary. Therefore, the knowledge given in the above sentences belong only to what is afoot in our universe. Beyond it, there are such endless needs and truths and unattainabilities that even the word infinity is a far cry to express it; and the universe cannot afford them and universe comprehension cannot reach them.

Actually, as has been openly stated in the first parts of the book, the purpose of all these universe events and universe occurrences is the realisation of the states of the truths – which we call spirits that we never know about their qualities – which are accepted as the evolution belonging to our universe and symbolised by the concept of need. And the unitary which we cannot completely comprehend is the expression of this realisation. Everything comes to the universe from there; the universe is governed from there. The plenary beams of light which conduct the universe and make the universe exist by becoming every speck of universe gush from there.

*
* *

In short, the unitary is a total comprehension, necessity and possibility of universe which cannot be grasped by the beings and which can be reached by them only after entering there. To tell mankind further than this is impossible and unnecessary.

YOU, WHO CAN BE YOU WITH MATTER

AND NOTHING WITH EVERYTHING

AND CAN ADAPT TO THE HARMONY

OF THIS EVERYTHING, LONG FOR THE

MOMENT WHEN YOU WILL BE OF

THAT HARMONY

The Earth is an organ within the solar system. As all organs, it also has certain life-cycles, developmental stages, transformations, and innumerable states of equilibrium which are disrupted and rebalanced by the uncountable influences it receives from the surroundings and above. And the explanation which we will make here about the forthcoming revolution – which is the last of the countless revolutions the world has been through so far – will make the knowledge in the last part of the book easier to understand.

*
* *

Approximately 70,000 years ago, there were mainly two great continents in the world. One of them was filling the space where the Pacific Ocean now exists. This was a vast piece of land, wider at the north and narrower at the south. Mankind call this the Continent of Mu. The other one was a vast continent which occupied the space where the Atlantic Ocean is now. There were a great number of islands, archipelagos, pieces of land which today the Himalayas occupy and other small continents filling in between these two vast continents. That was the landscape of the world of those times. Therefore, back then, there was a different constitution of terra instead of the current state of geography.

*
* *

Upon these continents, humans who were much more advanced and civilised than the mankind of today's world had been living. Their knowledge and technical prowess were way beyond those of mankind in today's world. For example, they had discovered radioactive substances, radios, televisions, electronic gadgets and other technology, which have recently started to be discovered in today's world. This technology existed a long time ago – in comparison with the history of mankind in today's world – before the submerging of their world, and they had even discovered and begun to use atomic energy a thousand years before their own revolution.

Nevertheless, they also had relatively simple, even savage tribes besides these well-civilised and advanced communities. However, even those savages were in a much more evolved state than the savages that exist in today's world. In short, mankind in the last world had a civilisation which surpassed in every field that of today.

*
* *

This state of mankind who had reached the pinnacle of development in the world had developed in them such pride and an excess state of claiming omnipotence that this state led them to acts prone to disturbing the natural circumstances of the world by unconventional ways through increasingly embedding them in the coarse matter of the hydrogen cosmos. And as a consequence of this they gave in to luxury, riches, comfort, matter worship, selfishness and all kinds of desires; they immersed themselves in the coarse combinations of the hydrogen atom and expected to get all their happiness from these combinations; and this was a last strenuous exertion of the beings caused by the material advancement and developments which had reached the final limit – a kind of degeneration. This degeneration is very natural and a harbinger of every great revolution that occurs.

*
* *

In surrounding environments, developments advance communally. All beings that constitute that surrounding – from the smallest to the largest – develop and rise according to their degrees. For example, as mankind become the most evolved beings of the world, each of the other beings that live within the inclusion of world plans advances towards the higher stages of their developmental possibilities. And cancers constitute the most obvious example of this.

Towards the last cycles of the world back then some diseases had emerged for which mankind did not know the reason. One of

258

them was cancer. The increase of cases of cancer among mankind is the degeneration observed in the cells, depending on the reason we have just mentioned.

Each of the cells and organs in the human bodies is a material ground of life for the relatively primitive beings. They render their own developments in these matter fields and within the possibilities those field provide. A moment comes when these simple beings which develop in time cannot obtain the things they need to develop further out of the matter they are in. That is, these matter possibilities and conditions become too barren to let them gain further leaps. However, developmental leaps of the beings never stop and they always want to go further without any restriction.

Whereas this state is seen as normal progress in the milieus which have abundant possibilities, in the matter milieus where such possibilities become barren and insufficient fields are left for the wider and further leaps, it causes some acts and behaviours of the beings which are observed as abnormal, unusual and degenerated; accompanied with their strenuous efforts, uneasiness, confusion and bewilderment. And such were the states of the beings which governed matter milieus, that is, the cells that become cancerous at the periods just before the submerging of the continent of Mu. Milieus of material development belonging to the lot of these beings who exist in the body organism had become unyielding for their further advancement.

For example, a skin cell which constitutes the body has at best a certain field of functioning, assigned for it. The somatic state of the body is not suitable for this cell to surpass it. Such a surpassing does not fit with the harmony of the body. The primitive being that made that cell a developmental milieu for itself could obtain the development it needed as it perfectly functioned at the beginning. However a moment came that it completed this developmental cycle. It started to feel the need to prepare for the higher developmental milieus. Accustomed biological conditions and possibilities which that cell existed in were not in a state to respond to these needs of advanced activity. Therefore, the cell being became unable to fit into its body.

As a result of this situation, that primitive being that had used a normal skin cell in usual and proper ways then started to make a strenuous effort to orientate in a direction outside of the body order and harmony. This strenuous effort caused some states and situations of that cell within the skin community which were not in accordance with that community so that this naturally put into effect a disordered state in its development which is called cancerous. It is certain that this cancerous state of the skin cell, orientated to the activities outside of the harmony and order within the skin organism, is merely the last resort of the being who tries strenuously to complete a developmental stage and to pass into a higher stage but cannot find any possibility for it within the conditions it is in.

As to the body organism which seems here as if it was wronged; actually it does not lose anything and renders the automatic service and assistance it has taken on in the issue of preparing ground for the evolution of other beings. By doing this duty, in the face of the mechanism of destiny, it will also acquire spatial merits, which is a higher manifestation of destiny and so, benefits from the wider possibilities of the passing to the higher plan; and this means its leaping to a further stage, its development.

Therefore, there is no wrong or injustice. We have previously said that each individual of a one hundred person communal plan obtains his own evolution by working for those one hundred persons. Everybody, from the smallest to the largest, always gains leaps forward and rises by depending on another, exchanging with each other. In none of these acts directed to this ascension is there injustice, punishment, reward, malice, disaster for any being. Everything is the result of the acquired merits by the measurement of the mechanism of destiny and of the efforts spent on this path.

*
* *

Thus, during the last times of the previous world cycle, the beings had become very close or at the final limits of their developments within the matter milieus they are. This situation was such for all beings evolving in the matter milieus at every stage from cells which constitute the bodies of mankind and all other high world beings from plants, to animals and to humans. For this reason, cancerous diseases had increased. And again, for this reason, mankind become dissolute and begun to trash about with the need of going outside of the matter conditions which become unresponsive to their further leaps.

However, despite the fact that in order to satisfy their higher needs which spill over the conditions of world matter should they have directed their activities to those conditions beyond matter (these conditions have been previously explained) mankind could not do this and had attempted to seek their needs within the conditions of the coarse hydrogen atom world which they live in. When they could not find the happiness they sought there, they strenuously made effort to console themselves by burying deeper into those matter. And this situation put into effect the scene of the degeneration of mankind, their becoming cancerous; and this is a necessity and natural characteristic which is generally seen, at the beginning of every revolution, of every evolutionary cycle.

In order to explain it well, we give an example. Imagine a penniless man dreaming of being a millionaire and expecting all his happiness from these millions; and after eight or ten years, he possesses that much money. When he sees that the happiness he expected to come with the millions did not come in spite of his current riches, what will he do? When he sees that the expected happiness did not come with the money, he will try to forget his frustration by burying himself in his money; and this will cause him to be confused and bewildered. Whereas he could understood that this happiness will not come with money and he could seek it elsewhere. But he cannot do this. When he cannot find the happiness he sought and sees that he gets completely distanced from it, he falls into more unhappiness.

In short, mankind during the previous world cycle who completed their cycle by using the last possibilities of world matter did not want to think that expecting superior results from the world matter which become unable to offer possibilities for further leaps of the beings would be like pressing oil out of marble; and despite all the efforts they made they could not find the happiness they sought in matter and could not reach any satisfactory or consoling result for their needs of further leaps. This situation confused them more, put them into insoluble confusion, irritated and degenerated their states in matter. By the efforts and wishes to satisfy their essence-needs of their essence-beings of which they do not know and cannot find out about, mankind took the wrong path and got stuck into world matter.

The meaningless pride, fruitless obstinacy, failures which emerged as every venture remained abortive that occurred in them as a consequence of this situation created confusions, disappointments and turned them into a riddle, even incomprehensible to themselves. Then mankind became restless beings who attack here and there in vain, without comprehending what to do. This small observation, which we will remind you among the innumerable daily samples of small examples from such states of confusion and bewilderment into which mankind falls in similar circumstances, will be sufficient to give a simple idea about this topic. A child, who liked to kill birds with his slingshot a few days ago, comes upon the carcass in the road of a bird which died on its own and feels pangs and tries to bury it, spending lots of effort. However, this pang of his does not stop him from killing other birds with his slingshot a few days later. It is possible to expand the scope of this small example among mankind and to obtain possibilities of expanded observation about the states of confusion that mankind is in.

And all these states were the expressions of reaching the threshold of a revolution. For surely there would be a reciprocity of the merits of the beings – who had now felt their higher needs and started to writhe about amidst those needs – which measured, calculated and appreciated in the mechanism of destiny; and this was a great revolution of the world, which would allow them to reach higher spaces which they deserved; and this was the reason that the world was at the brink of a great revolution.

*
* *

As we said about the being of the cancerous cell, this writhing of mankind was not meaningless. The meaning here was expressing that the essence-being could not be contained any more and started to feel the need to reach higher developments, leaps, results and acquisition.

On the face of the mechanism of destiny; no merit is left ne-glected, no willing which is orientated towards further leaps and in accordance with original necessities is rejected, no strenuous effort or writhing is in vain; and especially no need of the essence-being is left unfulfilled. All of these are minutely measured, calculated in the mechanism of destiny; and out of new fields of possibilities, that is, of the milieus of development which are most suitable to these needs, occur the manifestations – as in the manner we previ-ously explained – which are spatialised with the original time measurements; that is, the destiny manifests.

So, the mankind of the previous world cycle – who had been ma-tured and entered into a state of inability to benefit from world-matter – were in such expectation of the high spaces and high realms which will fulfil their high destinies and further needs. And the ones who had not yet attained this degree were seeking the milieus suffi-cient for their simple states and needs. Thus, for all those needs to be realised it was necessary for the world to change and consequently, for the new spaces, that is, the new destinies which will fulfil the new needs to emerge. Indeed, it would not be appropriate for the indigent mankind in these two groups which are separated from each other by major differences to exist in the same milieu.

*
* *

So, as a result of these high developmental necessities, the world was preparing for the realisation of a revolution, a day of transi-tion. This revolution of the world would occur, as it did in every cycle, first by disruption of its equilibrium and then by restoration of it. As of the initial indications of this disruption of equilibrium, at this or that part of the Continent of Mu, tremors, ruptures, vol-canic eruptions had started to be observed which could not be pre-vented by the power of mankind. These incidents continued for 80–100 years by increasing, intensifying and getting more frequent.

The destined day was approaching and mankind were running towards their deserved destinies. A great majority of mankind had prepared their merits at the higher spaces. And they would go there. The ones who would enter the moment of transition without preparation would yet remain in the world after the period of revolution was closed; and they would live in this world to cultivate their remaining sides for some short or long periods of time until they acquire their merits. These two classes of hordes of mankind which were unable to live together in regard to their needs were approaching a fork in the road in order to continue their developments on separate paths and spaces. When this day of transition which was imperative and determined by destiny would came to happen no power could stop it. Then everything would be a *fait accompli*, the measurement of the merits would be disclosed and the consequences of the beings acquired in the face of the mechanism of destiny and original time would be realised. Eventually, the day of transition arrived.

*
* *

One day, as everybody was busy with their daily life, all of a sudden the ground started to move in all continents, that is, all over the world. Still at the beginning of this quaking, most of the magnificent buildings, glorious temples, ornamental palaces collapsed and the majority of the big cities were devastated. A great number of mankind were trapped under the collapsed buildings and died.

Continents were destroyed; sea water rushed inland; the Earth was fissured; fleeing mankind in terror and fear died in their masses. This turmoil continued for three days and on the third day both of these two continents submerged; and so disappeared these two vast continents of the world; one into the depths of Pacific Ocean and the other into the Atlantic Ocean. The whole appearance of the world changed and took on its current geographical state.

*
* *

After the Mu period ended, the world regressed and became wild. The people who survived in the world regressed under two influences. One of these was the terrible – to them – events that occurred during the great cataclysm; these had a shocking effect on the nervous systems of the mankind and made them crazy. The

264

second was much more significant and encompassing. This was the imperative of a developmental plan the beings in duty in this act prepared in accordance with sublime necessities.

The world had started a new cycle. This cycle was a state of the world which was most primitive, akin to amorphous and simple. This was necessary to be as such. For, there were innumerable beings waiting to complete their subhuman developmental stages and to start their stages of initial humanity. They were to come down to the world as the most primitive humans and to start their developments. However, the world could not be a sanctuary, a ground of evolution for these primitive beings without going through such a revolution and going down to simpler states which may be suitable for the needs of the newcomers. For example, had they came into a world like the evolved one of today, not only could they not evolve here, they could not have even lived. Therefore, they needed the simplest matter and also the most primitive parents in order to render the developments they need.

From reasonable, more or less conscious and comprehending parents such a horde of cannibalistic and savage children could not be born and live among and evolve among them. This was impossible for children as well as for parents. These children were the beings who had their first step into the stage of humanity of the world life with their simplicity, primitiveness, inexperience and lack of manner. Because of this, they were coming into the world with the need to live within all characteristics of the savagery period which is the character of initial humanity and of going through all refining experiences of that cycle.

Thus, they needed wild matter, wild surroundings, wild plants, wild animals, and wild parents. Therefore, in accordance with the communal necessities of the general evolutionary and developmental mechanism in universe, for the ones who remained in the world to be able to do this parenting duty automatically they needed to regress to the states of mankind in the initial stages and to simplify. The world, by subjecting to a very long evolutionary advance starting from this simple and primitive period and by going through various developmental stages could reach today's level and civilisation of mankind, after 70,000 years.

*
* *

The submergence of the continents we stated above which coincided with the closing of the previous world cycle have been described in the books of religion by two great symbolic events. One of these is Noah's Deluge and the other is Judgement Day.

According to the Deluge symbol, the entire world is covered by waters; all living creatures die except those who remained in Noah's Ark and are saved. And after the waters recede, life in the world continues. The real meaning this symbol carries is that a cycle in the world is completely closed and a new cycle of humanity is opened.

As for the Judgement Day symbol; this symbol is much more encompassing than the Deluge symbol. Here, a last day of the world is to arrive and on that day the ending of mankind will be determined; the meritorious ones will pass into higher spaces and the ones who do not suffice will remain at tormenting places. And this clear expression of the Judgement Day symbol is the end of the world itself which we mentioned above.

Nevertheless, every religion carries the purpose of saving mankind from self-indulgence and conveying them to the understanding of duty. To achieve this purpose, every religion has utilised every means mankind can understand and regulated its commands accordingly.

Those of mankind who could reach the stages of religion at this cycle of the world, although they progressed further than the ones at previous stages, have not reached their current level of understanding and point of view as of today. Besides, in their essence-beings there were excess impressions of terror belonging to the previous catastrophe which was not so long ago. They were scrutinising the events emotionally rather than in regard to knowledge and comprehension; they were benefiting from events on this path; and the main component of this emotional side was – as we have said – fear. This feeling – which is even valid in the majority of today's mankind – was completely prevailing over consciences back then.

And religions have utilised the instincts of this fear for the development of mankind and established some significant evolutionary automatisms by them. In short, in earlier times mankind have started to do preparations belonging to the intuition of the knowledge of duty only under the influence of these fears and could more or less reach their current power of the intuition of duty.

Because of this, religions have seen that symbols of the Deluge and Judgement Day which illustrates the submergence of the world within the qualities of reward and punishment were necessary and beneficiary in order to give automatic understanding of the responsibility of duty to mankind who yet lived in the reality of fear, by utilising the fearful and sensational sides of these symbols. Thus, two birds had been killed with one stone. One of these was to give to mankind at least the primitive intuition of a great truth; and secondly – which was more important back then – was to ensure that mankind embraced semi-comprehendingly some duties of humanity – even out of fear of punishment – and their entering into developmental harmony.

We may explain this better with this small and simple example: when thunder is heard, a mother may say, 'If you do not eat, Pa Thunder will get you!' to her young toddler who fusses about his dinner. Believing this and out of fear, the child immediately starts to eat so Pa Thunder does not get him; and the purpose is served. Here the intended end is to make the child do his duty, whose necessity he has not yet comprehended, by scaring him. He does this and grows up as he benefits; and when it is time he learns about what Pa Thunder is; and then he obtains more encompassing results from this knowledge. This applies to mankind as well.

Most of the time, great religious leaders have had to act as this mother did; and have accustomed mankind to the preparation of the intuition of duty through these processes which were suitable to the time and the space by commanding goodness, honesty, altruism, self-sacrifice and especially a great number of other forms of worship. And by means of this habituation mankind could rise to the level of today's intuition of duty.

Had not religions benefited from these fearful feelings of mankind through these symbols which have played a precious role in their development and had they attempted to disseminate the truth among people only with the purpose of expanding the cadre of knowledge as it is done today; they would be way too distant in rendering the feelings of duty which mankind have just started to intuit in this state. Moreover, for the mankind of those times it would not be possible to understand and believe the truths as they are.

*

* *

Today, the cycle of knowledge, logic and comprehension prevails, not the cycle of fear and feeling. Therefore, the symbols, allegorical explanations and expressions the great religions used imperatively in the past in the face of the truths do not give the intended results regarding today's comprehension. Today, we need to state the truths openly, as they are. For, mankind has now reached the last maturation points of the hydrogen atom cosmos; and they put their steps on its threshold in order to go out of the gate of this immense realm. And this threshold can be passed over only by the maturity of knowledge and comprehension.

These words carry clear expressions. The hydrogen stage is the beginning of the realm of beings which is a cosmos that follows a mechanical developmental stage which is dark, vast and long as infinity; and which belongs to the initial stage of matter in the evolutions of spirits. This cosmos constitutes an immensely micrometric and macrometric universe with all its spheres, solar systems, nebulae which are observed by mankind; and when we speak of the matter-universe, mankind see and accept this universe only. For, this is the cosmos in which mankind live and are bound to. Even though this cosmos seems infinite to them, it is actually a certain and small section of the universe – which contains the infinite developmental stages of matter substance – particular to the possibilities of the hydrogen atom that we call the hydrogen stage or hydrogen cosmos. And within this hydrogen cosmos, all objects, occurrences and realities which are subject to the mechanisms of time and space particular to themselves and defined as matter by mankind are gathered.

Among those ensembles, there are nebulae in uncountable numbers. These nebulae contain billions of solar systems. These systems are constituted of various matter-parts – that is, planets which revolve around a nucleus and constitute a whole with that nucleus. And one of the planets of these systems is the Earth. The world, in the point of view connected to the comprehension of the hydrogen stage, having no value as of a point within an immense matter-being, is actually not small and insignificant as it is seen within the hydrogen cosmos. The world is one of the last stations of this very long and semi-comprehending matter cosmos called the hydrogen stage. And one of the gates of this immense and infinite cosmos which opens to a more infinite universe of sublime duty and organisation is found at the stages of humanity in the world. Therefore, now the imperative of explaining the truths below that are needed to be known by mankind without needing any symbols at all.

Within the innumerable nebulae which constitute the developmental milieus of the hydrogen cosmos, there are billions time billions of solar systems. In every solar system there are various spheres. Around every sphere there is a magnetic field particular to that sphere. Out of the established relations of the spheres by adapting each other in a system, the particular magnetic field synthesis of this system is put into effect. These magnetic fields of the system are in relation and at balance with each other.

One of the spheres of the system revolves around itself in its place. This is called the sun or the nucleus. The others revolve around this nucleus. They are called planets. Contrary to the assumption, planets of a system are not parts which are broken off and separated from the sun of that system. They have been constituted – by the mechanisms we previously explained – separately within the nebulae which that system is connected to; and are connected to each other by the motions that occurred as the result of relations and equilibria of their magnetic fields in accordance with their developmental degrees. Therefore, it is not correct to place the sun at some place by assigning privilege to it and to place the planets another side. The sun also takes its place within the degrees of the system and mingles with its planets. And its degree is not superior to the planets but below most of them. However, as we will say a little later, in the sun, the larger gathering of the beings in duty, who take a role in the management of all planets results in giving to it an especial place within the system.

So, in this way, the sun and the planets of every system are satisfactorily graded and regulated for the needs of all beings – from the simplest to the most evolved – who are in that system to grow up.

Therefore, every planet of a system has taken on the function of preparing the beings for the superior possibilities of a superior planet than itself.

Besides the simple beings who evolve within a system, in all backward spheres and especially in the sun of the system, there are powerful beings of the plan of duty who are engaged with the duty of conducting all kinds of possibilities pertaining to the evolutions of the embodied beings who have reached the advanced developmental stages within that system. Those beings are not embodied by the matter of those spheres. Their bodies are made up with materials gathered from higher matter milieus that do not belong to the hydrogen cosmos. In this regard, it is inappropriate to call them bodies. They themselves gather this matter in a most suitable way for executing their obligations. And they do their duties by using this subtle matter as means among one or several spheres of that system which are suitable to their duties. They can exist on any sphere they wish, as long as it is not considered as incarnation. For example, if needed they can visit the Sun, the Moon, Mars or Jupiter. These are the beings of the plan of duty who execute duties in the applications of various orders of systems.

Nevertheless, as we said, besides these, in the spheres there are real inhabitants of those spheres who embodied to evolve. They are, as in the world, embodied beings who built bodies out of a sphere and by connecting them, they use those bodies during their lives in that sphere. These beings, in all other planets of our solar system, are simpler and more backward than the ones in our world. They jump up to higher spheres after developing through uncountable embodiments in the spheres they are in and eventually reach the most evolved sphere of their system. In our system, this evolved sphere is – as we have said – the Earth; and its most evolved being is man.

So, the beings in duty in a system we have just mentioned assist in various ways in the developments of the simple embodied beings in the systems. Eventually, the embodied beings who have completed the most evolved sphere of that system, for example the Earth in our system, enter into states of concluding the hydrogen cosmos and acquiring the merit for higher realms.

Therefore, billions of beings pass to the superior realms of duty in the universe from the billions of evolved spheres of the billions of systems of the uncountable nebulae of the hydrogen cosmos.

*
* *

The most evolved planet of our solar system is our world, the Earth sphere. And contrary to the assumption, in the other planets of the system, for example in Mars or in the Sun, there are not more evolved beings than the ones in the world. Although Mars is one of the evolved planets of our solar system, the beings here are less evolved than the ones in the world. One of the most backward planets of our solar system is Pluto.[19] The most evolved being of this planet is more backward than the most backward being of our world, which is fungi.

Likewise, the Sun is a backward sphere of the system as well. Actually, the beings in duty, who govern the other planets of the system and especially the world rather exist in the Sun because the simplicity of Sun matter makes it easier to manipulate. However, as we have said, these beings in duty can circulate in other planets as well. And they can execute duties in every sphere.

Thus, in our solar system, the place of gathering, where beings live who have completed the developmental stages of the hydrogen cosmos and, upon receiving their diplomas, are to be promoted to the higher cosmos, is the Earth. Our world has now started preparations for opening the gates of the cosmoses deserved by the mankind the world carries upon itself and who are about to complete their duties in this cycle of the past 70,000 years that followed the closing of the Mu cycle; and to close the gate of the hydrogen cosmos which exhausted its possibilities, behind them.

*
* *

---

[19] *Pluto*: Originally (from its discovery in 1930 until 2006) classified as the ninth planet from the Sun, Pluto was recategorised as a dwarf planet and plutoid, owing to the discovery that it is only one of several large bodies within the Kuiper belt, which is a region of the Solar System beyond the planets and similar to the asteroid belt, but it is far larger. (*Publisher*)

Life on Earth is a complete complex of motions and events. Mankind who is immersed and stuck within these events, sometimes sees around opposite events, contradictions and they assume them as disorder. However, this vision is wrong and a result of misinterpreting the events, especially because of the lack of knowledge about the causality principle.

The ones who look at the world through the power of knowledge which helps to connect the effects of the events to their causes are soon to see that there is an immense harmony and an orderly sequencing in its every state, every event and every being – from its smallest particle to its whole. Orderly and devised occurrences of the bonds of causality put into effect the great universal harmony. So, in order to observe this harmony, it is necessary to think upon the relations of causality and cause between all the events which lend mankind the intuition that every motion and event are directly and indirectly interconnected through infinite bonds; and to try to see and hear something in this field.

In order to ensure this thinking and vision, it is necessary to review the knowledge we previously gave that nothing is without a reason in the universe and everything concludes. There, we have given sufficient knowledge about the causality principle. The ones who follow this principle as they examine life on Earth can see many events and states of occurrences which are interconnected as one concludes another and another causes the other, within a successive and harmonious flux. Devices, schemes and actions which advance towards great purposes within this flux make mankind feel intensely the existence of a great harmony in the universe.

Take a small bird egg, for instance. Taken by itself, this simple bird egg has innumerable ordered and devised states which are connected to each other by immense results. Let us trace the life of the egg which is connected to this great harmony. In time, a hatchling is made out of this egg. In order for this hatchling to develop, it has to be kept at a certain degree of warmth for a while. For this, some influences are sent to the female bird from above, from a plan which is engaged with this deed. This bird has some instincts under these influences. As a result of these instincts, she patiently sits on the egg for a while. She ensures the seed in the egg grows up to be a hatchling by her body warmth. The order and sequencing governing a few links of the chain of cause and effect we listed so far are obvious. This is the expression of a great harmony.

To disregard or underestimate the hatchling which is just out of the egg and not even a drop in the immense universe is very wrong. It should be remembered that this hatchling is a part of the universe as well and for it to live and grow up, the parts of universe assigned to its lot work continuously. Nevertheless, the hatchling is still a simple, inexperienced beginner. It does not know how to eat or fly, it does not recognise its enemies, it does not see the dangers, it cannot determine from where or how it will obtain its food. Therefore, as a newcomer to the world, if it is left alone it cannot live and it dies. However, it needs to live and do some deeds.

Because of this, someone is needed to teach and make it to do these deeds; and this someone will be the female bird which helped it to come to the world. However, this female bird cannot think of this and appreciate this need of her hatchling. Then, the intervention of the beings in duty in the evolutionary order starts and such influences are sent to her that because of the instincts put into effect by those influences the female bird cannot but feed and teach her hatchlings and this time even sometimes putting her life on the line until they can take care of themselves. The hatchling needs to live and for this, influences are needed to be sent to the female bird from above. For, that hatchling has come into the world to fulfil the developmental need of its being in the state of a bird in the world. And by this means, it will render all necessities of the bird body and gain all of its refining experiences – within an automatic mechanism – and be a vehicle for the applications of some other beings around it through its relations with them. The necessary devices for all these deeds will be established with the assistance of the beings in duty; and so the bird will give and take whatever it needs to give and take to and from the world.

After all of these have happened, it is now necessary for it to leave the bird body. For, it now has started to feel the need of reaching the possibility of further development. In order to ensure this possibility, a new device is needed. Those beings in duty render this device as well. Among the various vehicles which will remove this bird from the world when it needs to leave the world in order to enter another body, they turn to the most suitable one – which is as well for the evolutionary harmony of other beings.

For example, a cat which needs to live, but cannot find food for days and is hungry, will benefit from this event and is well suited to the device mechanism above. Therefore, beings in duty start to descend into that hungry cat and lead it to activities towards the eating of that bird. By this means, the cat will both feed itself and develop the capabilities it needs. The same influences also descend to the bird which needs to leave the world now and drags the bird to the exact place of the cat. Under this influence, the bird cannot see the cat and directly lands where the cat may easily reach it. The cat catches the bird and eats it. Now, the flux of the event has forked into another branch, that is, into another being's plan as well. However, let us leave it aside and continue with the end of the bird.

We have taken only a few of the life events the bird has gone through from going out of the egg until it dies; and we have shown their cause and effect bonds and devices which advance towards certain purposes in a perfect order. And other than this, it can have many other direct or indirect relations with plants, animals and even humans in its particular communal plan. All of these continue without violating even a hair's breadth the frame of the general developmental harmony. Among them, besides the states which seem good, there are also apparently bad, disruptive, disordered states, such as upon landing on the ground to feed, the poor bird is abruptly eaten by a monstrous cat; but after the knowledge above, what is observed here is not the disharmony but, quite the contrary, the most perfect mechanism of harmony and order.

Thus, by this device, this bird will now come to the world in another body which is superior and suitable for development. Now that being, after it left the world through the devices we mentioned above in order to come into the world in an other animal body which has more abundant possibilities, again everything – parents, educators, environs, climate conditions, helpers etc. – are prepared for it. Whatever is needed for the development of that being, they are put into effect by the being in duty to it within various devices and arrangements. Arrangements and devices are adjusted to each other in order to determine and assign its various relations with other beings both from its own species and outside of its species who will enter the communal plan – which is automatic – of that being. For instance, if it is to be a dog, among the devices preparing the developmental possibilities in dog life, a man who needs to die by rabies is ensured to own that dog. All of these occur within the harmony of the great order which conducts the general evolution in the world.

It is time for the dog to go. It will die. In accordance with the plan, he gets rabies. In the meantime, the man who is its owner has completed his deeds in the world and becomes ready to leave the world in order to continue his development in new bodies. Again, in accordance with the device and plan, the rabid dog will bite him, he will become rabid, and so both will die. All of these are interconnected devices which advance in great harmony.

As it is seen, that being's advance in life which is apparently defective and at opposite sides of each other at first in its relations with the environ in its simple life as an egg, then the stories of the cat in the bird's life and later the man in the dog's life actually follow an ordered advance which is suitable to the harmony of general evolution and development. And this advance has caused an adult bird to gain the initial instincts belonging to the duty of motherhood; and has ensured that a cat lives on through the body of the bird and develops some capabilities; it has caused a man to get rabies through the body of the dog and consequently caused some results to occur in his individual and communal plan.

All of these are for the occurrence of the most necessary states these beings have needed for their evolutions. So, this situation is the manifestation of a small part of the great harmony which belongs to the world. Although apparently contradictory to each other, these devices which are made to advance towards a single purpose are actually of the necessities of the great evolutionary order and consequently of the universal harmony.

We have taken that being when it was a simple egg. Then, after it has established infinite relations and bonds in such innumerable bodies with other innumerable beings; and after it has increasingly expanded the scope of its field of connection, finally, one day, it has elevated into a human body and acquired the power and ability to use it. Until that moment comes, it has created billions of events in the universe through its billions of relations with its environment and the exact, unfailing interconnectedness of these events puts into effect the most vivid observation of the ordered devices of this harmony.

In the communal plans which a man will establish with its environment, family, friends, other people, society, nation and eventually directly or indirectly with the whole mankind, there will be uncountable relations and bonds influencing him; and these bonds and relations which will continue influencing throughout all the lives of his humanness will bring about consequences within innumerable devices and combinations which concern the whole mankind and even the universe; and his next life which is now universal will continue on towards the unitary in complete reconciliation with the devices and order of the universal harmony.

Here we have shown that on the path of a simple bird egg which it will traverse until it becomes a universal being there will be its communal plan which is connected to its individual plans; relations of that communal plan with the other communal plans within direct or indirect devices and orders; there will be various environmental and natural conditions which are suitable to the necessities of all these individual and communal plans; these plans will be regulated by these conditions; a great number of beings in duty at very different degrees – some completely automatic, some semi-comprehending and some with complete comprehension – will take on duties and work in these regulations, ordering and adapting; and above them, the beings of the higher and superior plan of duty will conduct them under their directives and controls as administrators, in accordance with the directives of necessities they receive from the unitary; and eventually, a day will come when that simple egg will become a powerful being who has taken a role like others in the administrative mechanism of the great plan of duty.

Here, the force which sees that this simple bird egg will become a great being in duty in the far future and which can regulate and determine the necessary preliminaries to ensure this higher state of it while it is still a simple egg, originates from this great harmony.

That is, determining the initial preparations of a being's future states which will occur after billions and billions of years and executing these preparations towards their goal without digressing even a hair's breadth is only possible by the force of a great harmony.

It is now clear that all these activities occur within the great harmony of the divine order which intends evolution in the universe and connects the universe into a single occurrence with all of its events. And despite their generally negative appearances on the face of the one-sided and barren comprehension of human beings, this order flows onwards within a complete and unswerving harmony.

*
* *

Motions belonging to the developments and evolutions of all beings can occur only under the light of these orders and devices within this universal harmony. Every device, every event meets the evolutionary imperatives of the divine necessity which covers all beings. Therefore, as it is in all realms of universe, our world also which is included within this divine necessity is of course within this great harmony. Because of this, as a bird's getting torn apart by a hungry cat is how necessary for the development of both the bird and the cat, and is in order with the evolutionary plan of universe, likewise, a chief's dragging a nation into war for this or that apparent reason and his causing the death of a great number of mankind or their living in starvation, misery and suffering is that much necessary for the separate respective developments of all beings involved and a harmonious event in the general evolutionary plan of universe.

In the former one, both the bird and cat have been dragged automatically to this deed; in the latter one as well, this chief and the ones who follow him participate automatically in the harmony established towards the great target on the same path. As a result of all of these, surely innumerable developmental leaps will be done and infinite possibilities of progress will be opened for those human beings. Here, the apparently disharmonious, disordered and defective scenery of the grappling, battling and clashing is actually the expression of a harmonious state, which ensures the possibilities of development in the suffering, anguishing and tormenting ways mankind deserves and wants through an order beyond their comprehension.

*
* *

In all states and events of nature, states which are suitable for all kinds of needs of the beings are put into effect in accordance with the general harmony of evolution. This harmony and order in the cosmos is the manifestation of the divine necessity, which prevails over the destinies of beings on the evolutionary path. This necessity is fulfilled by the gradually expanding functions of those beings in duty at every level in the great universal organisations in accordance with the directives coming from the unitary.

In this way, all realms, the whole universe is a complex of innumerable events, occurrences and flux which are in a close embrace with each other within a great harmony. Harmony is the universe itself.

*
* *

The ones who look around carefully at the world even with shallow vision, can see uncountable manifestations of this great harmony reflected in nature.

When looking down at the Earth from high above, everybody can see the harmony of the converging of the lands with the seas. Converging the lands with the seas without giving even the slightest harm to the lives of millions of living beings is one of the manifestations of the evolutionary harmony which manifest on world matter. The seas do not exceed their boundaries against the lands as if they are in deep respect. The lands keep their stand against the seas with a calm imperturbability. All of these are regulated by the beings in duty in accordance with the life conditions of the living beings in the world and with the general harmony. A slight disturbance of this harmony, for instance, the rising of sea levels for 8 or 10 metres brings about results which may cost the lives of many living beings in many places. However, in places where this should not be happening, this harmony is never disrupted.

*
* *

Seasons make a nice example of this harmony which is established for the continuation of life and the development of beings in the world. Seasons follow each other within a great order and arrangement, without exceeding certain limits in the degrees of heat which stays within the possibilities of living of the ones with life. The automatism in their flow is established by the great beings in duty. By this means, there are not abrupt jumps, for instance in the mild climates, from very hot summer days to the coldest days of winter. Degrees of air temperature gradually climb down and up from the uppermost limit to the lowermost and from the lowermost to the uppermost limit, and by changing a few degrees a day within spring and autumn flows, summers turn into winters and winters turn into summers; and the limits of air temperatures, above and below, do not reach up unendurable levels for those who live in the world. This state is a calculated device which is regulated by the sublime plans that obey the great harmony of cosmoses.

Degrees of hotness and coldness of the seasons are full of materials which respond to all kinds of needs of the beings. Again, here there is a great harmony of order. And all these orders and devices are established on the path of preparing infinite sources of possibilities to the world beings within the general evolutionary flow of universe. Innumerable beings in duty were given duties in these establishments in order not to divert an inch from this harmony.

The humid weather conditions of the spring which are sweet and necessary for life cause the waking up of many plant and animal bodies. Everything gets refreshed, rejuvenated. The summer season is the maturation period. All fruits ripen; each one with life discloses the inherent forces within itself. This is a season of productivity. Autumn meets the needs of some beings who completed their duties within a certain period of time and now need a temporary sleep or death and rest in order to prepare for their new lives. In the meantime, the leaves turn yellow and fall. Trees start to go back to their secret lives. Many animals retreat into their dens or shells and dive into sleep or death which prepares them for the future in order to prepare themselves for their new awakening in the next spring.

Winter is a season which contains all kinds of evolutionary material of all embodied beings. In this season, mankind encounters many tests and trials, experiences and observations. Working and making effort under relatively harsh circumstances help mankind to mature and strengthen. All these occur within interconnected devices through mutual exchange and support. Each of these is of the orders and devices which constitute the general harmony of the world and do exist within this general harmony as closely interconnected.

The order particular to each season is established. This order is executed as adjusted to the life possibilities and degrees of endurance of the beings living in that climate. Plants, animals and humans of hot climates find the life conditions they need in that climate. Seasons faithfully obey this harmony. Under no circumstances do icy mountains exist in tropical regions and roasting deserts do not exist in arctic regions. This is because such situations are not suitable for the living possibilities of the bodies which inhabit those places.

At the moment mankind is face to face with an untimely death because of a drought when the soil is dried and cracked, animals cannot find water to drink; beings in duty, who are engaged in activities suitable to the great harmony, immediately take action and start to send their influences to that region. By means of these influences clouds gather, rain waters fall down to the soil to revitalise the ground and a perfect and harmonious automatism becomes established in order to prevent harmful conditions. Waters in the ground evaporate with a certain degree of heat and retreat back to the skies and, when needed, fall again as rain. So all these states and advances continue on their path within an order, suitable to the harmony of the general evolutionary flow without even diverting an inch.

*
* *

Nights follow days with certain intervals. In this regard, each region on the Earth has an adjustment, a periodical order according to the season. In certain seasons, the durations of nights and days always stay fixed. All of these are states that occur within unfailing devices.

In the world, states and orders occurring in every event and situation and within an ordered rhythm and great harmony are the manifestations of the general harmony of the world. There is not a disordered, defective thing. All events are made manifested as regulated and assisted in degrees in the evolution of each being.

The world is a small part of the universe which is a vast harmony. None of the things that occur here can go outside of this harmony. If it does, it cannot exist. For, harmony means the events becoming harmonised, adapted and complementary at each point of the great evolutionary path. And this expresses that all motions which constitute the events become completely merged and fused with each other. Nevertheless, every being, every matter-part, every vibration is each a motion complex. We have previously mentioned that no particle of the whole universe can be free of the beams of light. This divine light is the harmony itself; and all motions of the universe can exist only by the power of this divine light. We have stated this point as well. Therefore, to break away from the harmony means to be free of motions; and for any matter or being which is free of motion, its existence or permanence cannot be considered. Thus, wherever motion exists, there is certainly a manifestation of universal harmony.

*
* *

Seen from the perspective of mankind, all things which appear such as goodness, bad, disorder, meaninglessness, lowness, highness, disrespect are relative. These are but barren judgements which are concluded because of mankind's lack of vision about the universal order and harmony. A lion's attacking a defenceless fawn and feeding it to his cubs; big fish eating small fish; uncountable killings and preying in the plant, animal and human realms which continue from the moment the world is built; mankind's destroying their own peace and ease by attacking each other, inviting their days full of uncountable torture and suffering by their own acts and deeds and eventually, making the world a hell, a dungeon for themselves: such states which are seen as outrageous are actually necessary, imperative and certainly beneficial states which occur under the control of the beings in duty connected to the administrative mechanism in accordance with the necessities of the great harmony.

They flow on within the great order and harmony of the cosmos which advances in accordance with the purpose of preparing the ever new developmental stages of all beings and mankind. Mankind can and will see this state only in relation to their evolution. None of these is unnecessary, outrageous and unwarranted within the evolutionary order and general harmony of the universe. These concepts of outrageousness and needlessness are relativities based on one-sided views which are accepted and valued by mankind because of the imperativeness of the world life which manifests, again, within the evolutionary harmony. Indeed, the ones who observe the world objectively by separating from the feelings for a moment can see this truth clearly at that moment.

When they look at the insect kingdom they soon appreciate that in spite of all those fights and battles among them a great harmony ensuring their growth and development always exists; and within this harmony, these fights and battles carry great significance as well.

The struggles and fights of the inhabitants of an anthill engaged with their fellow creatures in defending their nest are not in vain and unnecessary. Others attacking them and their responding to the attackers are devices which automatically make those beings acquire capabilities that are needed to be taught by the ant life. All these states are the parts – of the great order of nature which comes from the original directives – that are accrued to these ants, bees and insects so those beings can do the simplest and automatic preparations for the states of gathering, organising, acquiring merits for communal plans and eventually, one day, to join mankind who has taken the path of the sublime plan of duty.

By the means of their organisations automatically established in this way, they do faithfully a great number of deeds and duties without harming each other for surviving, breeding their generations, preserving the well-being of their community and – hidden behind all of these activities – for the sake of ensuring their development. And they do not slack and neglect their deeds at all. We said they do these deeds without harming each other because these world bodies which eat each other at any moment according to the world comprehension actually help each other through these acts unknowingly and without comprehending; and this is to be, as such is an imperative in their communal plans. So, as is observed in sometimes positive and sometimes negative ways, the state of complying to and participating in the necessities of the great order and harmony flows on within the whole realm of plants, animals and mankind, from the smallest to the largest.

*
* *

In mankind – provided that it always stays within the cadre of the great order of nature and evolutionary harmony – much wider and encompassing variations of the state of complying to the harmony of the communal plan necessities are observed. For example, the harmony which manifests as a great peace and calmness among mankind in some places is not different and apart from the harmony which advances in many other places as annoying and harming, strangling and killing each other. All this turmoil which is seen as disharmonious and defective in the view of mankind is the manifestation of universal harmony which is devised and regulated according to various degrees of merit, developmental needs and power of mankind, in accordance with the world order. Therefore, the world life which embraces all with life – starting from grit and stone – and the motions and events belonging to them must be taken as a whole, with this aspect of it.

It is like an immense orchestration whose sounds, when taken separately, resonate as discord and grate on the ear but become harmonious, beautiful and even necessary states and values for the perfection of the orchestration when they are heard within the whole of it. If a man who does not understand about knowledge of composition and orchestration attempts to tune an instrument which apparently sounds jarringly to his liking, he may disrupt the harmony of that orchestration. However, the whole state of the world is within a harmony which has an infinite scope that cannot be compared with such an ordinary orchestration. In this regard, the world is an immense composition which has been established with all its constitutions. And the ones who put into effect this composition are the great composers in duty, who have adapted to the original necessities coming as filtered from the unitary. That is, they are the great organisers.

*
* *

And mankind who has been crawling within the powerful devices of the great order and harmony of the world up until today, has now reached the pinnacle of their evolutions in the world. The ongoing devices of the great universal harmony are not in a state of allowing much further evolution of human beings who have been cultivated so far within these devices in the world. For, mankind is in a state in which they have rendered all their refining experiences within the possibilities of hydrogen cosmos, have overcome all developmental stages belonging here and completed their cycles. Their essence-beings make strenuous efforts to reaching new horizons, new environs and new illuminated lands filled with developmental possibilities. They have the longing and intuition to attain the widest possibilities of the great universal harmony and becoming of that harmony.

Although mankind cannot completely attain the comprehensions of this intuition of theirs in their states as humans, mankind today lives in the densest and darkest confusion of this writhing about. It cannot yet forecast where it will go and where it needs to go but it trashes about with the need of going surely somewhere, of reaching an illumination, of arriving at a spacious environ, of breaking through the heaviness of the matter conditions it is in by its uncontained acts and without knowing the reason or true nature of this. When it cannot find even a particle of the happiness it vehemently pursues without comprehending its quality, out of frustration it tries to console itself by burying itself into the temporary pleasures of material toys.

However, its thrashings about, which seems to have no use other than increasing its confusion, is actually preparing for it the paths to happiness it seeks, anticipates and needs on the face of the mechanism of destiny. And in order for mankind to attain this happiness they vehemently expect, the necessary devices are certainly on the way of establishing within the great harmony of the cosmos. These further devices are appreciated and determined within the harmony of the divine order in accordance with the imperative of effectuating necessary forms according to the new wants and needs which reached maturation and with the gradual changing of the current world order.

Therefore, regardless of however catastrophic the all incoming changes may seem in the face of human comprehension, they will occur under the devices and orders which are most suitable and perfectly responding to the needs of human beings. The events to be started soon will prepare the last suitable scenes for human evolution which could be possible in the world; and will close the curtains on the last act of a suffering stage of the world which has been continuing for ages.

*
* *

None of the needs of any being in nature is met with neglect. Orders and devices which are suitable to all evolutionary needs and wants are immediately established, because the universe is for evolution and there, fulfilment of all evolutionary needs is an imperative. As to the forms and directions of the new schemes and devices to be established on the face of these needs; we have said that human beings have entered the state of candidacy for more superior lives and reached the gates of the infinitely illumined lands. However, for mankind to attain these high and illumined lives which they deserve these gates must be opened. So, a small deed remains to be done for mankind to be able to migrate to these unique lands of happiness which they longingly pursue, drenched in blood and sweat, and this is but to open wide these gates which are ready to be opened by giving it a flick and barging in. However, the realisation of this will be possible, again, within the flow of some events which are very ordered and harmonious. And this is to be as such is necessary for the well-being of mankind.

Certainly, many humans will benefit from the great preparations which are ensured by the harmonious devices within this immense order and consequently, they will not miss the opportunity to flow away within a great atmosphere of joy in order to soar in the infinite lives of the etheric[20] cosmoses in the realm of infinite possibilities.

---

[20] *Ether*: The substance assumed to be filling the void between atoms and the whole universe; with no weight and conducts heat and light. Today it means, according to the theosophists, the states of matter which are not perceived by the five senses of man; lighter in density compared to solid, liquid and gaseous states of matter and higher in vibration, subtler and more fluid. (*Publisher*)

We have now stated clearly that in the radical changes which are about to start to occur soon in natural conditions, nothing will be purposeless and imprudent; and even the smallest event will be put into effect within an unfailing and infallible device and harmony by the superior beings in duty in accordance with the necessities coming from the unitary. And the opening of the gates we just mentioned above means the comprehension, internalisation of this truth and willingly and happily complying with the devices that exist accordingly. Therefore, the new harmony which will occur with the changes in the natural conditions on the Earth has an extraordinarily great value and significance in regard to granting these possibilities of deliverance. Remember that these states which will be apparently disordered, worrying and even disturbing are actually valuable means which will help mankind to acquire high gains and are for the benefit of mankind. For, the countenance of mankind which will be changed and the harmony which will be established by the new devices will occur only after the closing of a world cycle. So, because of this, there are the last preparations the world will go through.

These preparations have two aspects: the first is to make mankind gain their still lacking knowledge, observations and faith by telling them that this world cannot be a convenient habitat for them any more; and the other aspect is to put into effect a new world which is convenient for the simple bodies who will come later.

*
* *

Now we start to explain the qualities and forms of forthcoming natural changes, that is, of the events that are about to manifest; in short, of the great world revolution that is about to happen.

Some simple events which we may term as the first indications of this forthcoming closing of the great world cycle have already started. These are some atmospheric changes which do not yet have significance in the vision of the mankind and are assumed temporary disturbances due to the blind forces of nature. These states will gradually increase and continue without ceasing while making their greater signs felt strongly. For example, the due hot days of summer will not arrive somehow; abnormally hot weather in the middle of winter and cold weather in the middle of summer will start to be observed. Besides long-term droughts in some places, constant rainfalls at other places will create floods and significant damages will occur. Strong winds will blow becoming dangerous and in some places, they will result in great havoc. Meanwhile, earthquakes will occur; violent seismic upheavals will reveal themselves in this or that part of the Earth among the natural events which mankind will define as disasters.

On the seas, unaccustomed events will occur. For example, on shores where no tides occur, the sea will sometimes rise 8 to 10 metres and invade the land. Some cities which are unused to and unprepared for such high tides will be under the threat of floods and suffer great losses.

In various locations of the world, from place to place landslides will occur; and some towns and places will experience quite frightful and worrisome moments. Similarly, during those earth disasters some places will fissure and smoke and flames will flow out.

In short, all of these great winds, floods, seismic upheavals, earthquakes, the surges of the seas, inundations and ground fissures will gradually trouble mankind and increase their losses. However, none of these will be out of the harmony or out of order; all of them will be expressions of the gradual advances of the steps regulated to the targets we have just mentioned.

These states will continue for more or less 40 or 50 years in the world stealthily but unceasingly, and not in sufficient potency for mankind to be able to penetrate their true significance. Nonetheless, they will increase in intensity while following a gradual advance which has a preliminary quality for further stages. The ones who have read and embraced the knowledge in this book will not have any hardship to intuit the meanings such states, indicated already at the beginning; and they will acquire the possibilities of preparing themselves for the great day to come with ease, heartfelt peace and even joy.

*
* *

Approximately fifty years later these events will begin to make themselves felt much more strongly and to acquire characteristics which are very disturbing, scary, suffering and arduous for mankind —more correctly, for those who have not properly prepared themselves. Nevertheless, because these events would still not be sufficiently intensified to impose their true significance on mankind, the majority of mankind will be far from understanding the true meanings of these events and be simply clueless about what will befall them. For example, some bizarre changes in climates will initially begin gradually; cold places will gradually get warmer; and some regions will be scorching hot unusually. As the result of such states freakish winds will create terrifying hurricanes and because of these great damage will ensue. Earthquakes will occur more often and intensify; ground fissures and eruptions will increase; and as the years go by these states will make themselves felt more explicitly.

Some cities will be obliterated by major tremors and in their places, vast indentations or lakes will appear; in some places widespread and continuous droughts will begin; mankind and animals will die in great numbers; wooded, green and fertile areas will turn into wastelands and will even become dry deserts and will turn into inhabitable areas for mankind who had been inhabiting those places for ages, and they will flee in order to look for more fertile places and will begin to migrate. Consequently, from place to place mass migrations will begin and this will create major strife among human communities.

The swelling of the seas will increase; and world matter will not fail even a moment to tell the mankind in a proper language that they should not expect more, even expect nothing any more from it by displaying its terrible countenance to mankind. In short, the world will gradually become barren, disagreeable for mankind and will lose its suitable characteristics for life. And after all, as we have previously explained, the cancer cases which will increase entirely towards the end of times are one of the significant evidences which will explicitly show mankind that world matter does not respond to needs any more. Shortly, starting from the fiftieth year, besides the consequences put into effect by the droughts, some compelling natural events including wide-scale migrations from place to place will cause major unrest in the world; and the gradually souring countenance and harshening conditions of nature towards mankind will swiftly increase the degree of this unrest.

*
* *

These states will continue up to the hundredth year by increasing; and after the hundredth year, the events and changes that started in the world will begin to give some meanings to mankind about the real nature and implications of all these events. The states which continued up to now as simple changes, will now begin to develop within a complete turmoil and in an explicit way which expresses the changing of the old world orders and devices.

Ice sheets in the colder regions will start to melt and as some cold regions get warmer, distinct changes will begin in the climates of the world. Within these states which seem in complete disorder there are orders and devices which are preparatory for the realisation of the forthcoming days of deliverance and good news for mankind.

As the world gets increasingly warmer, in some places major differences in the seasons will appear. There, scorching heats will prevail in summer and winter; the cold weather will be in excess. And towards the last days, seasons will completely change; the current mild climates will become hellishly hot like the tropical regions; and formerly cold climates will become the hot regions of the world. Consequently, many cities will become uninhabitable because of the hot weather; on the one hand, hellishly hot regions and on the other unendurable aridness of the former vast fertile lands which has now dried and turned into deserts.

Following the hundredth year, great natural events will commence, and they will cause the mass deaths of mankind in parts; and states which are deemed as great disasters by mankind will follow each other. Nevertheless, despite the death in such large numbers, the population of the world will not decrease but on the contrary, increase. For example, the world population which has reached 2.5 billion today, will increase up to 6 or 7 billion by then.[21] The main reason for this increase is the coming back of all the beings to the world who have left the world until now and accumulated in the spatium. All beings of the spatium will come back to the world in order to live in this last world cycle and benefit from the great possibilities and knowledge of that period which are preparatory for future lives. And this will cause the occurrence of births at large scales from place to place. Actually, the rush of the ones in the spatium towards the world and the increase of the world population have already begun.

Here we state that mankind of those times in the last days of the Mu world we have previously mentioned were prepared in the same ways. These portents we have mentioned had displayed themselves there as well and taught many things to mankind. Now, the same devices are starting to be repeated for mankind as well. The ones who compare the parallelism of the knowledge we have previously given about the events before the closing of the Mu world with the events about the closing of this last cycle of the world see that there have been almost no alterations between them.

*
* *

We summarily state the final states the climates will take at times very close to the ending of the world:

The northern parts of Russia will become extraordinarily cold in winter (-60 °C to -70 °C) and in summer, it will have temperatures of mild climates (0 °C to 25 °C).

North Greenland, Scandinavia, European North Russia, the Caucasians, Afghanistan, Tibet, China, Japan and Alaska will be quite hot in summer (45 °C) and quite cold in winter (-50 °C)

In south Greenland, England and all countries of Central Europe, from the northeast part of France: in England, northern France, Denmark, Belgium, Holland, Germany, Switzerland, Austria, Czechoslovakia, Hungary, the entire Balkans, the north-eastern part

---

[21] The world population in 1959 – in the year this book was written – was around 3 billion; by 2012 it had reached 7 billion (source: GeoHive.com). (*Publisher*)

of Italy, Turkey, northern Greece, Iran, Pakistan and the northern part of India there will be summer temperatures of tropical quality (50 °C to 70 °C) and winter colds below zero (-20 °C to -8 °C).

In the south-western part of Italy, Sicily, southern parts of Greece, the Mediterranean region, the whole of Africa, Madagascar, Arabian Peninsula, the southern part of India, Malacca, Indonesia, New Guinea, the Philippines islands, Australia, New Zealand, the southern part of Canada, the whole of the United States of America, California, Mexico, Venezuela, Colombia and the northern part of Bolivia there will be continuous hot temperatures in summer and winter; temperatures in these regions will continuously vary between (40 °C and 70 °C) .

This situation belongs to the final stage of the world. Climates will be entering gradually into these states only fifty years later. That is, world climates will not be abruptly passed into final degrees of temperatures which we gave here but gradually across the years.

*
* *

Towards the final moment of world revolution all natural events will intensify, tremors will increase; floods, deluges, major landslides, land fissures and great earthquakes which can devastate a few cities at once will continue following each other; and mankind will encounter another and more terrible disaster not long after the previous disasters. In the mean time, naturally, there will be deaths en masse; pandemics will occur; life on Earth will cause much suffering and be arduous.

Reasonable, knowledgeable and well-prepared mankind, when they can see this situation, will understand very well that world matter is not sufficient for world mankind; and the world is making this truth dawn on mankind. And so a moment will come when the majority of mankind will understand that there is no place left in the world for them to live. And this will be the most perfect order and device of the world which has been established so mankind may see the truth with complete clarity; and through the power of this order and device, mankind will acquire the strength to open wide the gates with great longing which separate the two realms we have mentioned above; that is, they will begin to attain the light of their comprehension.

*
* *

This turmoil will confuse mankind by increasing and becoming inextricable; and finally a moment will come and from that moment on, the world that has been in the throes of death will soon close its eyes to its former life. At this stage, the world will look like a boiling cauldron. During this final stage, which will continue for only a few days, all continents and the seas will be in turmoil. The ground and the skies will shake.

In the meantime, the ground will be fissured and come apart. These parts will continuously shake as if dried leaves were rocking back and forth before an immense wind. They will go up and down. The earth beneath every foot will shake. Vast cracks will occur. Out of these cracks the blackest smoke and toxic fumes will gush. These fumes will gradually cover the Earth. It will get dark around. This smoke will be in the form of clouds of fume containing the vaporous toxic gases made out of burning coals in the substratum of the ground mixed with waters. It will waste the mankind en masse. In some places, the width of these crevices, which are at enormous lengths, will reach to 30 or 40 kilometres. And large pieces of land, together with their cities which mostly have already been destroyed, and large mountains will begin to topple down into these wide open pits of fire.

For example, Turkey may be buried in such a crevice with a 50 kilometres width with all of her parts up to Lake Van. These enormous and vast abysses of fire will be opened here and there all over the world; and the hills, mountains, valleys, plains and vast pieces of land, together with all their devastated cities and damaged developed areas on them, will roll down into these abysses. And the remaining survivors of the inhabitants of those places will be buried in these fire pits altogether. Meanwhile, some fire pits will spurt out lava as hot ashes all around and these will fall down on mankind as rain of fire. At the same time, enormous and dense clouds will cover the skies of the world. Ceaseless lightning, with violent thunder, will

292

strike through dense black clouds of fumes and vapour and touch down all over the world, illuminating all around.

On the one hand, as the thunder muffles the screams of mankind, the underground roars, the din as the gases and lava spurt out and overflow from the blown up fissures and opened cracks, as mankind unconsciously yells and cries out amidst the suffocating and burning fumes, the opening of the fire pits and abysses, the pieces of land which shake like dried leaves, lightning; on the other hand, oceans surrounding the continents will rise as never seen before and the seas will heave as enormous mountains which contain billions of tons of water will begin to attack upon the continents.

This situation is now the last hours of the world; the face of the Earth is sinking. That is, a world life, which has completed its cycle, is about to close forever and ever. Thus, the oceans attacking the continents will begin to cover all lands together with all of their devastated cities, opened fissures, forests, valleys and vast grounds. They will run after mankind like herds and swallow them. In places where the sea waters join with the fire pits and fissures, great explosions and immense vapour clouds will occur. In the meantime, continents will crack across and all devastated regions which have been once ages old civilisations with all of their artefacts and monuments will topple down into these pits of hell and will vanish in a few hours.

Over the places they are buried into fire pits the enormous sea mass of the oceans will immediately cover them and all continents of the world will soon be obliterated. New oceans will replace them which are thousands metres deep; and consequently, one more world cycle, together with all the civilisation and material wealth it has attained so far will be closed down and become of the past which is destined to be forgotten.

And in the midst of this turmoil, most of mankind will go to a cosmos which will respond to their needs; and the remaining few will be stranded and bewildered on the pieces of rock which have survived the great cataclysm in order to pass into the new world. For, some higher parts of the old continents, which sunk into the depths of the seas, will stay at the surface as large pieces of rocks in order to constitute the islands at varying sizes and archipelagos of the future.

*
* *

As the face of the Earth sinks, from the sea bottom which was upside down, enormous pieces of land will rise up and consequently, new continents will be constituted out of these. These new continents will be an ages long study subject for the geography experts of the next world cycle.

We have said that mankind of the new world cycle will be constituted from the remaining mankind on the higher parts and hills of the continents during the submerging of the world of today. At the new continents which rose up from the sea bottom during that time there will be no mankind yet. Since there will be no soil on the islands where mankind who will pass into the new world from the world of today must inhabit, those people will be contained in these islands which are only rocks and surrounded by seas. Consequently, after all of these events which happen and finish in a few days, the calm will return; and the general equilibrium which has been disrupting for years in the world, after going through this final crisis of a few days, will be restored as according to the new world conditions, everything will be done and over with, and the sun will rise from the horizons of the new world with the same brightness and begin to go on rejuvenating it.

*
* *

As for mankind, of those who passed from this world to the next one, although at first keeping their body structure, major regressions will occur in their mental states, intelligence, comprehensions, feelings and memories. They will lose their consciousness and go insane. Those people will forget all knowledge and concepts belonging to the former world cycle, great human civilisations and their own individual, family and communal lives. There will be nothing left from their past knowledge, neither from their sciences, techniques, capabilities, habits nor anything from their previous identities; they will act only upon instincts as in a state of a very primitive man.

And their leading instinct will be fear. During the great world transformation terrible events, which will go on for days before their eyes, the horrifying and raucous sinking of the world, will cause an enormous instinct of fear which will continue for a very long time in their beings. However, because they have lost all their knowledge about the past and are in a complete unconsciousness and incomprehension at that time, they will never know either the reason or quality of this fear but will only live continuously under its pressure. Moreover, conditions of the world milieu, which they just entered and which gets increasingly barbarised and vulgar, will increase and fortify their instincts of fear.

Feelings of fear will gather this primitive mankind as groups of fives or tens. They will be afraid of everything; and when they are scared they will get closer and embrace each other. Their glances will be fearful; and in their every state and act, all manifestations of fear will be seen. From time to time and when they are afraid of something in general they will shout out some meaningless, unconscious sounds; they will run around without thinking. For, they will not know how to speak yet and even be devoid of the merit of communicating with signs. For example, when one of them starts to shout, the rest will go along, especially by the instinct of fear, and shout as well; after shouting for a while, when their fears are soothed somewhat, they will again become silent altogether.

These poor people who have passed from the former world into the new world and remained hungry, naked, without tools and gadgets or anything and especially without wits, thoughts and consciousness, and who can only move around by the instincts of fear and hunger, will spend very harsh and stern moments on those rocks and among wild animals. They will not find food, will be out of clothing, will be unable to see even a tree cove to seek sanctuary and will be exposed to all natural events in an environment surrounded by rocks. Sunlight will burn their skins, cold winds and temperatures will bruise their naked bodies. They will run from the attacks of wild animals; and in groups of fives or tens will nestle in between rocks or stone coves. And all of these states will excessively increase the instinct of fear which already exists in them.

Since their comprehension and intelligence are yet a far cry from the state of ability to make weapons for the hunt or defence by chiselling stones, mankind at these initial times will not be entered even into a stone age. They will try to fulfil all of their needs – which are merely instincts – with their naked bodies which are not donned with any kind of tools and naturally, through instincts. For example, out of the needs the feeling of hunger bring out in them, together they will attack the seemingly weakest of the animals; and again, they will attack the weakest of their fellow mankind; dismember and eat them. Cannibalism will be the most natural and imperative act for the lives of mankind at these initial times; and they will start their first world lives by eating each other, that is, by cannibalism.

*
* *

We have said that the new world will be constituted by the islands and archipelagos belonging to some parts of the submerged old continents which have remained on the surface as well as by the new large continents which have emerged, rising up from the sea bottom. Likewise, we have mentioned that these islands where the mankind who remained from the past world will be nothing but rocks and have no soil. Therefore, around the first mankind there will not be plant life yet. And, the state of the new world which is in this situation will soon become wild. Everything will become simpler, primitive and barbarised. Mountains and hills with rounded peaks which existed in the old world will not be seen in the new world; instead of those, mountains and mountain ranges with pointed peaks which are like saw teeth will be formed; steep valleys will be seen; everything will become sharpened, poignant and stern.

We previously mentioned that it is imperative for the beings to adapt the environment they live in. Because the beings to come into the world will build their bodies out of the matter of the environment they are in, it is natural that those of mankind who have passed into the new world will become coarser as their generations breed and adapt to their coarse environment. Resulting from their adaptation to this coarse environment, their bodies will quickly get coarser. This state of coarsening which will be seen in the bodies of mankind and the animals which passed from the old world into the new world will increase by the generations, depending on their needs belonging to their primitive surroundings and will continue for a long time. For example, as the generations go on, larger sized animals will appear; they will be wild and because there is no soil and consequently no plants on the islands, the calm herbivores of the past world will not be seen in those places.

As such, as the first generations of mankind who have passed to this new world go on, their body formations will change and a state of coarsening will begin in those as well. Body structures and shapes of this first generation of mankind, who have to fight, grapple and clash with the harsh and stern nature, wild animals and with each other will be radically altered in accordance with the new needs raised out of their life struggles. That is, as the generations go on, bodily formations which are suitable to this coarse environment will emerge with all of their characteristics. In contrast with the past world, tall and slim human figures will be no more; on the contrary, the bodies of humans will be low and spreading, their bulk will get large, their muscles will be toned, their chests will widen, their arms will extend, their feet's capability of function will increase, their toes will lengthen because these will work as fingers, their arms and legs will strengthen and the skulls will take shapes accordingly.

Since the load of the brain of that day will be obliged to serve more sensual instincts than the intellectual life, it will be free of the mental activities of a civilised man, and there will be no need for a perfect brain and the formation of a skull which serves the protection of this brain; consequently, the brows will get smaller and retreat backwards with the reducing of the skulls. On the other hand, because of the imperative of eating flesh, only the jaws will develop, teeth will be sharpened and pinpointed and strengthened, mouths will get large, coarse and protruding. For protection against the violent weather elements, hairs on the skin will increase and thicken.

This state of coarsening which will start with the new generations to come after this transition will continue for 300 years. During this period of time, the new generations which will come into the world as humans will consist of the beings who have completed all developmentary stages belonging to the lives of the stages of animality and sub-humans in the other planets of the solar system and will now have acquired the merit of building human bodies and are in need of coming to the world as humans. That is, in this period of coarsening, the children of mankind who have passed from the past world will be beings who have just completed the subhuman stages of other planets and by entering into this world have just stepped into the initial stage of humanity. After all, this wild environment has been prepared for them. One of the duties of mankind who have passed from the past world into this new world is to give birth to these beings that will pass to the humanity for the first time from these stages of animality and subhumanity and to parent them.

*
* *

During the time mankind will spend upon these rocky islands, at the new continents which no one inhabits yet, the soil will exist; torrential rains will fall on those places for days and months and consequently, in some parts of the continents wild virgin forests of tall trees with large trunks will grow.

And after this coarsening period of mankind which will continue for around 300 years, they will gain the power of leaving the rocky islands they inhabit and go to these continents and will start to utilise their forests, plants and other possibilities. For, before that time, neither their thoughts and powers nor the possibilities and tools they live in will allow them to leave from the places they are at. However, after a period of 300 years of coarsening, mankind will gradually leave these islands by the primitive and simple stirrings towards development and by the further few needs which will occur –albeit simple, again – in their instincts and they will begin to pass to the closest parts of these continents; and consequently, they will enter a very long and slow tempo of development afterwards in order to render all the ensuing necessities of the establishment of a new world.

During this period of development of humanity of the new world which will continue for 60,000 years, mankind will go through long eras like the ages of stone, iron, bronze; they will overcome some ages like antiquity, middle ages; in short, as it has happened with mankind who have passed on to this world from the Mu world, among these too, gradually instincts will pass to in-tuitions, intuitions to comprehensions; and by the development of true comprehensions, they will gradually pass to communal and higher communal plans.

In the mean time, among the ones who remained in the next world because they could not cultivate themselves until the final stage of transition of the past world, if there are ones who quick-ened their developments and have swiftly prepared for the plan of duty; they will completely leave the world without waiting for the end of the world, provided that they can render the duties they are given –according to their merits – from above (it is absolutely nec-essary to accomplish a duty in order to pass to the plan of duty) after 5 or 10 incarnations, that is, during 8 or 10 centuries; then they will reach to the places where the other happy mankind went to the higher plans during the past world revolution.

And the rest, in order to wait and prepare for the days of the new revolution which is to come 60,000 years later, will begin to live again within innumerable individual and communal tests and trials, troubles, struggles, wars, combats, deaths, murders, diseases, captivities, prisons, dungeons, inquisitions, mad houses, hospitals, sufferings, hardships, poverties, hungers, heavy duties; in short within all the uncountable developmental materials which prepare the human evolution of the world life and are to be gone through across each world cycle history. In the mean time, they will run af-ter many realities named truths by struggling among apparently opposing beliefs, realities, knowledge, faiths, religions, sects, schools and convictions with sometimes automatic and sometimes semi-comprehending efforts; and they will fall into many disap-pointments, deceptions, mistakes and failures.

Meanwhile, they will encounter the formidable struggles of life; they will work, they will toil after the attractions of transient but powerfully luring pleasures while trying hard not to forget their true purpose and goals, they will arrive at the threshold of the next new world revolution which will come 60,000 years later, through the very slow and arduous advancing and only then will the power of leaving this world completely be attained.

For, within this very slow developmental tempo, most of mankind will be able to understand and learn the meaning of matter, its limits of possibilities, for what purposes it is, in which degree and ways it can be beneficial and serving to mankind. In short, at the end of every developmental cycle, the world school will close its gates after the graduates it has educated in order to hand them over to the higher institutions, and will open its gates to the newcomers in order to educate them in place of the outgoing ones; and consequently, it will be rendered one of its infinite functions which is cyclical. This is the destiny of not only the world but all worlds, all cosmoses and universe.

*
* *

Here we would like to repeat this: regardless of how tumultuous and terrible these states seem – that is, the state of formidability in the appearances of the great world revolutions – this is only seemingly. Here there is nothing to be afraid of, to be terrorised, to evade or to begin to worry about. For, these horrible scenes belong only to the realities which the world matter are subject to. And they will remain in the world with them. To the other side, to the higher plans, none of it, even the particle of a particle will pass into it.

And death is actually a moment of time which does not inflict suffering and pain. The scene of the events causing death does not actually belong to the essence-being. These are states belonging to the body and the world. The human having died will leave all of these at that moment and will even forget their memories. Therefore, hot fires of volcano vents, rampageous attacks of the sea masses, violent tremors of the earthquakes, thundering and lightning are means of death which are merely toys for the ones who are destined to go from here. This is because the sole thing this cataclysm which has broken out in the world can take from mankind is their coarse bodies which they are already willing to leave here.

And mankind are already consentient for this. For, humans to be capable of the attaining forthwith the joyful atmosphere of the higher and happy realms which they may begin to intuit even at that moment, depends on the arrival at the second of death when they will leave their bodies; and they, according to their ability to comprehend, will await the arrival of this second right away. This is a moment of happiness, joy and deliverance. This is the moment of completion of the world school which has thousands of years' history of suffering, of the arduous stages of learning which have passed under heavy conditions successfully and completely. This moment is a moment when the conditions of successful or failed lives together with their various fears, sufferings and even torments which are full of hopelessness and disappointments will end; and when everything will pass to the illuminated, clear and powerful fields by walking on the happiest, swiftest and easiest paths. This is a moment of deliverance in every sense.

In this tumult which seem so terrible, on this day of judgement which displays such horrible scenes, transition from the coarse hydrogen cosmos which is a life of shackled imprisonment full of suffering and hardship of tens of thousands years to a higher realm which is bright and happy will occur. And to ensure this transition, the only deed left to be done by mankind in the world is to wait for this moment which is as short as the duration of an inhaling and to go through this simple, easy and small application as exhaling that single breath.

Here the real disaster will befall those of mankind who cannot die – more correctly, who lose the merit of dying at that moment but are sentenced to live on and again keep guard over a simplified world which will continue on for thousands of years – which is neither a prosecution nor a punishment. This is merely the realised consequence of their desires and passions for matter which they sought, pursued and even worshipped throughout a whole world life on the face of the verdicts of the sublime mechanism of destiny.

We have repeatedly said that all of these events to occur are subject to great orders and devices and nothing occurs arbitrarily and in random. The meaning of these words is that all of the events which occur in the world have and are regulated in accordance with the directives and necessities coming from the unitary. Everything is done by the related beings in duty to the plan of duty, in ways and forms judged by the appreciation of the mechanism of destiny and under the directive of the original necessities and with the assistance of the original time, in accordance with the degrees of merit which the beings acquired themselves by working. Therefore, everything to occur is based on major calculations and very subtle and encompassing technical rudiments.

*
* *

Now, we give the necessary explanation about the technical mechanism which supports the knowledge we gave above about the sinking of the world. Before we engage this explanation, we will revisit a scientific subject we have previously mentioned.

Each of the billions of systems filling the nebulae is constituted by a nucleus which is called the sun and the planets revolving around it, that is, the matter-parts of that system. We had previously said that within such a system, each sphere has its own particular magnetic field. Likewise, we had explained that although these fields – which are in distinct characters particular to the matter-part they are subject to – are in close communication with each other within a system; they never mingle with each other and thus, any matter-part which belongs to a sphere cannot leave the magnetic field of that sphere and enter the magnetic field of another sphere; and in case such a state occurs in the face of an enforcement, it is imperative for that object to adapt the quality of the new magnetic field it entered and in order to do this it has to change its own quality mandatorily. So, consequently, various magnetic fields of various spheres within a system interact in accordance with the necessities of the general structure of that system and are in a state of complete equilibrium.

Forms, lengths, shortness, axial directions of the orbits of the matter-parts, that is, spheres and the nucleus within the system; the velocities of the planets' axial rotation and of their orbital periods are appointed by the states of motions which will occur in consequence of the development of that system and the states of equilibrium among them; and these motions are possible by interactions among the parts and under the control of the higher influences. All of these – as we said – depend on the developmental and evolutionary degrees of the systems and they change in accordance with these degrees. That is, the occurrence of the influences between the matter-parts of a system in forms to put into effect the motions in this or that way vary in accordance with the states pertaining to the evolution of that system.

In short, there are various matter-parts rotating around a nucleus. Each of these matter-parts has its own magnetic field. According to the developmental degrees of that nucleus and the parts which rotate around it, the states of interactions between these magnetic fields vary. So, the whole of the states of equilibrium which is established as a result of these interactions puts into effect a magnetic fields synthesis and we call this the solar system.

Therefore, each system has a state which contains a complex magnetic fields synthesis; and this is particular only to that system. Consequently, it is necessary for it to be in a state of equilibrium with the magnetic fields of other systems as well; and this equilibrium of magnetic field extends as it gets complex and widened into the nebulae in between. Therefore, between the magnetic field complexes of a nebula there are also encompassing states of equilibrium accordingly.

*
* *

Changes to occur in any sphere which is included in a system are possible by the influences to be sent to the magnetic field of that sphere. That is, infinite changes needed in a sphere occur through influences to arrive at the magnetic field of that sphere from the sun of the system or from elsewhere; and these influences are sent directly or indirectly by the beings of the plan of duty who are engaged in that system.

If changes in scale of a great revolution are needed upon any sphere – as the ones in the world we have mentioned above – then the need of sending more intense and forceful influences arises. Therefore, let us explain where this strong influence, which will put into effect this great world revolution that will evidently take place, comes from and how it renders its function.

The first strong influence which will reach the solar system for this event will come from the magnetic field of a planet which is almost four hundred times that of the Earth, of another system which is at great distances from this system.

This planet, while larger than the Earth, which has much simpler and heavy matter than the world, has an accustomed orbit it follows around its own sun which is quite distant from the solar system. And as it traverses its orbit, it has diverted from the part of its orbit which coincides with the solar system which the Earth is subject to and started to advance towards the solar system by making a vast curve. This situation has been realised through the influences continuously sent by a plan – in accordance with the directives coming from the unitary – engaged with the large and small revolutions to occur in many systems pertaining to this advance.

Consequently, upon its great curve this planet will reach a certain point which is plotted for it – by that sublime plan of duty – close to the solar system, and later it will change the direction of its advance – that is, its curve back to its own system and when entering the original orbit of its system, it will continue its accustomed orbit around its own sun. This planet's diverting from its accustomed orbit and extending its journey in an unusual way with a great semi-curving towards the close quarters of the solar system whilst returning back after a certain point without colliding with the Sun is of course not a coincidental event but is a result of a sublime necessity coming from the unitary.

This planet has currently left its orbit and advances towards the direction of the solar system and gets nearer at each moment. This planet, which is still impossible to observe right now, will be observable with the naked eye from the Earth 150–200 years later. Now, let us elaborate on the consequences of this planet's unusual journey.

*
* *

This journey of the planet we mentioned is the necessity of a general evolutionary process which concern many systems. Firstly, this planet itself will encounter and collide with the magnetic fields of many other systems, until it gets closer to the solar system. With each collision, enormous tremors, instabilities and upheavals will occur on its own structure; and the beings of that planet which are much simpler and primitive compared to that of our world will only be able to accelerate their development by means of those enormous convulsions.

304

Secondly, this planet will cause disruptions in varying degrees in the equilibrium of the many other systems it will encounter until it reaches the solar system; it will make their states topsy turvy and consequently, it will prepare possibilities for the development of many other spheres. Finally, its magnetic field will influence our solar system in the way we will soon explain; and our Earth which is the most developed sphere of this system will get into most violent consequences of this influence. Now, we begin to explain the working mechanism of the influences which cause the emergence of these consequences.

*
* *

Earth does not rotate on its orbit around the Sun in a vertical axis. This axis is tilted at 23° 27' to the vertical position and it completes its daily cycles by rotating around this direction. At certain places of the world, which rotates under these conditions, for example, at its poles, there are the located and continuous icy regions and between the poles, an established equatorial climate. The top and bottom points of this axis assumed in the direction of this tilt constitute the south and north poles of the world. That is, the points where these poles exist correspond to the two end-points of the axis the world rotates on. As the world rotates around its own axis, the motions it makes are zero at these points. And this is a result of the state of the general equilibrium that is established within the whole of the world, through innumerable imbalances occurred through the value differentiation of the magnetic field values in opposing characters which are constituted by the world parts in accordance with the duality principle we previously mentioned. Today, this equilibrium, despite it registering more or less slight deviations, is in a stable state. As a result of this situation, the current geographical climates, seasons and states of day and night are brought about.

Now, let us trace the planet which gets near to the solar system. Currently, this planet is at a very great distance from the solar system. Consequently, its magnetic field is not yet in direct contact with the magnetic field of the solar system. However, from the moment this planet – which is four hundred times the size of the Earth – has left its orbit and started to advance towards the solar system, some indirect influences of it have started to affect the solar system. That is, the magnetic field of our solar system which is in relation with the magnetic fields of other systems which this planet is now in contact receives the influences of the aforesaid planet through this way. However, because this planet is still very far away and its influences arrive through ways involving the intermediaries; its consequences in the solar system are very weak today.

Nevertheless, this planet continuously gets closer to the Sun. A moment will come – almost fifty or sixty years later from today – that the magnetic field of this planet will enter a state of direct contact with the magnetic field of the solar system. When this state occurs, the very heavy and dense magnetic field of the planet will make a powerfully oppressing influence over the magnetic field of the Sun. This heavy influence the whole solar system with all its planets receives will put into effect various reactions upon the planets – more correctly, upon their magnetic fields.

We said that the influence coming from the sojourner planet is very coarse and heavy. Therefore, because there is an enormous incompatibility between the subtle and complex magnetic field of the Earth which is the most evolved sphere of the solar system and the coarse magnetic field of this planet; the most violently convulsive consequences and reactions of the influence coming from the planet to the solar system will be seen in the Earth sphere. As a result of this situation, the Earth's current stable axial tilt of 23° 27′ will increase 13° under the pressure of this coarse magnetic field of the planet and the axis of the world will be tilted at 36° to its orbital plane. The initial shift of the poles begins with the sojourner planet's first direct influences to arrive at the solar system.

The concept of pressure here should not be taken literally. That is, it should not be thought here as if the world is impacted or bent with a push coming from outside. To explain this, let us first take the motions of a sphere which rotates around its own axis. This sphere rotates around a straight line called axis which connects the two stable points we call the poles. The occurrence of the polar points here is the result of the sum of the total equilibria put into effect by the opposite values in the structure of the sphere and its magnetic field, that is, by the motions.

Motions at the poles are zero. On the other hand, where the motions are most is the belt region, which is the exact middle of the distance between two poles which we call the equator. So, the mean ratio between the velocities of the motion, which is the most in the equator and is the least at the poles is the result and manifestation of the total sum of the motion equilibria in the sphere – as we said. Therefore, when disruption or alteration occurs in these equilibria within the sphere for any reason then the zero points, in other words, polar points can be displaced. That is, poles can shift slightly or radically – depending on the intensity of the degree of the equilibrium change – upon the sphere to the back or forth, left or right relative to their former locations. And in accordance with the equilibrium principle, the equator immediately changes its position, takes its proper place around the sphere relative to the new poles. Occurrence of this situation means that the sphere which rotates starts to divert from the former rotational direction in order to rotate in a different direction on the axis which occurred between the new poles.

And the thing that will happen in the Earth is the same. After the influences coming from the outside planet to the magnetic field of the Earth and in turn, into its structure, disrupt the initial equilibrium by affecting the inner motions of the sphere; these changes in the equilibrium continue on through new states and new motions that start to occur in the Earth – in accordance with the consecutive value differentiation mechanism – up to the boundary where the equilibrium is to be established completely. As the result of this, the existing north and south poles at the known locations of the Earth shift. Since the poles – as we just mentioned – are the result of the general equilibrium of the sphere; as these are displaced, the equator of the sphere immediately changes its place to take its required location on the surface of the sphere according to the new situations of the poles. Therefore, the axial direction between the sphere's new poles to occur will start to change after the shifted positions of the poles relative to its former axial direction.

For example, as the Earth's North Pole starts to shift gradually towards the south at the part in Siberia, the South Pole will start to shift towards the north within the same degrees at the opposite part at the direction where the cape of South America is located. As

307

the result of this, equator will take its place around the Earth at same distance from these two new poles, that is, its location will change relative to the poles. In this case, because the Earth always rotates around its own axis between the poles and this axis is more tilted than the former one; this situation of the Earth displays the scenery which is a little bit more tilted relative to the former one.

Actually, the Earth sphere has not changed its position. For example, Francis Joseph's Land[22] will be at the same place where it has been in a tilted line relative to the orbit of the Earth. However, the polar point which has been there will now be located not there but much lower relative to this archipelago. Similarly, Taymyr Peninsula[23] will also not move an inch from its former locations relative to the Earth's orbit. However, the former North Pole is above it, but the new North Pole will go partly below this peninsula and will occur below it. Similarly, in the Southern Hemisphere the South Pole is to be arranged according to it. For example, the South Pole which previously has been at much lower parts of Alexander Island,[24] although this island would not change its place relative to the Earth's orbit, has now shifted to its higher part.

So, the direction of the new axis of the Earth which occurs relative to its new poles has become slightly more tilted to its former equator relative to its former axis; and the new equator has changed accordingly and moved up to a surface vertical to the newly occurred axis.

Thus, as a consequence of the disruption of the total motion equilibrium of the world by the influence coming from the planet, the North Pole will shift south at the Russia side and the South Pole will move up north at the direction of the cape of the South America. Certainly, in accordance with this situation, the oblique degree of the axis between the newly situated North and South Poles – relative to the former axis of the Earth – will increase relative to the obliquity degree of the former axis; and this increase will be at an angle of 13°. The locations of these points in accordance with the

---

[22] *Francis Joseph's Land*: an archipelago located in the far north of Russia. (*Publisher*)
[23] *Taymyr Peninsula*: a peninsula in the far north of Russia, in the Siberian Federal District, that forms the northernmost part of the mainland of Eurasia. (*Publisher*)
[24] *Alexander Island* : the largest island of Antarctica. (*Publisher*)

current geographical positions are: the new North Pole will shift to a point where the current polar circle joins with the 100th meridian. And the South Pole will rise up in the direction of the cape of the South America and reach the point where the current South Polar Circle joins with the 80th meridian. Naturally, then all meridians and parallels as well as the equator will shift and they will take their places upon the Earth according to the new poles.

*
* *

The direction of the former axis had diverted from its vertical position to the Earth's orbit at an angle of 23°. Since the new tilt to be added to this axis due to the polar shift is 13°; the obliquity degree which the new axis will gradually tilt and reach as the final limit will be 23° + 13° = 36°. Since the Earth's rotation around its own axis will always occur around its own axis; rotational directions of the Earth around its own axis will change as well according to this changed tilting.

Therefore, the polar points will occur according to the new rotational ways the Earth's magnetic fields will engage on because of the necessity of their disrupted equilibria; and the axis will emerge accordingly. These polar points – where the motions of the Earth are at zero as it rotates around on its own axis – will be the points which are antipodes[25] of each other, that is, the points of two hemispheres which are diametrically opposite sides; and these are the points we indicated above. However, this situation belongs to the final stage and will not occur at the first direct contact of the planet with the solar system. At the beginning, the North and South Poles will start to shift very gradually toward these points. The initial influence of the planet which manifests in this way will begin vaguely 50 years later and will continue very gradually between 50 and 100 years; and some slightly obvious climate changes will begin 50 years later. Nevertheless, this situation will still be not to a degree which preoccupies mankind.

*
* *

---

[25] *Antipodes*: Any point on the Earth has an identical point at the opposite side. For example, the North Pole and the South Pole are antipodes. (*Publisher*)

Changes at the equilibrium states which follow the initial disruption of the Earth's equilibrium by the initial influence of the planet, will continue on until the moment the complete equilibrium is established through the successive value differentiations which will go on between the motions of world parts.

And this will occur as such: after the initial equilibrium disruption, former poles will get warmer. Consequently, the ice at the former North Pole which exists on the seas and the ice at the former South Pole which sits on the land will thaw as well because of the warming of those places. With the melting of the ice at the North Pole, the volume of the seas at this region will decrease; and with the melting of the ice at the South Pole over the lands, immense water masses will pour into the seas and contrarily, the volume of the waters in the South Sea will increase.

Consequently, as a result of the imbalance in the seas around the two poles, a great water current will start from south to north; and this situation will begin to impose new influences over the Earth's magnetic field but stronger than the influence of the incoming planet does and will cause the Earth's magnetic equilibrium lines to change more and more; and these will lead to other motions; and thence, the poles will then begin to converge on the points we indicated above, no longer by an external influence but by the influences resulting from the equilibrium changes which will occur through the successive value differentiation mechanism of the Earth in the wake of this influence.

Therefore, the first influence which causes the poles to shift upon the sphere will come from the sojourner planet; and then, the influence which will complete this deed will continue with the value differentiation mechanism of the motions of the Earth's own structure. Consequently, the equilibrium changes the Earth with its disrupted balance will go through until it reaches a state of complete equilibrium will increase much more in the years following the hundredth year and ensure the swift convergence of the polar point to the places we delineated above.

*
* *

At the time the polar points gets near to this final state, these changes will occur at the tropics[26] as well: the Tropic of Cancer will be 36 degrees latitude north of the new equator relative to the Earth's new axis against the Sun; and likewise, the Tropic of Capricorn will be 36 degrees latitude south of the equator.

*
* *

From the hundredth year on, climates will gradually get near to the states expressed by these final degrees of temperature. When the final state is reached, the equilibrium of the Earth will be abruptly disturbed; and as we said, the world will be upside down within a short time with a semicircle turn. That is, the North Pole will replace the South Pole and the South Pole will replace the North Pole. However, as we have previously said, we again state that these changes will occur not in the form of an impact to the sphere and its becoming topsy-turvy but in the form of the pole shift.

*
* *

When the world is turned upside down by making a semicircle turn through the mechanism explained above, it is natural that the new axis of the Earth will take on a new direction according to the rotational state which will occur by the newly established equilibrium of the world. So, the events in the final stage of the world's sinking which we have mentioned, that is, the moments of the world's submerging and judgement day will correspond to the radical disruptions in the equilibrium during the Earth's becoming abruptly upside down which starts suddenly after the poles reach the final points we indicated by first shifting gradually, which is completed within a few hours as the North Pole shifts to the south and replaces the South Pole and on the other hand, the South Pole replaces the North Pole.

---

[26] *Tropics*: A region of the Earth surrounding the Equator. It is limited in latitude by the Tropic of Cancer in the northern hemisphere at 23° N and the Tropic of Capricorn in the southern hemisphere at 23° S; these latitudes correspond to the axial tilt of the Earth. The tropics include all the areas on the Earth where the Sun reaches a subsolar point, a point directly overhead at least once during the solar year. (*Publisher*)

However, the upheaval of the poles after this semicircle turn of the Earth will not put into effect a distinct change in the new world, even no change at all. For, after the poles are upside down there will be no constituent belonging to the former geographical states, comparing the points where the new poles will be established with the former countries and the geographical situation will be out of question. Therefore, the new world to be born, regardless of which degree its axial tilt will be, will have a north pole and a south pole like today; and its poles belonging to the previous cycle will be of something of a past forgotten forever, together with all its geographical constitutions.

*
* *

It should never be forgotten that the influences which put into effect all these events and consequences descend directly or indirectly to the magnetic field of the world from the sublime plan which is engaged with providing the states the world needs – as we always repeat – in accordance with the original directives filtering from the unitary. Doses of these influences are sent with their exact values, neither a little more nor a little less; and so the original necessities are executed.

Therefore, all these acts are not unplanned but are put into effect within certain criteria and orientated to the purpose of application of an immense evolutionary plan. And all of these are devices which are full of wisdom and established within the immense harmony and order of universe on the evolutionary path. In this day of utter confusion there is not a disaster as it is seen. Things that happen here will ensure on the one hand, the transition of mankind to the realms they deserved who successfully completed their evolutionary cycles in the world and turned their backs on world matter which does not satisfy them any more; and on the other hand, they will fulfil the needs of unprepared mankind who long for returning back to coarse matter and could not shake themselves free of coarse matter, assuming that happiness would only be gained by becoming buried in that matter.

The mechanism of destiny appreciates the degrees of merit, in accordance with mankind's efforts on the path of attaining the spaces they choose, want and need by their freedom which is taken

312

as a basic in evolution; and they execute their necessities accordingly. Consequently, at the stage of the world's closing, everybody will find what he seeks, his needs will be responded to, he will reach his place at the merit steps of the evolutionary ladder and by this, the ones who progress will progress and those who regress will remain in their place.

Therefore, in spite of their horrible and formidable appearances, these closing scenes of the world will be the greatest moment of liberation, the arising of the most joyful and happiest day, the breaking of the greatest redeemer dawn which was expected for ages.

Here we have shown that the world, by completing another developmental cycle since the closing of the Mu cycle, is about to add another one to its openings and closings which have been repeated hundreds of thousands of times. This situation which has been determined for the world in the face of the sublime principles will continue again and again; and consequently, each time the world will prepare the ground for mankind to become completely free of the world and leave in masses in order to pass to the higher realms which they need and have acquired the merit for after completing their evolutionary preparations particular to the world by utilising all developmental possibilities of its one cycle.

*
* *

The place that mankind who have been completely freed from the world by dying in the great world cataclysm, will directly go to, as we mentioned, is a semi-subtle higher plan relative to the world which we call the plan of love.

In this plan the prevailing reality is love. More correctly, mankind who will pass there will live there for a while in order to perform various applications of love in that plan and consequently, to become able to completely adapt to the higher necessities of the plan of duty. Thus, the semi-subtle realm or the plan of love is above all an intermediary plan. That is, it is an intermediary plan which ensures the transition of mankind who have been freed from the heavy burdens of world realities to the very subtle plan of duty through an easy, sweet and happy advance.

313

In order to be able to pass to a higher stage after the completion of every stage of material development, it is imperative for all beings – plant, animal, human – to go through such intermediary plans. For, the functions of these plans are very significant. For example, at some stage an animal being has attained the merit of utilising a body in a higher stage, that is, the human body, after properly completing the stage of animality. This lasts for a very long time and the animal being cannot immediately leap to humanness from the stage of animality. For, even if it has properly developed in its own right, there are still very significant and profound differences between using the animal body it has used so far and using a human body.

So, that being, after going through certain transitional stages between the body realities, will be able to adapt completely to the necessities of humanness and to adjust using the human body properly. Therefore, it needs to live in a plan which will allow it to do such a transitional preparation. And this is its semi-subtle realm. Here, that being encounters some situations which prepare it to the necessities of humanness and after doing its transitional application in those situations for a while, it steps into the human realm in order to start from its most primitive stage.

However, he still cannot immediately enter into the state of an independent human being. First, it enters a state of ability to build the components of the human brain; and afterwards, by living in the human brain cells for a long time and rendering the applications of human body management as required, that is, upon acquiring the merit of using a human body independently; it connects to the world by bonding to a human body in order to use that body for its following evolutions; and it embodies with a body in the state of human and later – as we previously said – it completes all evolutionary stages in the world with its human body.

*
* *

The semi-subtle realm which the mankind needs to go through in order to pass into the super-human plan is incomparable in scope and extent to the intermediary plans which are needed to be gone through while passing from the subhuman realm to the stage of human. Intermediary plans have their own particular means to prepare the beings from the lower plan for the higher plan. These means belong to neither the realities of the plans they have left nor the realities of a higher plan. These are merely vehicles which ensure the transition of mankind who will pass from the lower plan to the higher without any shocks in the face of the differences which exist between these two plans; in other words, their adaptation to the unaccustomed realities of the higher plan in the shortest way; and these vehicles, in one aspect, contact the realities of the plan left behind and in other aspects, display some states akin to the next plan. However, they are actually neither the realities of the plan left behind nor the realities of the plan to be passed to; they are merely a preparatory mechanism particular to the intermediary plan.

*
* *

The preparatory means of the semi-subtle realm, that is, of the intermediary plan which the mankind will enter after the world is love. The love in here, although it is not the love as it is understood and felt in the world, nonetheless has an aspect which is close to the one in the world. Although the love in the world is different than the concept of true love in the plan of duty, nonetheless it has the value and quality which can be a preparatory step to that love. Because of this, thanks to this preparation he has done in the world, a human being who acquired the merit of entering the realm of love, that is the semi-subtle realm, will participate in this great mechanism of love which is completely different from the love in the world and incomparable to it in its scope and extent.

The thing that being should do in this plan is to utilise the miscellaneous variations of this very encompassing and extended love in order to benefit from their possibilities which are preparatory for the higher plan of duty. Therefore, the quality – which cannot be understood by world mankind – of the love in here displays very powerful states which ensure the beings in the intermediary plan to adapt to the higher realities of the plan of duty. For, completely accepting and adapting to the plan of duty is not an easy task. Success in here has technical issues which entail many efforts.

*
* *

The efforts in the plan of love are completely different from the efforts spent in the coarse deeds in the world. None of the hardships, troubles, suffering, torments, tortures, diseases and deaths which always stand against the mankind during the efforts in the world exists here. The effort in here occurs – in accordance with the increase in the comprehensions of the beings (which is realised swiftly in the plan of love) – as filled with pleasures and happiness which are much more enjoyable. As a matter of fact, the sparkling intuitions of this great happiness which emerged in the essence-beings of the mankind while they were still in the world attract mankind to itself.

However, mankind cannot attain this happiness in the world in spite of their longing. Nevertheless, mankind always pursues and raves about it throughout their lives without knowing its quality and without having the ability to describe it. And from the moment they leave the world, they will jump into the lap of this happiness – which they longed for, pursued for ages but could not get a hold and even could not specify its quality – in the plan of love; and then they will satisfy themselves in the real sense, in other words, then they will understand what contentment means which they have never been able to attain in the world.

The first primitive steps of the love which prevails in this plan begin in the world with the name of love and by occupying the whole life of the semi-subtle realm, end at the threshold of the plan of duty. Therefore, this great and encompassing love will also reach its final stage towards the plan of duty and complete its function there.

*
* *

This function of love is very necessary and significant in regard to its ensuring beings adapt completely to duty. For, this function of love provides the great possibilities of enablement of entering into duty.

The plan of duty is a completely different sublime plan. Since we have previously given the necessary knowledge about this plan

316

we do not repeat them here. We will suffice to say this that the plan of duty is a plan which is throughout harmonious and ordered, a togetherness, a complete and pure cooperation and coordination. Not even the slightest disharmony, contradiction or contrariness exists. For the beings who will enter there it is necessary that they have absolutely and exactly adapted to this harmony, and it is even imperative that they have become part of that harmony; and this can be possible by many preparatory stages which need to be gone through on this path.

After all, the harshest, most primitive, hardest and most suffering stages of the levels in the preparation for duty are gone through by mankind in the long cycles belonging to the world's life. Afterwards, in the semi-subtle realm, that is, in the plan of love, the last stages of this preparation which lead directly to the plan of duty will be completed willingly – as we have just said – with much ease, comfort and happiness. Consequently, through the sublime mechanism of love in this realm, the power to adapt the harmony and necessities of the plan of duty will be acquired. Therefore, the sublime love in this plan is a sweet and basic means of reaching the great plan of duty.

*
* *

While the beings live within the variations of love in the semi-subtle realm, there is as well the earthly cravings particular to this place which will stand against the beings. We will soon talk about the quality of this earthly craving. In the plan of love, it is imperative for the beings to abolish and become free of these earthly cravings of theirs which prevent them from preparing for the great plan of duty, as soon as possible. And this will be ensured, as we have said, through miscellaneous applications of love; this is enjoyable work and occupational field for the beings, quite unlike the strife and suffering that need to be gone through during the abolishment of coarse earthly cravings in the world.

And as a consequence of these sweet occupations, eventually these obstacles will be abolished; and the beings will step on the first steps of the great plan of duty within an imperceptible flow.

317

For this, there is no need in there for major shocks, tumultuous transitions and deaths as in the world. For, such states will actually be out of the question for the beings after they have left the world. Consequently, the beings who have completed and passed the plan of duty will step on the first steps of the plan of duty and they will be given duties right away.

*
* *

Now, we will elaborate on the preparatory state of the mechanism of love in the semi-subtle realm.

Mankind's leaving the world means their leaving their physical bodies which consist of coarse hydrogen combinations belonging to the world and returning to their original state, the state of being. The beings who use human bodies – as we previously said – are a very subtle state of matter which is so distanced from the concept and reality of world matter that it cannot even be called matter. Such a state cannot be matter in mankind's view, because a being has no material quality in the sense accepted and recognised by mankind. Because of this, we previously termed the beings a complex of influences.

Consequently, when the being who is an influences or energies complex leaves the world, that is, its body, and while it is in a completely bodiless state, it catches a semi-subtle matter combination and connects to it in order to utilise as an influence vehicle in the plan of love. At that moment, this combination substitutes its coarse body in the world. This matter exists in a semi-subtle state between world matter and subtle matter of the plan of duty. However, it draws near to the world by its coarse side as well as to the plan of duty by its subtle side. Therefore, we call it semi-subtle matter and the place which is made up of these matters the semi-subtle realm.

The beings of the semi-subtle cosmos can build realities akin to the concepts of time and space in the world out of these matters by utilising their sides which are close to world matter. And also they can live in these real images they have built. The degrees of subtlety of the matter which are helpful to them in building these spaces may well be perceptible in setting by the very sensitive tools of the world.

318

Since these beings have not yet entered the plan of duty, no duty – even automatic ones – is given to them. Because of this, they do not intervene with the evolution of any beings and interfere with their activities. They do not have such an authorisation yet.

For a being who has entered the semi-subtle realm, the real purpose is to reach the plan of duty. For, matter states in the plan of duty are subtle matter and in order to do duty in that plan, the beings need to be free of remaining connected to a single semi-subtle matter combination.

So, the beings in there have a very powerful means to overcome this obstacle; and that is love. Therefore, love in the intermediary plan is a sublime vehicle helping to overcome the semi-subtle matter of that plan through sweet and joyful struggles which are devoid of any kind of suffering and sadness.

*
* *

Entering the plan of duty means accepting some obligations of duty and possessing the power and possibilities to execute the necessities of these duties. Therefore, the being in the plan of duty needs to use various matter which are suitable to duties. However, a being who has not reached this state yet deeply internalises the semi-subtle matter combination it caught after it left the world and cannot leave from it. And when it cannot leave from this matter, it cannot have the possibility of various subtle matter and as a result of this, it cannot render any duty. This is because it needs to utilise various subtle matter and milieus in order to do that duty but its semi-subtle matter which it cannot leave prevents this.

Therefore, for the beings in there to be able to pass to the plan of duty, it is necessary to leave this semi-subtle matter forthwith which they initially caught, that is, which they use like a kind of body for themselves. They must be able to do this so they can use different subtle or semi-subtle matter as they wish in order to execute the necessities of a duty which may be their lot and which they can change immediately in accordance with necessities.

So, their most powerful tool which will help them in leaving their semi-subtle matter, which they caught as soon as they passed to the semi-subtle realm and could not let go, will be love. These beings, in doing various applications of love, will be freed of remaining connected only to a single semi-subtle matter; they will be able to leave that matter when they want to and will be able to use different matter instead of it. Therefore, as we have just mentioned above, this semi-subtle matter which is initially caught by the beings who have passed to the plan of love becomes a kind of earthly craving of them which needs to be overcome during the completion of the preparations in there. By setting this matter aside, they overcome their earthly craving and from that moment on, they reach the first steps of the plan of duty. And the vehicle which helps in attaining the success here is love in all kinds of variations.

*
* *

In this plan, a certain length of time needs to pass from the beginning to the attainment of a complete accomplishment. Duration of this period varies in accordance with beings. For some it is quite long, whereas for some it may be short. It is difficult to determine this period with world time. For, time which is used as a measurement for this period is a time beyond the world's comprehension. Therefore, it is much more encompassing than world time. For example, if we accept the longest period to be passed there as 300 years as measured by world time; this period can be 3000 years or more with the perceptual time of this place. And there is still no certainty about it. The time of that place cannot be compared with that of the world, because these values always vary in accordance with comprehensions.

In the deeds of the super-world, comprehension time and comprehension space prevail. However, it is because the beings of the plan of love will use the side of the semi-subtle matter which is closer to the world during their initial time there, that is, during the times when they are still strongly connected to semi-subtle matter they can live in realities closer to the world. Likewise, although comprehension time fully prevails outside the world, the beings who use semi-subtle matter can build spaces as well, which are more or less akin to world space by utilising the sides of these matter which are close to the world.

Nevertheless, as these beings properly increase their comprehensions by doing applications of love in there and as they free themselves from remaining connected to semi-subtle matter; their time and space as well start to acquire encompassing characters of perceptual time and space accordingly; and at the moment they are completely free of this semi-subtle matter combination, no activity is left in them belonging to the material realities; and then, by using the matter they wish in required places according to the duties they will take on, they can utilise all kinds of time and space realities which that matter is subject to.

Because they do not have continuous connection to certain matter after they are freed of the semi-subtle matter, they have in their subtle beings the enabling power to use and let go of the matter they want. Therefore, a being in the plan of love who is able to let go of its semi-subtle matter and to pass to the plan of duty means that it does not remain connected to any matter but remains as the essence-being, that is, in a state of developed energies complex; and that it is able to use any matter it wants whenever it wants with this energy; and that it is able to influence and intervene in the realms to which this matter is subject, and to execute many deeds and do many duties in those places; and a being in the semi-subtle can only attain these possibilities by carrying out various applications of love which is sweet, joyous and full of pleasure and enjoyment.

*
* *

Now, let us describe the semi-subtle realm. This is a realm constituted by the energies belonging to the highest combinations of the hydrogen atom which is the nucleus of our matter cosmos. These high energies which do not exist within the accustomed realities of our current world constitute the coarsest atoms of the semi-subtle realm. Here, we see it necessary to caution against allowing a misunderstanding:

The semi-subtle milieu should not be mistaken with the state we call the spatium which is previously mentioned as the place which beings who have not yet been freed from the human body realities will enter as usual between their deaths and births. The spatium is not a milieu or a space. This place is only a state of the being's severing its interests and relations with its surroundings while the being temporarily separates from the bodily bonds and returns to its essence-being. It is still a man in this state of its and he has not got out of the world, but he is a man who has severed all of his interests with the outside and remains in a state of privacy with his essence-being only. At that moment, any space for him is out of the question. His space remains as merely a perceptual point where its being has gathered around, as we previously mentioned.

Whereas, the semi-subtle realm which we now talk about is a milieu and space which is the supra-hydrogen cosmos and a very subtle and encompassing milieu compared to it. This milieu is only particular to the beings who have been absolutely freed from the world; it is a matter state constituted out of the subtle energy particles which are emanated spontaneously – always under the control of sublime beings in duty – by the most superior and evolved hydrogen combination of the world.

The first vehicle which is used and bonded by the beings who passed to this realm is a certain matter combination made out of semi-subtle matter, as we said. The beings increase their adequacy and merits by using this combination as well as by struggling with it on the path of love. And because there is no dense matter similar to that of the world, tiring, tedious, arduous, difficult and slow progressing activities – as in the world – do not exist in this plan. Due to the wide scope of possibilities of semi-subtle matter, with the smallest effort the beings in this cosmos will obtain results which can only be obtained after working very hard for many years in the world with much stress and tiredness. Because of this, there are no coarse states in this plan such as hard work, tiredness, suffering, strife and struggle contrary to the way it is in the world.

In here, all desires become realised with a small push of will, with only a wish, as if they occur automatically, spontaneously. For example, the being can build a space for itself and live in there as it wishes due to the rich possibilities of semi-subtle matter at its hands. Again, it can create the forms its wishes with the same matter it uses by a simple act of imagination; and turn them into objective values for itself. During all of these applications, that being does not feel any of the things called tiredness by mankind.

In accordance with the necessities of semi-subtle matter in this plan; the disorders pertaining to coarse body organs such as disease, health, tiredness, laziness, impotence, aches and pains etc., and to the higher organs of the body such as mental exhaustions, idiocy, insanity, sleep and fainting spells, coma, anxieties and coarse desires etc. cannot come into the cadres of matter of that cosmos. There are no such things in the semi-subtle realm.

Similarly, in the semi-subtle realm there are no realities particular to the world such as beauty, ugliness, youth or old age in the physical sense. And especially, the most basic and imperative reality of death, to which world matter is subject, does not exist at all in the semi-subtle realm. Instead, there are only imperceptible and very sweet transitions and changes of form from one stage to another. The possibilities of matter at the hands of the beings in there give them the comprehension of space and time which the world could not yet attain. By this means, they can build and dissolve the images they wish by themselves. They do not remain imprisoned by fixed images, unlike in the world. The life in here, with its one aspect, is more or less similar to the life which mankind calls etheric. However, the prevailing factor in the basic structure of this life is love.

*
* *

In the books of great religions, the symbol of heaven has been used to give mankind the intuitions of the semi-subtle realm. This is a beautiful and powerful symbol. However, as is valid with all symbols, here as well, it should not be stuck only with forms. For, it should be remembered that these symbols have been placed in order to address various human comprehensions of every cycle and consequently, to reach some ends and purposes. So, the symbol of heaven which is stated in the religious books expresses this semi-subtle realm mentioned here, in which the reality of love prevails.

In heaven, some images have been mentioned belonging to a comprehension of time and space which is akin to world time and space. According to this, those who have entered heaven can move as they like without hardship and tiredness. Unlike in the world, they can go wherever they want and they will find the things they want ready before them. This situation expresses the possibilities of the semi-subtle milieu which we have just mentioned. For, as we have said, in the semi-subtle realm as well, beings can immediately create the space or images they wish for without tiring and spending any effort and they can act as they like. Their wishes and thoughts are realised as if spontaneously. So, these are the meanings intended by the symbol of heaven.

Variations of love which exist in the plan of love, to an all-encompassing and sublime degree that cannot be understood by mankind, have been explained in the concept of heaven through material symbols of love which are helpful for even the most inexperienced of mankind to be able to intuit some things even in simple meanings. In the symbol of heaven, sublime realms and attainment of divine wisdom in those realms are mentioned. These expressions carry the meanings of the convergence on the sublime harmony which the beings of the semi-subtle realms – after they go through the most sublime love complexes – will reach in the advanced stages and that we call the plan of duty. Adaptations and unions in there with divine truths, that is, with the lights of the unitary which we call harmony, are symbolised in the symbol of heaven as the reunion with the divine lights.

*
* *

The life in the plan of love allows beings to be gradually freed from the semi-subtle matter to which they are connected which prevents their reaching the sublime subtle plans of duty. Love, in order to reach this goal, unifies beings as groups. Gradually, a complete harmony and togetherness is established among groups. Consequently, beings are swiftly prepared for the necessities of the plan of duty which are total agreement and harmony. The love which gathers the beings into groups and ensures complete harmony and agreement among those groups will certainly be of a more profound state than it is in the world.

*
* *

The plan of love is an etheric realm which entails efforts and activities full of happiness within its vast scope of love – which is not known by mankind – and prepares the beings for ever higher plans. The subtlety of matter which is told in the most fantastic fairy tales appear quite coarse compared with this realm. Moreover, besides the great pleasure and enjoyment given to the beings by this subtlety of matter which lays all kinds of possibilities before them, the happiness bestowed on the beings by the extent of love which is unknown to mankind is high and deep, comparable with nothing in this world. For, in there, there is no question of facing the anxieties for beings, as it always is in this world, which might be anticipated after every pleasure deemed as happiness. On the contrary, in there, a true happiness is followed by a greater happiness; a true peace which has been attained is followed by a more meaningful and encompassing peace.

The states which start at the initial stages of the plan of love and which have aspects more or less akin to world time and space become subtler as the preparations of beings progress and they start to distance themselves from this closeness to the states in the world. This situation is an expression of beings becoming gradually freed from semi-subtle matter with which they were bonded. As the bonds with semi-subtle matter loosen, the states of perceptual time and space are entered; and aspects of the semi-subtle realm similar to the world are abolished. Convergence of the groups on the plan of duty increase and the imperatives of the necessities of the plan of duty become more distinct. In the groups interconnected with love, various manifestations of love particular to this place support this situation. The beings who are freed from subtle-matter combinations become completely free and acquire the possibilities of changing matter as they wish by using various matter. For, by then, the state of remaining connected to a semi-subtle matter combination which prevents this has been abolished.

Consequently, beings who advance towards the plan of duty by preparing as groups take on their first duty with their groups of five or six individuals with a total understanding of duty and within the possibilities of perceptual time and space. This means that they have entered the plan of duty.

Therefore, the transition to the plan of duty occurs with a quite sweet preparation, as imperceptible and within a gradual flow; not like the transition from the world to the semi-subtle which occurs tumultuously, together with violent tremors and deaths. Afterwards, these beings begin to rise by climbing towards the pinnacle of the cone of light which carries the divine necessity from the initial stages of the plan of duty onwards, with an increasing speed of maturation due to the ever widening of their groups and to the increase in comprehension which becomes identical through the widening of these groups.

*

* *

This is the sublime end which awaits human beings who will pass to the plan of love. Therefore, this transition from the world to the semi-subtle realm will allow beings to come together with the contentment of happiness which they have kept alive for ages in their essence-beings; and pursued and strove for its vague intuition without reaching any comprehension in the state of being human at all and could never be satisfied. And the value and power of the human being is in his knowing of his existence and of the Force in this transition.